REFUGEES, RACE AND THE LEGAL CONCEPT OF ASYLUM IN BRITAIN

Cavendish Publishing Limited

London • Sydney

REFUGEES, RACE AND THE LEGAL CONCEPT OF ASYLUM IN BRITAIN

Prakash Amritlal Shah LLB, LLM, PhD
Lecturer in Law,
University of Kent at Canterbury
Formerly Lecturer in Law,
School of Oriental and African Studies
University of London

Cavendish Publishing Limited

London • Sydney

First published in Great Britain 2000 by Cavendish Publishing Limited,
The Glass House, Wharton Street, London WC1X 9PX, United Kingdom
Telephone: +44 (0)20 7278 8000   Facsimile: +44 (0)20 7278 8080
Email: info@cavendishpublishing.com
Website: www.cavendishpublishing.com

Shah, Prakash

Refugees, race and the legal concept of asylum in Britain

1 Asylum, right of – Great Britain 2 Refugees – legal status, laws, etc – Great Britain

I Title

342.4'1'083

ISBN 1 85941 601 2

Printed and bound in Great Britain

PREFACE

The research for this book was done by the writer while at the School of Oriental and African Studies (SOAS) in the University of London. The Law Department at SOAS is probably the most unique of places to pursue a course of legal study. One of the benefits of studying at such a place is the contact that one has with persons who approach legal study with a totally unconventional perspective, in that one immediately becomes conscious of one's limitations as basically a Western trained legal scholar. Not only that; one is surrounded by people who have knowledge about the Asian and African world that is probably unsurpassed in the United Kingdom and this fact makes one quite self-conscious, if not necessarily rigorous enough, about writing about people from those regions. The years spent studying and teaching at SOAS witnessed a process of transformation for this writer. I started out as a person who, like almost all Western trained law students, was taught to believe that the civilisational values embodied in legal thought were based upon a uniform conception of justice that could be extended to all persons without distinction. This belief was always tempered, however, by a barely articulated semi-consciousness that all was not necessarily sound with these premises, this awareness no doubt influenced by my own experiences as a young East African Asian adult growing up in a society that appears to have in-built mechanisms to marginalise things Asian and African. Then came the opportunity to meet Dr Werner Menski, a South Asianist, who taught, *inter alia*, courses on Ethnic Minorities and the Law and Comparative Immigration and Nationality Law at SOAS. I eagerly took to the style of his teaching and tried to absorb the content of his courses. Dr Menski is unique among legal scholars for his empowering method of teaching and communicating, and made myself and many of my fellow students (he is known among some as 'Guruji') feel that we had 'something to say'. What that method is still remained a mystery as I took on the role in subsequent years of teaching on those same, and other, law courses at SOAS. But he had set me upon a path to investigate more thoroughly issues surrounding the legal position of ethnic minorities in Britain.

This book is in no small measure directly due to Dr Menski, who blew up Western legal mythology before our eyes and began the painstaking task of reconstructing the trajectories of ethnic minority legal experiences. There have been many other colleagues, students and friends who through their suggestions and advice contributed to this work and will forgive not being mentioned by name. Special thanks are due to the colleagues at the Law Department of SOAS who were constantly encouraging and to the School at large; to Navtej Singh Ahluwalia for allowing many issues to be thrashed out in late night discussions; to Curtis Francis Doebbler for his encouragement to write on UK asylum law; to Yohannes Petros whose uncompromising ethical stance became water in a desert; and to Cara Annett at Cavendish Publishing for seeing this project through. Due respects are to be paid to my parents who are constant sources of support and inspiration, and thanks to my brother and sisters for their patience and understanding.

Prakash A Shah
Kent Law School
University of Kent at Canterbury
October 2000

CONTENTS

TABLE OF CASES

TABLE OF STATUTES

TABLE OF STATUTORY INSTRUMENTS

TABLE OF INTERNATIONAL INSTRUMENTS

ABBREVIATIONS

AC	Appeal Cases
All ER	All England Reports
BCAR	British Council for Aid to Refugees
BDTC	British dependent territories citizen
BOC	British overseas citizen
BPP	British protected person
BRC	British Refugee Council
CA	Court of Appeal
CUKC	citizen of the United Kingdom and colonies
DC	Divisional Court
EC	European Community
ECO	Entry Clearance Officer
EEC	European Economic Community
EU	European Union
EVWs	European Volunteer Workers
HL	House of Lords
IAS	Immigration Advisory Service
ICIHI	Independent Commission for International Humanitarian Issues
IGCR	Intergovernmental Committee on Refugees
Imm AR	Immigration Appeal Reports
INLR	Immigration and Nationality Law Reports
IRO	International Refugee Organisation
JCWI	Joint Council for the Welfare of Immigrants

KB	King's Bench
LJ	Lord Justice
PC	Privy Council
QB	Queen's Bench
UKIAS	United Kingdom Immigrants Advisory Service
UNHCR	United Nations High Commissioner for Refugees
UNRRA	United Nations Relief and Rehabilitation Administration
WLR	Weekly Law Reports

CHAPTER 1

INTRODUCTION

This book presents several cases of group migration to Britain which are taken as examples of refugee movements, and analyses the reactions of the British legal system which, in turn, conditioned the quality of asylum which the refugees received. They include gypsies who have come to Britain periodically when attempting to escape persecution on the European continent; Protestant Huguenots, also fleeing from persecution on the European continent; Africans who tried to escape slavery; various European refugee groups, mainly political exiles; groups of Jews who sought to escape victimisation in countries of East and Central Europe; Asians who fled or were expelled from East African countries; refugees from Vietnam; Tamils from Sri Lanka who were more recently joined by other groups of Asian and African refugees. Specifically, the practice of immigration control in Britain is analysed in relation to the migration of these groups, and it is argued that, in this context, the legal system has consistently been favourable to European refugee groups, while it has consistently rejected, or been hostile to, the presence of Asian and African groups.

1.1 REFUGEES

The concept of 'refugee' is relevant when the migration of an individual or a group of persons becomes problematised. Although migration has been a reality throughout known human existence, it is only very recently that migration *simpliciter* and refugee phenomena have been treated as distinct entities in public, academic and legal discourses. There exist many 'primary' institutions dedicated to administering the lives of people classed as refugees as, increasingly, migrations which are classed as refugee phenomena are brought into political spaces at local, national and global levels. These primary institutions take many different forms. They can be of putatively global or international reach, such as the United Nations High Commissioner for Refugees (UNHCR), or be brought into being by the consent of several States for a specific situation such as the United Nations Relief and Works Agency, mandated to contain the Palestinian refugees who were forced to flee after 1948. They can be national institutions such as the Home Office, Refugee Council or the Refugee Legal Centre in Britain. They can also take the form of non-governmental organisations (so called NGOs) which may have local, national or transnational reach; they tend to perform some tasks of governing the lives of refugees and may be linked through funding to governmental agencies (see Ferris, 1993). These actors tend to generate their own definitions of what or who refugees are. It is the existence of a multiplicity of definition-generating bodies which underscores the fact that the definition of 'refugee' is contingent on the situation and the interest that propels the body into action and gives it its *raison d'être*. Above all, legally authoritative definitions tend to prevail, although, in practice, they may be deviated from, again depending on the interests of the actors.

Even more recently, dedicated academic institutions have been set up to study specifically 'refugee' phenomena – for example, the Refugee Studies Programme in Oxford University established in 1982, now with its own *Journal of Refugee Studies* (JRS). This marks the coming into being of a discrete social scientific discipline in the form of 'refugee studies'. Such academic institutions are adjunctive to, and they mainly serve, the 'primary' actors in the refugee field already mentioned. In the first issue of the JRS in 1988, Zetter (1988, p 1) provides some reasons why the issue of refugees has become so important:

> But in the present century it is the word 'refugee' which has increasingly been deployed to describe the millions of uprooted people who have been forced into exile or displaced within their own countries because of intolerance, war or other human factors. 'Refugee' constitutes one of the most powerful labels currently in the repertoire of humanitarian concern, national and international public policy and social differentiation.

Yet, from a social scientific point of view, the prevalent legal definitions are found to be inadequate, and considerable thought has already been expended in the effort to come up with a workable definition of a 'refugee'. Again, Zetter (1988, p 5) seeks a distance from definitions arrived at in legal or administrative contexts. He would also exclude from the agenda of the JRS migrations which are seen as solely or largely generated by voluntary and self-determined decisions. He would place into the 'refugees' category displaced persons and asylum seekers within the context of *enforced* movement. For Zetter, the 1951 Geneva Convention on Refugees and its 1967 Protocol, the most widely ratified international law instruments, establish only a *de minimis* definition, and he points out that the scope for re-evaluation has still to be kept. Among others, Zolberg *et al* (1989, pp 1–33) also point to the inadequacies, for analytical purposes, of definitions based upon international legal norms. Instead, they point to the common element of the *fear of violence* as the prime cause of refugee movements. Richmond (1993) qualifies the usefulness of the model proposed by Zolberg *et al*, by pointing to the fact that fear of violence itself does not account for different behaviour in violent circumstances, nor for compelling circumstances which do not involve violence or the threat of it, but which are still extremely coercive. He proposes a complex, multivariate model of analysis centred on the concept of 'ontological security', which is seen as the prime motivator of refugee flight.

Five main determinants – political, economic, environmental, social and bio-psychological – are combined in pairs to give 25 finer categories which can be said to lie behind refugee movements. Therefore, while refugee phenomena are characterised by some circumstances which compel migration, it is difficult to delineate these with exactitude, and any definition will necessarily be open-ended.

1.2 RACE AND ITS VARIANT SIGNIFIERS

When making an attempt to introduce the concept of 'race' into a field of academic discussion, it appears obligatory to begin in an apologetic fashion. This is mainly due to the fact that, while discussions about race as an attribute of human beings have historically been central, they have been driven underground and disregarded as an appropriate point of departure in official discourses. Yet, in his study of race and international relations, Füredi (1998, p 5) writes that 'race was central to the identity of Western political elites. It was inextricably linked to the Western notion of 'civilisation', which on the ideological level at least informed international relations'. But he shows that cultural superiority expressed in the form of race became a source of anxiety by the end of the First World War. 'Racial thinking' became regarded in the Anglo-American world as having the potential to disrupt the world system; and, by the end of the Second World War, it was so discredited that considerable resources were expended to eliminate discussion of it in international affairs. Füredi (1998, p 2) notes, significantly, that the greatest influence on this shift took place as a result of resistance to Western domination.

> Ideas about race relations evolved in an attempt to minimise the danger of racial conflict. The impulse of pre-emption influenced the emergence of the early race relations industry. The main policy outcome of this discussion was the need to contain reactions to it. This attitude cannot be described as anti-racist. It expressed fears about racial conflict and demanded a pragmatism that amounted to a kind of voluntary self-censorship ... This lack of openness meant that it became all too easy to overlook the significance of race in international affairs.

Since the Second World War, however, fears about racial conflict to which Füredi refers were vocally expressed by Enoch Powell who, in 1968, publicly expressed a metaphorical prediction of rivers of blood through communalism if immigration of non-whites into Britain continued; 'the black man will have the whip hand over the white man' (Hiro, 1991, pp 246–47). The Powell experience indicates that, even after decolonisation, deep-seated fears of racial conflict could still be brought to the fore, and that they remained potent in the metropolitan centre itself. Nevertheless, proving Füredi's thesis, Powell was quickly dismissed from the shadow Cabinet, and the Heath regime later oversaw the policy of containing the immigration of Asians from East Africa, a policy that had been decided upon by the previous Labour Government.

In line with the censorship which today prevails over the direct raising of the perceived problems created by racial differences among groups, various other notions have come to replace 'race' as a category understood in a phenotypical or biological sense. Thus we encounter the respectable and prominent use of 'culture' or 'ethnicity' and now 'religion' (this last, particularly against Islamic traditions) as primary indicators of difference. Paul Gilroy (1993, p 65) makes the same point in another context when he speaks about the 'new culturalist racism as but one example of what might be called ethnic absolutism'. Further, indicators of difference are seldom used exclusively by themselves, but they interact with certain other oppositions that are made at the local, national and global levels. For example, labels of 'fundamentalist', 'polygamist' and 'patriarch', 'traditional', 'poor' and 'less developed' are opposed to qualities ideologically upheld in Western thinking such as 'liberal', 'monogamous' and 'equality seeking', 'modern' (even 'post-modern'), 'rich' and 'advanced'.

Such a 'culturalist' stance was taken by Margaret Thatcher, the former British Prime Minister, whose statement in January 1978 underscored the shift in terminology from 'race' to 'culture', and from 'war' to 'swamping':

> People are really afraid that this country might be rather swamped by people with a different culture. You know, the British character has done so much for democracy, for law, and done so much throughout the world, that if there is any fear that it might be swamped, people are going to react and be rather hostile to those coming in [Hiro, 1991, p ix].

Reacting in 1989 to the prospect of the Hong Kong Chinese being granted British citizenship with the right of abode in the UK, Norman Tebbit, a prominent MP and former Conservative Party chairman, echoed Thatcher by evoking images of Britain becoming swamped by people of a different history, culture and religion (Hiro, 1991, p x; Shah, 1995b, p 100).

The tendency to avoid questions of race also centrally affects more serious academic thinking in the field of immigration. Cohen's (1994) study on British reactions to the immigration of their presumed 'others' includes a discussion of asylum and can be cited as an example here. Cohen (1994, p 1) expresses a terminological reserve at the beginning of his study in the following sense:

> Those who are hostile to the expression of an exclusive British identity – or to the narrower English identity with which it is frequently conflated – often denounce a high level of xenophobia as 'racist'. While I use the term in the text, I do so with caution ... My wariness derives from a belief that the expressions 'racist' and 'racism' are often used thoughtlessly, as mere epithets. If so abused, the terms can serve to mask the dynamic and chameleon-like inventions and re-inventions of a complex social identity.

> We will need a finely tuned rapier, not just a clumsy blunderbuss, to penetrate the enigmatic nexus of unease, affinity, antipathy, empathy, conflict and distaste between the British and the rest of humankind.

When Cohen discusses the issue of asylum he cites 'reasons of State' and 'ethnic solidarity' as a mask for granting asylum on humanitarian grounds. By 'reasons of State' he probably means the various factors – 'economic', 'demographic' or 'political'. While his analysis certainly bears this out, he does not go on to explain why some groups of refugees experience (sometimes extreme) hostility from the State and why, in fact, their physical presence is not regarded as an economic, demographic or political asset. Rather than attempting to mount an analysis based on the racial origins of those rejected peoples, which other parts of the study would have supported, he simply bemoans the level of power assumed by State organs in the field of asylum (Cohen, 1994, p 97).

Cohen later explains his reasons for opting for a discussion based around the concept of 'otherness'. He first finds unsatisfactory the various meanings given for the term 'racism', stating that they have moved from biological or phenotypical, to being conflated with other indicators of difference which to him are socially, culturally or ideologically constructed. Cohen's preference for examining British reactions to their others appears more grounded in a reflexivity which he admits: '... discussions of Otherness easily admit more liberating possibilities of self-examination and auto-critique' (Cohen, 1994, p 199). However, in pursuing his concept of Otherness and, more fundamentally, by dismissing non-'racial' indicators of difference as merely constructed, Cohen misses the chance to investigate the continuities behind the older, explicitly racial classifications and the newly constructed 'culturalist' ones, as well as their relevance to the concept of asylum. In doing so he fails to deal with the fundamental question: which people are seen as permanently other than the British?

Some points of caution are nevertheless in order at this stage. Emphasising the centrality of race as a factor in the State's response to refugee movements is not to imply that solely racial factors are at work in the desire to control or not, as well as in the manner of control. Political and economic factors may provide other ways of exploring whether such other instrumentalities are at work in the State.[1] On the other hand, the portrayal of refugees or migrants as economic liabilities or as assets may itself reflect biases that are actually racially determined, but expressed in economic terms. This is evident from some of the data presented in this book, although this question is not explored in detail.

1 For a brief analysis of political factors at work in the construction of asylum law, see Shah (1999).

Another problem arises in the use of broad categories such as 'European' and 'non-European', 'white' and 'non-white'. These admittedly wide classifications should not be read to imply that even some European refugee groups have not had to face hostility from the State. The case of Jewish refugees arriving in Britain from the late 19th century onwards did result in the passage of the first permanent legislated controls on migration in Britain. This was after the politicisation of the 'alien' presence in Britain which more or less pinpointed the Jewish presence as a liability to the nation. However, one of the main aims here is to examine the State's response to European refugee migrations *in relation to* its reaction to non-European migrations. This will give a clearer picture of the extent to which, in Gilroy's words, a kind of 'ethnic absolutism' is at work in the processes of controlling refugee migrations.

1.3 ASYLUM AND THE LAW

The concept of asylum has sometimes been associated with the protection given to fugitives under the auspices of religious authorities in the form of 'sanctuary' (Carro, 1986). However, a contemporary account by Rabbi W Gunther Plaut (1995, p 11), still motivated by religious and ethical considerations, defines it thus:

> Asylum is a term which ... signifies refuge offered by a country. In the past, particular places served that function, such as an altar, a temple, or a church, a city or a ship. Today asylum generally indicates a nation where a refugee may find temporary or permanent shelter.

Grahl-Madsen (1980, p 52), one of the foremost international law scholars on the subject, defines asylum in a very similar manner, as:

> ... a right of an individual to stay in the territory of the State granting asylum: not permanently, but so long as he is in need of it; that is to say, so long as he remains a refugee, or until he acquires a right of residence in a third country.

Official accounts retain obeisance to the principle of asylum as having a long historical tradition in Britain. A Home Office memorandum of 1984 is an example of this:

> The UK, like most other Western European countries, has a long tradition of granting refuge to those who have fled their own countries to escape political or religious persecution ... an historical account ... would need to go back at least to the 16th century when the grant of asylum to those persecuted for their religious beliefs became commonplace. But it is worth noting that the first piece of modern immigration legislation – the Aliens Act 1905 – provided that anyone who sought asylum on political or religious grounds should be granted entry and should not be refused leave to land even if he was likely to fall a charge on public rates. In the same way today a valid claim for asylum

> overrides the normal requirements of immigration control that other immigrants must satisfy in order to enter or remain here.[2]

The present study is focused on the laws relating to the control of immigration. In this context, the two broad historical studies, by Bevan (1986) and Dummett and Nicol (1990), should be highlighted. Both are particularly useful in explaining the development of immigration (and nationality) laws in the UK and they particularly show how racial considerations have been instrumental in shaping those laws. Bevan (1986, p 11), for example, is forthright in saying that: 'Racial purity is frequently defended in terms of the necessary homogeneity of the host society. It has been a central plank of recent UK policy that coloured immigration has to be restricted to assist national racial harmony.' Legal practitioners, in particular Macdonald and Blake (1991, pp 8–19), also acknowledge that immigration legislation in the UK has generally been crucially informed by racial considerations. More focused studies of immigration law have reinforced the view that the racial composition of the UK has been uppermost in the minds of policy makers. Sanjiv Sachdeva's (1993) account of the 'primary purpose rule' in British immigration law leaves no doubt about that in the area of family reunification for South Asian spouses since the 1960s. An analysis of the development of British attitudes towards decolonisation in Hong Kong similarly shows that a paramount consideration was the maintenance of a fictive racial purity in Britain, in line with Norman Tebbit's views (Menski, 1995).

Still, the official position has been to emphasise that racial discrimination is not the intent of the immigration laws, by guaranteeing 'colour blindness'. For example, paragraph 6 of the Immigration Rules which were published in 1990 (as HC 251) told us that: 'Immigration officers will carry out their duties without regard to the race, colour or religion of people seeking to enter the United Kingdom.' More worrying still is the refusal to tackle head on the issue of race in a recent book by Jackson, some-time Vice-President of the Immigration Appeal Tribunal, at a time when the question of asylum assumed a central position in law-making and legal practice. Jackson (1996, p 1) writes:

> Immigration Rules in the UK are said by some to be both racist in purpose and racially applied; by others to be racially neutral but appearing to apply primarily to non-whites simply because predominantly they form the categories who, because of poor economic conditions at home, seek entry into this country. Regrettably the structure of immigration control in the United Kingdom has traditionally been and continues to be the result of reaction to

2 Home Office Memorandum (1984–85), *Third Report from the Home Affairs Committee, Refugees and Asylum with Special Reference to the Vietnamese*, p 67. See, also, Zolberg *et al* (1989, p 5), who account for the term 'refugees' and locate its first recorded use in 16th century Europe.

> events as they are seen to be, rather than planned development. Whatever the underlying reasons for control, there is no doubt that extensive control of entry into and residence in the UK is here to stay.

Jackson thus avoids dealing with the uncomfortable issue of race although successive studies have already amassed a considerable amount of material to demonstrate its key role in informing the law and practice of immigration control.

The question of asylum increasingly began to assume a prominent part in publications on British immigration law particularly since the early 1980s (see Grant and Martin, 1982, pp 322–46; Supperstone, 1982, pp 84–85, 111–12; Macdonald, 1983, pp 237–47). Most books concentrate on legal-rationalist explanations of refugee law, using existing doctrinal material and case law (for a more recent example, see Jackson, 1996, pp 322–88). Unfortunately, such approaches, while vital for lawyerly arguments, do not provide historically grounded explanatory frameworks. As a consequence, there is a failure to elaborate critiques which question the fictive racial neutrality that legal discourses endow the State's control of refugee movements. It will be assumed here that legal rationality does not provide a useful tool for understanding the racist dynamics of the legal frameworks that have been applicable to refugees. On the other hand, it is assumed that 'law' acts an instrument of, and a legitimation for, the exercise of State power.[3] This exercise will cause some difficulty for lawyers today who have to negotiate an uneasy role as intermediaries between refugees and the State, and who are constantly compelled to rely on legal-rational arguments as advocates and actors in the process of legal reform.

The prevalence of studies based on international refugee law should also be mentioned here. Although international co-ordination on asylum is a relatively recent phenomenon, the main basis of obtaining asylum in the UK and other Western countries is currently the Convention on Refugees of 1951 and its 1967 Protocol. Various texts attest to the importance of these instruments (Robinson, 1953; Weis, 1953; Grahl-Madsen, 1972; Goodwin-Gill, 1983 and 1996; Hathaway, 1991). Yet, the existing commentaries tend to be formalistic or jurisprudential analyses, and do not generally discuss the racism inherent in the control of refugee movements. At times, however, an implicit racism is reintroduced through the use of legalistic categories. For example, Hathaway (1991) provides a consolidation of doctrine and case law almost exclusively from Western States. He makes an artificial distinction between refugees who fear migration prompted by a fear of persecution on

3 Adopting this assumption should not be taken to mean that State law provides the only means of legal ordering. On the other hand, it has to read with the acknowledgment that legal ordering by a State may in fact seek to displace or disregard other legal orders in existence. This is particularly shown by legal studies on the presence of ethnic minorities in Britain (see Pearl and Menski, 1998, pp 51–83; Jones and Welhengama, 2000).

the ground of civil and political status and who are thereby protected within the 1951 Convention system and 'most Third World refugees ... [whose] flight is more often prompted by natural disaster, war, or broadly based political and economic turmoil than by "persecution", at least as that term is understood in a Western context' (Hathaway, 1991, p 9). This is another way of saying that Third World refugees are not entitled to protection under international refugee instruments drafted for European refugees.

Such subtly phrased distinctions which are justified through arguments based on international law are also supported by the UK domestic courts. In the *Adan* case, Lord Lloyd recently declared that 'it is academic writers in the field who provide the best hope of reaching international consensus on the meaning of the Convention' and, referring to Hathaway's work, allowed the Home Office to continue denying refugee status to Somalis in Britain.[4] It is interesting that here was a group of 'Third World' refugees who would, in fact, have qualified as statutory refugees under the relevant international instruments; albeit that the House of Lords chose to depart from previously accepted doctrinal points related to their interpretation (Shah, 1998a). In another recent case, Waite LJ spoke of the need:

> ... as part of the price of achieving international acceptability, to impose limits on the definition of refugee status by abandoning a general recognition of rights of asylum whenever they are seen to be justified on broad humanitarian grounds and imposing instead a formalistic requirement to fulfil specific category qualifications.[5]

In the same case, Staughton LJ provided a quasi-constitutional rationalisation for a restrictive interpretation of international law:

> This restrictive attitude [in the Convention and Protocol] must be the deliberate choice of States that adopt the Convention, and in the case of States with a democratic system of government, must ultimately reflect the will of the people who are already citizens of those States. One may criticise that attitude but one cannot deny that it exists. The tension between humanitarian concern on the one hand and self-interest on the other has produced in this country the whole elaborate apparatus of immigration control, with immigration officers, adjudicators, appeal tribunals, judicial review and a greater burden on the Civil Division of the Court of Appeal than any other topic.[6]

Thus, refugees have, in effect, been nationalised through the liberal democratic process, which has given rise to an entire system of controls and employment for so many personnel with authoritarian power. However, what exactly the self-interests Staughton LJ refers to are, we are not told, nor whether they resemble Cohen's 'reasons of State', or Jackson's 'circumstances

4 *Secretary of State for the Home Department v Adan* [1998] Imm AR 338.

5 *Secretary of State for the Home Department v Shah* [1997] Imm AR 584, p 598.

6 *Ibid*, p 603

as they are seen to be', again underlining the potential of legalistic arguments as a cover for racist practices. Nevertheless, the relevant point for the present is that international laws are also not adopted or applied in a vacuum, and can be utilised for restrictive purposes. This study therefore avoids the temptation of discussing whether a certain domestic law or practice is, or can be argued to be, against an international law.

1.4 SCHEME OF THIS BOOK

Several cases of group migration, from the Tudor to the Victorian periods of British history, are considered in Chapter 2: gypsies and Huguenots; refugees from the French Revolution; Africans who were admitted as free persons after fighting on the British side in the American War of Independence; and various groups of political exiles from different European countries. The discussion is related to the debate on the existence in these earlier periods of a Royal Prerogative power to exclude those regarded as 'aliens', and the last section (see 2.5) carries a discussion of how the dominant legal approach was rewritten in response to immigration of mainly 'Asiatics' to the white settler colonies. The first permanent controls on immigration into the UK were instituted in the Aliens Act of 1905, after the problematisation of the migration of Jews from Eastern Europe to urban centres in Britain. The treatment of Jewish migrants under this legislation is considered in Chapter 3. Simultaneously with this attention on the settlement of Jews, small groups of gypsies were also arriving in Britain, and their contrasting treatment is also considered in Chapter 3.

Chapter 4 documents the treatment of refugees, mainly Jews, fleeing from spreading Nazism in continental Europe prior to the Second World War, and the admission of 'displaced persons' from Europe and demobilised Polish soldiers after the war. In addition to the regulation of immigration under the domestic legal regime, the significance of the emergent internationalisation of the refugee protection system is discussed. This includes the institution of the Intergovernmental Committee on Refugees before the Second World War and the United Nations Relief and Rehabilitation Administration and the International Refugee Organisation afterwards. A discussion of the significance, at the time, of the Refugee Convention of 1951 is also presented, together with the UK's approach to European refugees during the deepening Cold War.

The situation of refugees from the British Commonwealth is covered in Chapter 5. The transformation of the applicable regime from a paradigm of imperial control to one centred on immigration control is first described. Two case studies, of Asian migration from Kenya and Uganda, are then discussed, with an evaluation of the Commonwealth Immigrants Act 1968 and the quota voucher scheme applied to control their entry. Challenges to the restrictive controls in the domestic courts and in the European human rights institutions are also discussed. The limited scope of the Refugee Convention of 1951 was expanded by the Protocol of 1967. The relevance of the Protocol, both at the international and domestic level, is evaluated in Chapter 6. Chapter 6 also carries a discussion of the changing legal regime applicable to refugees up until the early 1980s, by which time a general shift in the origin of refugees had been identified. The chapter concludes with the case of refugees from Vietnam who were admitted outside this general legal framework as part of an international scheme.

There follows, in Chapter 7, a detailed discussion of the arrival and treatment of Tamil refugees from Sri Lanka. The reasons for their migration and the problems encountered in their gaining legal recognition at the domestic level are covered. The case of the Tamils also provides another instance of refugees resorting to the European human rights institutions after experiencing difficulties at the domestic level, and the European litigation is discussed in light of the hostile reactions against Tamil settlement in Western European countries generally. The final substantive chapter carries a discussion of developments in the 1990s when three major pieces of legislation – the Asylum and Immigration Appeals Act 1993, the Asylum and Immigration Act 1996 and the Immigration and Asylum Act 1999 – aimed at controlling the admission and recognition of refugees were passed in the UK. The reasons for enacting this legislation, and its impact upon refugees, is considered in light of the increasing emphasis on controlling migration into Western Europe at the European Union level.

CHAPTER 2

ENGLAND'S 'FREE AIR'

2.1 GYPSIES AND HUGUENOTS

This account begins with the gypsy groups who arrived in Britain in the 16th century. Having travelled from Northern India, they came from the Balkans, upon being uprooted from their settled communities and occupations and pushed towards Western Europe (Holmes, 1988, p 24). The case of the gypsies who came to Britain appears to be paradigmatic in several senses. First, they are an early example, in the so called 'modern' period of English history, of a distinct non-European people recorded as having migrated to Britain more or less forcibly due, in their case, to the persecution they faced in other European countries. Secondly, the treatment of gypsy groups arriving in Britain is marked by a hostility which has reproduced itself through the centuries, right down to the present day. The small gypsy groups which arrived in the early 1900s, and again in the late 1990s, were treated in remarkably similar ways.

There are some sketchy records of Henry VIII's distaste for gypsy groups in the histories of gypsies by Kenrick and Puxon (1972, pp 25, 45) and Fraser (1992, pp 114–17). In an Act of 1530, Henry declared of gypsies that 'from hensforth, no suche Psone be suffred to come within this Kynge's Realme'. If they did, their goods would be forfeit to the Crown and they would be ordered to leave the country within 15 days, on pain of imprisonment. One such case was of Paul 'Faa' who was ordered to leave the country in 1537. In May 1540, a number of gypsies were shipped to Norway from Boston, Lincolnshire and, between 1530 and 1554, some 14 other deportations have been recorded, together with injunctions from the Privy Council to sheriffs and justices of the peace to exercise vigilance. Further, an abortive piece of anti-gypsy legislation was also passed in 1545, towards the end of Henry VIII's reign. Although no particular dates are given for the incidents, according to Kenrick and Puxon (1972, p 45), France and England pushed gypsies back and forth across the English Channel. From England, they were deported to Boulogne and Calais and, having moved away from the port towns, they were hounded again by the French authorities. Although the more recent historical studies have indicated the presence of gypsies in 16th century England, the legal literature has apparently not acknowledged these events, and has not therefore accounted for them in legal speculation about the powers inherent in the Crown to prevent people from coming to Britain or to expel them. For example, Craies (1890, pp 33–34), who made a forceful argument against the idea that the Crown possessed any such power, admitted that: 'I have not been able to trace any case of the exclusion or expulsion of aliens from England in the 16th century, except in the case of Jesuits and one or two plotting ambassadors in Elizabeth's reign.' This is an early expression, not so much of 'colour blindness', but of legal silence, indicative of exclusionary mechanisms directed against some racial groups which could operate outside of legal debates altogether.

The treatment the gypsies received can be contrasted with that given to refugees who came to Britain in the context of religious strife among Christian groups on the European continent. The contrast holds not only because of the quality of their reception, but also because of their subsequent metamorphosis into the exemplary group of refugees to which the English State extended the principle of asylum. In 1535 and 1536, Henry VIII granted naturalisation papers to 45 Huguenots, soon after he had freed himself of papal jurisdiction. In the Low Countries, the Spanish Viceroy, the Duke of Alva, began, from 1567, to persecute Protestants, reaching a peak in the succeeding decades. The consequent admission of Flemings under Queen Elizabeth proved beneficial to English industry, and was at the time regarded as such. Elizabeth herself granted letters patent in 1564 for 'strangers from the Netherlands' who had landed at Sandwich to come to Norwich, whose mayor and sheriff had asked the Duke of Norwich to intervene with the Queen. Meanwhile, Protestants in France were under threat since the death of Henry II in 1559, after which a 30 year period of war ensued. In 1572, when the massacre on St Bartholomew's day claimed 70,000 victims in various parts of France, refugees crossed the English Channel; almost the entire population of Dieppe, together with many from Rouen and the surrounding areas of Normandy, came to England (Roche, 1969, pp 33–36; Chitty 1966). It has been noted that the Huguenots, of all the refugees who came to England, were:

> ... one of the most beneficial and widely welcomed by the native population ... with their intelligence, steadfastness, culture and love of liberty; they represented the seafaring and outward looking people of France, suiting England's new westward look across the Atlantic and also the new spirit of Protestantism [Roche, 1969, pp 36–37].

Not all the Protestant groups were welcomed equally in England, however. Anabaptists, a name which denoted a variety of revolutionaries and religious extremists, and other 'such-like heretics' who had come under the colour of avoiding persecution, were ordered in 1561 to leave the realm within 20 days or suffer imprisonment and confiscation of goods. In 1568, the Archbishop of Canterbury was ordered to compile a register of the Dutch immigrants who had fled Spanish rule and all who were found to hold Anabaptist views were to leave the country or be put to death. Catholics too were treated as undesirables or 'fifth columnists' and, in 1571, Queen Elizabeth exercised her royal prerogative to require them to withdraw from the realm; another order was issued in 1588 (Roche, 1969, pp 35, 39). The phobia against Catholics and

Spaniards continued until after the threat of any Spanish invasion had died away by 1597 (Roche, 1969, pp 35–40; Dummett and Nicol, 1990, p 57).

Nearly a century later, in the autumn of 1685, one of the principal waves of Huguenot refugees was seen in England, after the revocation of the Edict of Nantes in October. Since 1598, and after four decades of civil war, that Edict had enabled the co-existence of the Protestant minority with Catholic France. In the 20 years prior to 1685, attempts had been made to make it impossible for people to be born, work, marry and die as Calvinists. Many had started to leave before the Edict of Nantes was revoked. The total outflow is estimated at 200,000 between 1681 and 1720. Apart from those who settled in Britain, others went to the Netherlands, Switzerland, Brandenburg-Prussia, some went to Russia, the British colonies of North America and the Dutch colony in Southern Africa (Zolberg *et al*, 1989, p 6).

The case of the Huguenots has, since their settlement, continuously been used as a paradigmatic instance of refugees receiving asylum in legal and non-legal literature. According to the social/political scientists, Zolberg *et al* (1989, pp 5–6), the Huguenots' refugee character derives from the fact that they became the victims of the dynamics of absolutist State formation and:

> As persons whose flight can be clearly be attributed to the fear of persecution on account of religion, the Huguenots would certainly qualify as statutory refugees under the current definition. Indeed, they provide a historical model of the classic type of refugees, still relevant today.

Indeed, an indication of the legal relevance of the Huguenots has also been consistently claimed in England. In 1816, the example of the Huguenots' flight to England was used to argue against a royal prerogative to exclude aliens, which had been asserted in a bid to gain parliamentary approval for 'ancillary' deportation powers. If the power had existed, it was stated, then James II would have used it to prevent the Protestant subjects of his ally and friend Louis XIV from settling in England. James was known to entertain religious and political views which made it improbable that such aliens could have found an asylum in Britain, it was argued, had the Crown been invested with such a prerogative.[1] For Bevan (1986, p 53), a historian of immigration law, the acceptance by England of Huguenots in the 16th and 17th centuries 'can be seen as the start of that '*tradition of compassion*' for refugees which has lasted, however variably and thinly, until the present day'. By contrast, the treatment of the gypsies is not given such acknowledgment, an indication that

1 Lord Holland, Parliamentary Debates, vol 34, col 1067, 11 June 1816, and the Marquis of Salisbury, col 1136. May's *Constitutional History of England* (1906) declared: 'It has been a proud distinction for England to afford an inviolable asylum to men of every rank and condition, seeking refuge on her shores, from persecution in their own lands. England was a sanctuary to the Flemish refugees driven by the cruelties of Alva; to the Protestant refugees who fled from the persecutions of Louis XIV; and to the Catholic nobles and priests who fled from the bloody guillotine of revolutionary France ...' (1965) 6 British Digest of International Law 43.

the foundations of the tradition of asylum in Britain are built on British relationships with European refugees, and that this tradition of asylum has not been extended evenly among racial or ethnic groups. This trend continued right into the 19th century and beyond.

2.2 REFUGEES FROM THE FRENCH REVOLUTION AND THE NAPOLEONIC WARS

In 1793, France went to war with Britain, Spain, Holland, Prussia and Austria. In the same year, an Act was passed to regulate and expel foreigners, the first Aliens Act.[2] Lord Loughborough, who later became Lord Chancellor, stated that, whereas in 1588 the country had been threatened with religious fanaticism, now the country was threatened with an enemy inspired by the 'fanaticism of infidelity'. It seems that the form of immigration particularly objected to was that of political propagandists (Sibley and Elias, 1906, pp 38–39; Roche, 1969, pp 47–48). Aliens had to declare in writing their names, rank, occupation or description, and masters of any vessel had to supply these details to customs officers. No alien was permitted to depart from a place of arrival unless he had a 'passport' quoting the town or place where he proposed to go. Magistrates could demand of an alien his 'passport' and could detain him until the King's instructions were received. All aliens had to register with the chief magistrate or the justice of the peace, giving his name, rank, occupation or description, place of abode, and place(s) where he had resided in the past six months. A system of internal control to closely monitor movements was thus set up (Bevan, 1986, pp 58–60; Roche, 1969, pp 48–53; Sibley and Elias, 1906, pp 40–41).[3]

The powers under this legislation were altered by succeeding statutes, depending on whether there was a period of antagonism or rapprochement between France and Britain.[4] In 1798, another Act was passed which allowed the Secretary of State to arrest any person for being a 'dangerous person' and to detain him or order him to leave the Kingdom.[5] An alien had to further

2 An Act for establishing regulations respecting aliens arriving in this Kingdom, or resident therein, in certain cases, 33 Geo III, c 4.

3 Sibley and Elias (1906, pp 40–41) also mention that 'regulations for the discovery of aliens were imposed on the keepers of inns and lodging houses, to be enforced by the punishment of transportation'. See, also, Bevan (1986, p 59) to similar effect.

4 The measures since the 1793 Act and before the Act of 1826, as given by Sibley and Elias (1906, p 37), were 38 Geo II, c 50, 77; 41 Geo III, c 24; 42 Geo III, c 93; 43 Geo III, c 155; 54 Geo III, c 155; 55 Geo III, c 54; 56 Geo II, c 86; 58 Geo III, c 96; 1 Geo IV, c 105; 3 Geo IV, c 97; 5 Geo IV, c 37. They also state that these statutes were all limited in their duration, either for a period of two years, or until the cessation of hostilities (p 45).

5 38 Geo III, c 50. Alien merchants were exempt from the restrictions and, although they had to carry passports, they were 'given full liberty to pass and re-pass to and from all parts of the Kingdom' (Sibley and Elias 1906, p 40n).

state to 'the inspector of aliens' (a generic term) the reason for leaving the country whence he had come (Bevan, 1986, p 61; Sibley and Elias, 1906, p 56). The need to protect refugees was nevertheless underlined. The preamble of the 1798 Act alluded to persons who 'really seek refuge and asylum from oppression and tyranny', in what appears to be the first statutory mention of the right to asylum (Sibley and Elias, 1906, p 131). At the height of the revolution, there were some 80,000 French refugees who had emigrated to England (Roche, 1969, pp 47–48). After a brief Anglo-French rapprochement in 1802 with the Treaty of Amiens, Napoleon (as the First Consul of the French Republic) demanded of Lord Hawkesbury, the Secretary of State, that the British Government should remove:

> ... out of the British Dominions all the French princes and their adherents, together with the bishops and other individuals, whose political principles and conduct must necessarily occasion great jealousy to the French Government [Sibley and Elias, 1906, p 126].

Lord Hawkesbury replied that His Majesty:

> ... certainly expects all those foreigners who reside within his dominions should not only hold a conduct conformable to the laws of the country, but should abstain from all acts which may be hostile to the government of any country with which His Majesty may be at peace. As long, however, as they conduct themselves according to these principles, His Majesty would feel it inconsistent with his dignity, with his honour and with the common laws of hospitality, to deprive them of that protection which individuals resident in his dominions can only forfeit by their own misconduct [Sibley and Elias, 1906, p 126].[6]

With the return of hostilities, another statute, passed in 1803, repealed the Act of 1798 and gave the Secretary of State the power to expel aliens by proclamation on mere suspicion (Roche, 1969, pp 53–54, Sibley and Elias, 1906, p 37).[7] In 1803, an attempted deportation of about 1,700 French subjects seems to have been made, but not being permitted to land 'on the continent', they were ultimately allowed to take up residence in Britain.[8]

By 1816, the use of the powers in the earlier legislation declined as fewer people were declared as having been arrested and sent out of Britain and Ireland.[9] An Act of that year provided the Crown with a new power to deport individuals, but Lord Aberdeen sought to assure the House of Lords that the aim of the Bill was to exclude active mischief, not to shut out the oppressed or

---

6 Hawkesbury's reply of 28 August 1802 also dealt with the position of named persons whom the French Government had been unhappy to see residing in England. It is reprinted in detail in (1965) 6 British Digest of International Law 43, pp 45–48.

7 43 Geo III, c 155.

8 This event is footnoted in a return to Parliament of the number of persons arrested and sent out of the UK from 1793 to 29 April 1816 (Parliamentary Papers, vol XII, no 273, p 281 (1816)).

9 *Ibid.*

persecuted.[10] Lord Ellenborough, the Lord Chancellor, took the opportunity to cite the authority of Vattel, the international jurist, to substantiate the claim that *not only the British Crown*, but *all* sovereigns, had the authority to send aliens away.[11] Lord Holland appeared to be the fiercest critic of the new powers: he felt that there was something abhorrent to the feelings of Englishmen in placing in the hands of ministers the power of expelling aliens who disapproved of the principles of the House of Bourbon, and who sought asylum in Britain. How would ministers know that these refugees were violent or dangerous men?[12] He even deemed it to be in violation of the constitution.[13] The Marquis of Salisbury feared the fate of Spanish refugees who were being exposed to the vengeance of Ferdinand, as well as that of the French refugees.[14]

The power to expel aliens in the 1793 Act and in subsequent legislation was repealed in 1826, once the Napoleonic fever was over, and replaced with an Act for the Registration of Aliens,[15] which contained none of the earlier powers of exclusion. The registration requirement imposed in 1826 for all aliens was generally disregarded by aliens themselves after 1836 and was not enforced by the authorities (Porter, 1979, pp 3–4, 9).[16] In 1836, another Act reduced the requirements to an obligation upon the master of a ship to deliver to the chief officer of customs a list of aliens in his ship, and each passenger was obliged to declare his name, the country of which he was a subject and the date and place of his landing (Plender, 1988, p 67; Roche, 1969, pp 56–57).[17]

Thus, a system of national defence against perceived alien subversion was gradually dismantled over the 30 years. Hobhouse, an opponent of the earlier restrictions, had complained that they were:

> ... part of a new European system of general police ... part of that system which is to make Great Britain an accomplice in the conspiracy against the liberties of

10 Parliamentary Debates, vol 34, col 1062, 11 June 1816.

11 *Ibid*, col 1069.

12 *Ibid*, col 1083. Earlier, Holland had noted that 'deportation' and 'surveillance' were foreign terms, not to be found in an English dictionary, *ibid*, cols 1068–69. Some strong speeches against the measure were also made in the House of Commons, *ibid*, cols 78–81, 430–80, 617–33.

13 *Ibid*, col 1144.

14 *Ibid*, cols 1136–37.

15 7 Geo IV, c 54. A record of the numbers of persons sent out of Britain from 1816–1924 showed a further decline since 1816. In 1820 and 1822, no persons were sent away and the highest number was in 1818 when there were six persons removed (Parliamentary Papers, vol XVI, no 132, p 495 (1824)).

16 The authorities' non-enforcement of this provision was noted in the Report from the Select Committee on the Laws Affecting Aliens (Parliamentary Papers, vol V, no 307, pp 145, 153 (1843)), quoted in Porter (1979, p 3).

17 6 & 7 William IV, c xi. The requirement for an alien to declare his personal details was predicated on the assumption that it need not be done immediately on landing and could be done by writing rather than verbally (Roche, 1969, pp 56–57).

mankind, and is to degrade our English Minister for the Home Department into a mere runner for the continental cabinets.[18]

Such a statement is an example of the British nationalism that was to support the principle of asylum against perceived foreign interference for the rest of the 19th century, when it appeared to underpin a concept of 'Britishness' which could be opposed to continental despotism. It is in the second quarter of the 19th century that the historian of English law, Holdsworth (1938, pp 399–400), places the ascendancy of 'that sentimental vein in political thought, and more especially in Whig political thought ... which led many to object to a prerogative power which might be used to hand back escaped slaves to their owners, or revolutionaries to their despotic rulers'. Yet, while the history of escaped black slaves and continental revolutionaries contributed to the rhetorical development of the principle of asylum, it is apparent that, in practice, the two groups were treated wholly differently in Britain.

2.3 THE TREATMENT OF AFRICAN REFUGEES

Since the 16th century, England, along with other European nations, had actively participated in the slave trade, which created conditions of forced exile and labour for millions of Africans around the Atlantic Ocean. As historical studies show, the traffic of African people received sanction from, and yielded profits for, the centre of the English State. John Hawkins, upon his return to England after his first slavery voyage in 1562–63, formed an African company out of the leading citizens of London, and Queen Elizabeth provided a ship and became a shareholder in his second voyage (Bindoff, 1950, pp 252–53; Ramdin, 1999, pp 10–14; Rodney, 1982, p 83; Ruchames, 1967, pp 258–59). When an increasing number of Africans were seen in Britain, Elizabeth blamed them for the endemic poverty and hunger prevalent at the time and she twice attempted, albeit unsuccessfully, to have Africans forcibly removed from the island (Fryer, 1984, p 10–12; Walvin, 1971, p 61).[19] Ramdin (1999, p 14), in his book on the black and Asian presence in Britain, notes that in spite of Elizabeth's efforts to prevent the settlement of Africans in Britain:

> As the slave trade grew, in addition to direct importations from Africa, more and more black people entered Britain via slavery in the West Indies and the North American colonies where, especially after the War of Independence, the black slaves who had fought on the British side were promised their freedom.

---

18 Parliamentary Debates, 2nd series, vol 2, col 407, 12 July 1820, quoted in Porter (1979, p 71).

19 Walvin (1971, pp 64–65) has an extract of one such proclamation issued by Elizabeth in 1601, and Fryer (1984, pp 10–12) gives extracts of two letters written in 1596 by Elizabeth to officials in various cities, including London, to assist in the forcible removal of Africans.

The reception actually received by these 'freed' persons may be seen in the light of the continuing difficulty in establishing freedom once in Britain.

The celebrated *Somersett* case, which was interpreted in America and, to some extent, in Britain as having emancipated slaves in England, was actually more limited in its implications. In 1769, John Somersett had sailed from Boston to England as the slave of Charles Stewart whereupon Somersett escaped. However, he was captured and was about to be shipped for sale in Jamaica, when his friends took court action. Lord Mansfield LCJ, who ruled on the case, himself had an interest in slavery. He also owed his rise to the patronage of Talbot, Solicitor General, and Yorke, first Attorney General and later Lord Chancellor, both of whom had opined earlier in the century that a slave was not free the moment he set foot in England (Fryer, 1984, pp 113–26). Mansfield held for Somersett on the narrow ground that 'No master ever was allowed here to take a slave by force to be sold abroad because he had deserted from service, or for any other reason whatsoever' (Nadelhaft, 1967, p 194).[20] Ramdin (1999, p 15) states, in relation to the *Somersett* ruling, that:

> Even this decision was not enough to stop the taking of slaves by force from England, because the 1772 judgment did not provide adequate protective cover for 'free' black persons in England against unlawful enslavement. In effect, they remained vulnerable, having to wait another 62 years before ... they were emancipated like their fellow Africans on the plantations.

The reluctance to recognise the free state of black people in Britain was evident again in the case of the black soldiers who had fought on the British side in the American War of Independence (Fryer, 1984, pp 191–202; Ramdin, 1999, pp 17–24). Tens of thousands of black men had opted to fight or serve in other capacities on the British side in the American war, upon a British promise made in 1779 that freedom would be granted to them. After the conflict ended, thousands escaped to Canada, but many hundreds also came to London, where many suffered destitution. A relief programme was set up, eligibility for which was made conditional upon their accepting to be transported to Sierra Leone. This private money making scheme was helped by funding from the Treasury which was eager to see the black people removed. The coercion was tightened by the Lord Mayor of London who ordered the city's marshals and constables to round up any blacks found begging in the streets and to force them to be 'sent home'. The prominent

20 Many black people, determined not to continue in servitude, voted with their feet where they could. It seems that some magistrates since the early 1740s ignored the rulings of the higher courts by refusing to recognise black slaves as property and by setting black petitioners free. Similarly, some of the higher courts would entertain writs of habeas corpus to stowaways who had escaped from slavery in the West Indies and who were locked up on ships or in English ports. Thus, before the de-legalisation of the British slave trade in 1807, the process of emancipation had slowly begun to be recognised (Fryer, 1984, pp 203–07). The Scottish courts were, at that time, clearer in their view that the state of slavery could not be recognised under law 'in this Kingdom' (Fryer, 1984, pp 126–27).

black activist Olaudah Equiano had officially been appointed the commissary of the black poor, but he was branded a troublemaker due to his outspoken opposition to the 'repatriation' scheme and worries about safety of the journey. One voyage left England in 1787 with some 85 people dying on the way. Some 374 reached Sierra Leone, at which point they either died, were sold into slavery again or left homeless due to a conflict between an American slave ship, a British man of war and a local ruler.

By the 19th century, Britain built up a naval strength thanks to the exploitation of people in slavery and labour acquired through colonial expansion.[21] With the onset of the abolitionist phase in British history, which accompanied advocacy of direct imperial domination of Africa, the attitude towards slavery changed into a paternalistic humanitarianism which was directed against other Western powers' (Turley, 1980) and Arab States' (Howell, 1987) continuation of trading in Africans. This change of attitude also affected the legal debates on the right of asylum under English law. The cases that emerged demonstrate how the principle of asylum was applied by Britain against other States for the promotion of abolition in situations where slaves had found their way onto overseas British territories or had been taken on board British ships. On the other hand, there was only a gradual acceptance of the principle that slavery was not permitted on British soil, especially where the interests of slavers in the West Indies and the Americas were concerned. Meanwhile, the presence of black people in Britain was not tolerated, as the Sierra Leone experiment revealed. Despite the elapse of almost two centuries since the abolition of slavery, hostility against the presence of Africans remained a reality in late 20th century Britain.

2.4 THE EUROPEAN REFUGEES IN THE VICTORIAN PERIOD

As already seen, the principle of asylum was raised at several historical junctures to defend the possibility of settlement of various groups of European refugees, while quite the opposite tendency was evident in the case of African and gypsy refugee groups. It acquired a constitutional status from the Victorian period and, importantly, with reference to the right of various European refugee groups' continued settlement in Britain. Porter's (1979) study on *The Refugee Question in Mid-Victorian Politics* offers the most detailed analysis of the situation of European refugees in early to mid-Victorian

21 Visram (1986, pp 34–54) records the plight of 'lascars' (sailors who had been recruited from India) and Chinese men who manned British ships from the East since the 18th century. Once in Britain, they were often abandoned and literally froze due to inadequate means, clothing or accommodation. Several plans emerged to remove them from Britain, but nobody seemed to be willing to bear the financial burden.

Britain. He suggests, with a slight exaggeration, that the British authorities 'from 1823 right through the 19th century did not expel a single refugee from Britain, or prohibit a single one of them from coming in. Britain consequently was the most dependable of all European asylums, for everybody' (Porter, 1979, p 1).[22]

In the 1830s and 1840s, the various European refugees waged a campaign of words and were possibly involved in conspiracies abroad, but these grounds did not generally awaken a serious interest in them from the point of view of the British authorities. There was a fear of being watched among refugees, as indeed they were, by police informers, and they seemed conscious of the imminence of an Aliens Act if they overstepped the mark.[23] Radical German and Polish refugees formed links with the British Chartists and, for the duration of the Aliens Act of 1848, some of these links were underplayed due to the fear of possible action on the part of the authorities. On the whole, however, the refugees did not show an interest in British political movements. There was also not much love lost between the republicans, democrats and socialists, on the one hand, and the British upper and middle classes, on the other. There was a poor response to calls for help to alleviate the plight of the many indigent refugees, who had to compete with local poverty for charity.

In 1848, a sequence of risings in Italy, France, Austria, Germany, Belgium, Hungary and Switzerland (see, generally, Thomson, 1966, pp 204–34) led to a new wave of refugees coming to Britain (see Payne and Grosshans, 1963, on French refugees). Fears that Republican influences would radicalise the domestic population or incite riots inspired the British Government to finally enact an Aliens Act in the same year.[24] The Act gave a power to the Secretary of State and the Lord Lieutenant of Ireland to expel any alien who he had reason to believe (from information given to him in writing) threatened 'the Preservation of the Peace and Tranquillity of any part of this Realm'.[25] Any alien so expelled was entitled to know the reasons for his expulsion and to appeal to the Privy Council against an expulsion (with a facility to summon

22 Several groups of refugees were actually paid by the British Government (which tried to keep the matter secret) to go to the US. Between 1850 and 1858, more than 1,500 were induced to leave. The refugees received the cost of the fare to America and some spending money (about £10). In particular, this method was applied in the case of Polish refugees from Malta in 1850 and Poles and Hungarians released from Turkey in 1851 (Porter, 1979, pp 160–62).

23 Before 1851, intelligence on the activities of refugees was *ad hoc* and irregular. The police seem to have had little ability to infiltrate the refugee networks and spies had to be relied on. During the course of 1851, surveillance was made more systematic, regular and professional and there was deeper collaboration with foreign governments, either through direct police links, or through diplomatic channels (Porter, 1979, pp 150–60).

24 An Act to authorise for one year, and to the end of the then next session of Parliament, the removal of aliens from the realm (11 & 12 Vict, c 20).

25 Foreign ambassadors, children under 14 and any aliens who had lived in Britain for longer than three years were exempt from expulsion (Porter, 1979, p 86).

and examine witnesses on oath). The care taken to provide protection against expulsion contrasts quite favourably with the modern law of expulsion on the basis of national security, applicable to refugees and other non-British citizens (see Shah, 1998b). The Aliens Act of 1848, however, was not enforced against anyone and it was allowed to lapse in the summer of 1850.[26]

The presence of the refugees came into question as a result of the possible disruption to foreign relations rather than for considerations of domestic policy. In the 1830s and 1840s, only 'mild representations' were made or 'informal pressures' were applied to Britain about the activities of refugees on its soil. However, complaints made to Britain by the continental powers continued in the aftermath of the 1848 uprisings and began to push the refugee question to the front of the diplomatic stage. The temperature rose considerably when, through the early to mid-1850s, *coups, attentats*, or assassination attempts, occurred on the continent and were immediately assumed by continental countries to have been hatched in Britain, sometimes justifiably.[27] One published diplomatic note complained that the activities of the refugees (including the issue of coupons of loans by Italian refugees; conspiracies concluded in meetings among German, Italian and French refugees; the circulation of literature; and Kossuth's campaigns to enlist support for the refugees' causes), if allowed to continue under English law, amounted to a breach of the law of nations as declared by Vattel.[28] The British Government resisted such diplomatic pressure from its continental counterparts by playing down the threats which the refugees' activities in Britain could have on the latter's security. However, there was a more deeprooted reason for British reluctance to interfere with the right of asylum. It was genuinely felt, as opposed to Britain's view of itself as a liberal country, that continental countries invited protest and reacted with repression contrary to the natural order of things. The better approach would be to enable moderate liberal institutions to act as a safety valve and prevent dissatisfaction from overflowing into socialism and violence.

26 The Return showing the number of aliens directed to depart the Realm, states that no aliens were removed from Great Britain or Ireland under the 1848 Act (Parliamentary Papers, vol XXXIII, no 688, p 227 (1850)). It was formally repealed by the Statute Law Revision Act of 1875, 'an act of legislation that seems to have been clearly supererogatory, since, by s 7 of the [1848] Removal of Aliens Act, its duration was limited to one year' (Sibley and Elias, 1906, p 37n).

27 Porter (1979, p 200) suggests that the high point of European agitation against Britain over refugees had been in the months between the autumn of 1851 and the spring of 1853, when it involved several continental powers together. After that, the problem came up intermittently, mainly in the relations with France.

28 Further Correspondence respecting the Foreign Refugees in London, Parliamentary Papers, vol LIV, no 1464, pp 81, 85–87 (1852). The quotation by Vattel (from his *Law of Nations*, Liv 11, col v, s 64) read: 'All nations, therefore, are strictly bound to cultivate justice among themselves; to observe it scrupulously; to abstain carefully from everything which can prejudice it. Each should render to others what is due to them; should respect their rights; should leave them in peaceable enjoyment thereof.'

Other published diplomatic correspondence reveals the strength with which the principle of asylum was defended with other countries. In 1849, a number of the Hungarian revolutionary forces, together with Kossuth and a number of Poles who had assisted their cause, had taken refuge in Ottoman territory. The Austrian Government made representations to the Turkish Government, which had consulted the British and French ambassadors for their views. The British reply was unequivocal:

> Now, if there is one rule which more than another has been observed in modern times by all independent States, both great and small, of the civilised world, it is the rule not to deliver up political refugees, unless the State is bound to do so by positive obligations of a treaty; and Her Majesty's Government believes that such treaty engagements are few – if, indeed, any such exist.
>
> The laws of hospitality, the dictates of humanity, the general feelings of mankind, forbid such surrenders; and any independent government, which of its free will were to make such a surrender, would be deservedly and universally stigmatised as degraded and dishonoured ...[29]

Earl Greville, the Foreign Secretary, instructed British missions abroad on 13 January 1852 to communicate to foreign governments that:

> By the existing laws of Great Britain, all foreigners have the unrestricted right of entrance and residence in this country, and while they remain in it, are, equally with British subjects, under the protection of the law ... No foreigner as such can be sent out of the country by executive government, except persons removed by treaties with other States, confirmed by Act of Parliament, for the mutual surrender of criminal offenders.[30]

There were indeed few extradition treaties between the UK and other States in existence. The one with France dated from 1843. Between 1843 and 1852, 14 applications were made by France and only one was successful.[31] Another treaty was negotiated with France in 1852, but did not receive parliamentary approval, although this was the first time in British extradition practice that an exemption was provided for political offenders (Shearer, 1971, pp 14–15). The Permanent Under Secretary for Home Affairs stated in December 1857 that:

> The reason that the passing of Extradition Acts is so difficult is the extreme jealousy felt by the people of this country upon the subject of any interference by our police or magistrates with foreigners coming to this country, upon the mere allegation of their own government that they have been guilty of some crime [Porter, 1979, p 144].

29 Circular Despatch, 6 October 1849, quoted in (1965) 6 British Digest of International Law 43 p 44.

30 State Papers, vol 42 (1852–53), quoted by Vincenzi (1985, p 107). Porter (1979, p 149) notes the same despatch.

31 The treaty was confirmed by Parliament by 6 & 7 Vict, c 75 (May 1878, Vol 3, p 59n). In 1868, it was reported to the Select Committee on Extradition that the French had denounced an extradition treaty and that 'In the course of 20 years only one man had been given up.' Parliamentary Papers, vol VII, no 393, para 515 (1867–68).

The right of 'free ingress, sojourn and egress' was quite jealously defended by the press in Britain in the 1850s, when the diplomatic pressure applied on Britain was at a high level. The equality of the application of laws as between foreigners and the English was treated as a matter of pride. Demands by continental countries that Britain curb the conspiratorial activities of refugees were also criticised; conspiracy, it was contended, was too slippery a concept and could not be applied to the activities of refugees with any degree of accuracy, although Porter suggests that the strength of opposition to any action being taken against refugees was due mainly to the fact that such suggestions originated in foreign countries. The Victorians at this time also resisted the idea of 'passports', which were regarded as impediments to the right of free 'egress'. By the 1860s, the only Aliens Act in force stipulated that aliens arriving in Britain should show their passports – *if they had them, not if they did not*. It was never enforced, but not thought worth repealing. As to asylum, one newspaper regarded the 'right to exercise hospitality' as 'an inherent natural right – the boundary which the merciful Lord of Heaven and Earth has imposed upon the cruelty of man'.[32] These general attitudes were demonstrated in practice during the so called 'Orsini crisis' of 1858.

On 14 January 1858, ex-refugee Orsini's Birmingham made bombs exploded in Paris. This brought opprobrium upon Britain where there were still worries about the loss of the French alliance. Something had to be done to appease the French, but no law existed to expel foreigners. An Aliens Bill was contemplated, but the idea did not receive Cabinet support and had to be dropped.[33] A Conspiracy Bill was introduced into Parliament by Palmerston (who had been in favour of an Aliens Bill) on 8 February 1858. It would have classified conspiracy to murder as a felony, entailing life imprisonment, and it would have been given extraterritorial reach. However, the Government was embarrassed by revelations which made it appear that the Bill had been a result of French pressure and Palmerston had to resign his ministry (Porter, 1979, pp 171–90).

Four people were then arrested in Paris and, on 13 March 1858, Orsini and Pierri were guillotined. Simon Bernard, a Frenchman, who was thought to be the leader of the whole conspiracy, was arrested by English police on 14 February and charged with being an accessory to murder, which carried the

32 (1852) *The Standard*, 25 February, quoted in Porter (1979, p 112).

33 The draft bill would have given the government the power to send away any foreigner who might be suspected, on good grounds, of plotting, either to disturb the internal tranquillity of any friendly power, or to use violence against the person or life of any foreign sovereign. It was proposed to make the power accountable to a special secret parliamentary committee (the Foreign Secretary, Clarendon, preferred three Lord Justices) (Porter, 1979, p 175).

death penalty.[34] Bernard's advocate stated to the jury that its decision would have 'consequences most serious both to public and private liberty in this country, and to the cause of freedom and civilisation throughout Europe'. Lord Campbell, the Lord Chief Justice, had obviously anticipated that the jury would be conscious of more than the charges which Bernard had been brought to answer. He stated, in his summing up, that they need not be prevented from discharging their duty by:

> ... any apprehension that [their] verdict will interfere with that asylum which it has been the glory of this country to afford to persecuted foreigners. That is a glory which I hope will ever belong to this country. That asylum, however ..., amounts to this – that foreigners are at liberty to come to this country and to leave it at their own will and pleasure, and they cannot be disturbed by the Government of this country so long as they obey our laws, and they are under the same laws as native born subjects, and if they violate those laws they are liable to be prosecuted and punished in the same manner as native born subjects.[35]

The jury decided that Bernard was not guilty to a loud public cheer and the judges 'made a hasty retreat from the court'.[36]

The principle of asylum was thus pushed to its limit with respect to various groups of refugees from European countries. Legislative powers were given to the executive only intermittently and were exacting. Both the 1793 Act (and its extensions) and the 1848 Act were considered only to be necessary during extraordinary times. During 'normal' times, it was not thought proper that governments should have any powers at all to exclude or expel aliens, apart from limited extradition powers. When collusion between British and foreign governments was suspected, it led to the resignation of a minister, and the principle of asylum was given a boost which possibly prevented governments from legislating openly against immigration to Britain for a considerable time. When the Orsini crisis occurred, the British position for consumption at home was still that the right of asylum was a 'great principle of our constitution', which could not, in any circumstances, be infringed. The unconditional nature of the right to asylum could not be maintained indefinitely, however. As already seen, the principle came under pressure

34 Others who were arrested included Edward Truelove, for bringing out a pamphlet advocating tyrannicide, and Stanislaus Tchorzewski, for selling a pamphlet by Pyat justifying the *attentat* (Porter, 1979, p 191). Allsop, a British subject, had fled to the US and escaped prosecution because the British Government felt that it had insufficient legal basis under the Webster-Ashburton Treaty of 1842 to request his extradition at the insistence of France (Verzijl, 1972, vol V, p 304).

35 (1858) *The Times*, 19 April, quoted in Landa (1911, pp 261–62) and Sibley and Elias (1906, pp 133–34). In Parliament, Lord Campbell had earlier opposed any extension of the criminal law which might extend the power of the Government over refugees who had sought asylum in Britain, Parliamentary Debates, 3rd series, vol 148, cols 708–13, 4 February 1858, also quoted in (1965) 6 British Digest of International Law 43, pp 60–61.

36 (1858) *The Times*, 19 April, quoted in Landa (1911, p 262).

even with respect to the European refugees when there was a risk of diplomatic embarrassment. The international implications of granting unconditional refuge gradually had to give way to a more qualified doctrine of asylum when the Extradition Act of 1870 was passed. However, that Act contained an exception for political offenders and was really effective only against individual anarchists.[37] General measures were taken, on the other hand, signalling the openness to immigration, at least, of Europeans. By the General Repealing Act of 1863, almost all enactments passed against aliens since the reign of Richard II were deleted from statute. The Naturalisation Act of 1870, as Landa (1911, p 7) later claimed, enabled aliens to place themselves on a footing of equality with Englishmen after a few years' residence. Meanwhile, a wind of change was detectable in the common law doctrine of freedom of movement in relation to non-white migrants to the various white settler territories. This change shows that the idea of global co-ordination of migration on racist terms among some countries is not a new phenomenon, but something that may be being experienced in a new form in Europe today.

2.5 TWILIGHT OF THE COMMON LAW'S REIGN

By the middle of the 19th century, the predominant common law doctrine disallowed executive interference with people who migrated to Britain, and it was the case that such powers could only be given by Parliament temporarily during specific times of emergency. However, towards the end of the 19th century a shift in legal opinion began to take place as Asians and blacks competed with whites in the European settler colonies. The United States had begun to institute federal statutory controls in 1875 and had passed the Chinese Exclusion Act in 1882 which was supplemented by further restrictions on Chinese settlers throughout the 1880s (Plender, 1988, pp 68–70). Further restrictions, in the midst of heated debates about 'lesser races', were introduced throughout the remainder of the 19th century and beyond (Dinnerstein and Reimers, 1988, pp 63–84). The British Dominions and the smaller colonial territories had, by the 1890s, passed legislation aimed at controlling immigration, and did not necessarily regard British subjects as automatically entitled to migrate there (Manson, 1902). Exclusionary legislative policies based on racial grounds were tried and tested. In particular, blacks who had migrated to Canada from the US were to experience opposition to their settlement. In Canada and Australia, opposition

37 *Re Castioni* [1891] 1 QB 149 provides an example of a case where the 'political offence' exception was successfully claimed. In *Re Meunier* [1894] 2 QB 415, the courts approved the extradition of an anarchist, and did not consider that the political offence exception was applicable to them. By the late 19th century, the criminal laws were also being brought to bear on European refugees who were suspected of conspiring against foreign governments (see Kimball, 1973; Porter, 1980).

to the settlement of Chinese people led to specific legislative policies against them. Policy making was moving towards the institution of a 'white Canada' and a 'white Australia', which continued until 1962 for Canada and 1973 for Australia, under which only people from Britain and other (preferably Northern and Central) European countries were encouraged to come and settle (Hawkins, 1989, pp 3–41).

In *Musgrove v Chun Teeong Toy*,[38] the Privy Council faced the question of whether aliens had any legal right, enforceable by legal action, to enter British territory. Since the exclusion of Chun was held to have been legitimate under the Chinese Act 1881 of Victoria, the answer was *obiter*. Nevertheless, the Privy Council stated that it could not assent to the proposition that an alien who was refused permission to enter British territory could test the Crown's power to exclude him without parliamentary authority. He could only do so if he could establish a legal right, enforceable by action, to enter British territory: 'No authority exists for the proposition that an alien has any such right.'[39]

The *Musgrove* case gave rise to an academic debate in which authors either supported or contested the Crown's powers over aliens. Craies (1890), writing before the Privy Council decision was given, hoped that it would support the view that without a statute the Crown could not assert the authority to expel an alien. Haycraft (1897), writing after the final court gave its ruling, argued that the Crown had possessed the right to exclude and expel aliens, and that those who opposed that view only thought of the 'privilege' of asylum that had been granted to refugees:

> In the earlier part of this century the refugee was generally an interesting person enjoying the sympathy of some portion of respectable society, and not in any way akin to the indiscriminate political assassins with whom the governments are at war in these days [Haycraft, 1897, p 181].[40]

The basis of the Privy Council's view was, in fact, very tenuous given the many previous assertions to the contrary, while Craies's view of the position is more grounded in the canon of the hitherto accepted legal position. But the case is also interesting for the 'reception' into the common law of an international law discourse that had been evolving in a positivistic fashion. Both Pufendorf and Vattel had proclaimed that the right of asylum could not be put on a footing of an absolute or unconditional right. Pufendorf was admittedly more concerned to point out that the question of asylum should be read as subject to problems that may be brought by the large scale admission

38 [1891] AC 272.

39 *Ibid*, p 282.

40 Haycraft (1897, p 185) went further: 'Could it be argued, to put an extreme case, that, if a foreign government or society were to send over to this country a whole shipload of raving lunatics or convicted felons, at a time when Parliament was not sitting, the Home Secretary would be unable to preserve us from such an invasion because there was no time to obtain parliamentary powers?'

of aliens, while Vattel tended to emphasise the duty of humanity toward aliens. But both underlined the conditional nature of an alien's sojourn in a State (Sibley and Elias, 1906, pp 1–17). In *Musgrove*, the Privy Council stated that 'by international law this country has a right to keep the alien out.'[41] Almost simultaneously, while the Privy Council was considering *Musgrove*, the US Supreme Court drew inspiration from Vattel to declare, in the case of a Japanese person, that according to international law a State had the discretion to admit whomever it saw fit.[42] In these judicial pronouncements, the views of international jurists who took a less tenacious perspective of State sovereignty were totally ignored (Plender, 1988, pp 72–75). Therefore, whereas the common law had earlier been used to defend the encroachment of international demands to remove aliens from the UK, an international law doctrine that legitimised the power to control was now being incorporated into it.[43] The debate over the doctrine itself was soon largely obviated in that the control over the entry and residence of aliens was initiated by Parliament, in reaction to the politicisation of the mainly Jewish migration from Eastern Europe, culminating in the Aliens Act 1905. However, the *Musgrove* judgment has been identified as a turning point in legal thinking that has proved persistent to the present day, influencing a judicial perception that excluded aliens are not deserving of a detailed scrutiny of their claims (Vincenzi, 1985). What is significant is that such case law developed as a result of the exclusion of particular racial groups (blacks, Japanese, Chinese and South Asian) that were not considered as deserving of an equal right to free movement, and that judges in legal systems across the Anglo-Saxon world tended to accommodate legislative demands to exclude such people.

41 *Musgrove v Chun Teeong Toy* [1891] AC 272, p 277.

42 *Nishimura Ekiu v US* 142 US 651, p 659 (discussed in Plender, 1988, pp 70–71).

43 A further illustration of this thinking is the case of *AG for Canada v Cain* [1906] AC 452, p 546, where Lord Atkinson said for the Privy Council: '... it is conceded that, by the law of nations, the supreme power in every State has the right to make laws for the exclusion or expulsion of aliens ...'

CHAPTER 3

THE ALIENS ACT 1905, JEWS AND GYPSIES

3.1 AGITATION FOR CONTROLS AND THE ALIENS ACT 1905

After many years of economic restrictions and bouts of savage persecution against Jews in Russia and Russian Poland, the 'May Laws', which attacked the basis of Jewish economic life, were enacted in 1882. They were the straw that broke the camel's back, sparking off an exodus of probably one million people until the end of the 19th century. Other waves of refugees were generated by Bismarck's expulsion of alien Poles from Prussia in 1886 and the continuing repression of Jews in Romania. These groups formed part of a larger westward movement of people from Eastern and Southern Europe. Larger numbers of refugees left for the US, although many chose to stay in England. Up to 1890, most immigrants were initially from Germany, but they were soon overtaken by those from Russian Poland. A smaller group of Lithuanians, fleeing from Tsarist policies of Russification of religion and language, and the introduction, in 1874, of forced conscription, also settled in Britain, mainly in Scotland (Holmes, 1988, pp 27–30).

From the 1880s onwards, an increasing level of attention was directed to Jewish settlement in London and other urban centres in Britain, notably Manchester and Leeds. This problematisation of the Jewish presence eventually began to find its way into official circles. At the time, Arnold White, who became the key agitator in later years for aliens' restriction, was engaged in settling English families in South Africa. He claimed that as many foreign immigrants were arriving and settling in Britain as were leaving for the colonies (Landa, 1911, pp 8–9), and, therefore, 'the home population would be depleted of its best stock, and the core of the Empire would decay' (Gainer, 1972, p 108). In 1887, in response to such allegations, Lord Salisbury issued a Circular Despatch to Britain's representatives in Europe and the United States, requesting copies of laws or local legislation prohibiting the admission and the continued residence of destitute aliens. The resulting parliamentary paper noted that Britain stood almost alone in having no laws for this purpose (Roche, 1969, p 61).[1] It was also reported in 1887 that the total number of aliens

1 France had a power of expulsion by ministerial decree since 1849, and Belgium and Denmark, among other European States, had aliens regulations of varying severity (Roche, 1969, p 61). In 1892, when a Liberal Government was in power, the Labour Department of the Board of Trade was established and two commissioners were appointed to investigate how the laws in the US were operating (Landa, 1911, pp 15–16).

in the 1881 census was 135,640 (since then increased) and was less than the net English and Irish emigration in a single year (Landa, 1911, pp 9–10).

Nevertheless, the problematisation of the alien presence continued. Attention had been focused upon London, in particular, the settlement of Jews from Russia and Poland in the East End. Although it constituted merely one-third of the total foreign population, the agitators and the authorities made this community the almost exclusive focus of their attention, to the extent that the terms 'immigrant' and 'Jew' became synonymous (Gainer, 1972, pp 3–4). Perceived social problems in the East End were exhaustively studied. Among the issues raised were the extent to which the immigrants posed a threat to domestic labour and the labour conditions in the immigrants' main trades of clothing and shoemaking. Other issues raised were the extent to which 'natives' were being 'deprived' of housing; the conditions of sanitation in immigrant housing; stereotypes surrounding the customs and habits of the Jews; as well as their potential criminality (see Gainer, 1972, pp 15–143).

Two parliamentary committees also reported in the same decade. The first report was from a House of Commons Select Committee in 1889. It concluded that the number of aliens could not be calculated with accuracy and that, while the number was increasing, it was not so alarming. It was noted that aliens worked in a small number of trades and localities; they were moral, frugal and inoffensive as citizens; they were healthy, while neglecting their physical condition and sanitary laws. However, it found that the 'better class' moved to America while the 'worst' remained. It was thought that legislation such as America's may be necessary due to overcrowding in the great towns, population pressure and a tendency for the social and material condition of 'our own poor' to be reduced. The report recognised, however, that such legislation 'would pose great difficulties' and did not recommend it (Landa, 1911, pp 11–12). The second report was from the Lords Sweating Committee in 1890. It was rather less impressed with the deleterious effects on wages caused by foreign immigration and found that the evils complained of were found in trades not affected by foreigners (Landa, 1911, p 12).

One of the practical effects of the House of Commons report was the adoption by the Board of Trade of the former's recommendation that the collection of alien statistics be resumed. The power to do so was already available under the then disused Act of 1836. By 1894, another report was produced in which it was claimed that 'it is clear that we are now in possession of means of knowing the exact extent of this movement, and no change of character, magnitude or route can occur unobserved' (quoted in Landa, 1911, pp 16–17).[2] The statistics distinguished between *en route* passengers and settlers and, although they could not really give an accurate

2 The report cited by Landa is the Board of Trade (Alien Immigration), *Report on the Volume and Effect of Recent Immigration from Eastern Europe into the UK*, Parliamentary Papers, vol LXVIII, no 7406, p 341 (1894).

idea of the number of people who chose to stay in Britain, they were deliberately misrepresented in the continuing agitation (Gainer, 1972, pp 6–14). In fact, the proportion of transmigrants, about 800,000 in sum, to alien settlers in England from 1891 to 1901 is estimated at 15:1 (Gainer, 1972, p 2).[3] Jewish leaders themselves were concerned to avoid all the attention focused on their communities. At the same time, Landa (1911, p 15) noted that '[the] Jewish authorities did their utmost to direct the stream of refugees to the new world: thousands passed through England as transmigrants. But they were observed, and that was enough'. By 1901, the number of refugees in England is estimated to have been 339,000 out of a total population of 32 million (Gainer, 1972, p 2).

Parliamentarians then took to initiating attempts to legislate against aliens. Lord Salisbury, an ex-Prime Minister, introduced an unsuccessful Bill in the House of Lords in July 1894 which would have also excluded those classed as idiots, insane, paupers and those determined to suffer from any dangerous, contagious or infectious disease. The new Government of 1896 also put in the promise of an Aliens Bill in the Queen's Speech and, in 1898, another Bill, similar to the one in 1894, was introduced, but was also unsuccessful (Gainer, 1972, pp 156–59). In 1902, Balfour, the Prime Minister, appointed a committee whose terms of reference were:

> To inquire and report upon:
>
> (1) The character and extent of the evils which are attributed to the unrestricted immigration of aliens, especially in the Metropolis.
>
> (2) The measures which have been adopted for the restriction and control of alien immigration in foreign countries and in British colonies [quoted in Landa, 1911, pp 29–30].

The voluminous report[4] that emerged was described by a contemporary writer as 'of a character to satisfy the most ardent advocates of restriction' (Landa, 1911, p 30). It found that aliens were few in number and that there was little evidence that jobs were taken from English workers. The Commission recommended the setting up of an Immigration Department whose officers would have the power to make whatever inquiries necessary, that is, to determine whether persons were criminals, prostitutes, persons of 'notoriously bad character', lunatics, idiots or persons 'likely to become a

3 The same report (*op cit*, fn 2) found that the immigration into England was part of a large movement of emigration westwards from European countries (Landa, 1911, p 16). Landa (1911, pp 40–61) carefully gives a breakdown of the number of persons who could reasonably have been estimated to have settled in the 1890s and 1900s. He shows the glaring disparity between the publicised figures and the actual returns which were discernible from the census and from the Board of Trade's Annual Reports on Immigration and Emigration.

4 *Report of the Royal Commission on Alien Immigration*, divided into four parts: vol I: the report, Cd 1741, Parliamentary Papers, vol IX, p 1 (1903); vol II: minutes of evidence, p 61; vol III: appendix to the minutes of evidence, p 935; vol IV: index and analysis to minutes of evidence, p 1041.

charge on the public funds'. Power to refuse leave to land was to be vested in a court of summary jurisdiction. Convicted criminals were also to be deported. Further, if within two years of arrival, a person was ascertained or reasonably supposed to be a criminal, prostitute, pimp, a person of bad character, a public charge (except through ill health), or a person without visible or probable means of support, it was recommended that that person was to be deported at the expense of the shipping company that brought him (Gainer, 1972, pp 159–60). This last reference is an early indication of the imposition of responsibilities upon carriers to control travellers deemed unacceptable, and later found its way into the 1905 Act.

The Commission also recommended the prohibition of housing immigrants in areas where it was deemed that they contributed to overcrowding, and that any change of address during the first two years should be notified. If a person did move to a prohibited area, he would be subject to being ordered out and be guilty of an offence. This was an early example of a debate about a dispersal scheme that was to be applied again in the latter half of the 20th century. The registration of aliens was also recommended. At the time, however, it was regarded as a civil servant's nightmare, and the Under Secretary at the Home Office, Sir Kenelm Digby, who also sat on the Commission, refused to do anything with the majority's report. However, the idea of registration did not disappear from the scene altogether and, less than 10 years later, it was introduced for all aliens (Gainer, 1972, p 160).

Two further Bills, both unsuccessful, were introduced in 1904. A government attempt at legislation would have given the Home Secretary the task of deciding the fate of every alien passenger detained at the ports. A Criminal Aliens Bill introduced by the Liberals would have provided for the expulsion of alien prisoners on conviction and would have made it unlawful for any person who had been convicted of a crime in a foreign country, within the scope of any extradition treaty, to be found within the UK. Finally, a Bill was laid on 18 March 1905, which became the Aliens Act 1905. The Royal Commission's recommendations on overcrowding and registration had been jettisoned while the Liberal Opposition concentrated their attention on securing the right of asylum for religious and political refugees. The Act came into force on 1 January 1906, by which time the Unionist Government that had introduced it had been replaced (Landa, 1911, pp 32–34).

Section 1 of the Aliens Act defined 'undesirable aliens' as: (a) those who could not show themselves in a position to obtain the means of 'decently' supporting themselves and their dependants; (b) lunatics, idiots, persons suffering from infirmity or disease likely to make them a charge on the public rates 'or otherwise a detriment to the public'; (c) persons sentenced in foreign countries for non-political crimes; and (d) persons against whom expulsion orders had been made under the Act. Immigration officers, appointed under the Act, could refuse leave to land to immigrants who appeared to be undesirable and the individuals concerned could be detained. Landa (1911, p 194) drew parallels with British Imperial practice, citing the example of New South Wales some years previously where a prison governor had bemoaned that: 'The Alien Restriction Act is responsible for the reception of 17 persons who can scarcely be classed as criminals, but they undergo the same discipline and disabilities.'

Refugees were excepted from being refused leave to land on the grounds of want of means or the probability of their becoming a charge on the rates. According to s 1(3) of the 1905 Act, such a person had to prove that:

> ... he is seeking admission to the country solely to avoid persecution or punishment on religious or political grounds or for an offence of a political character, or persecution, involving danger of imprisonment or danger to life or limb, on account of religious belief.

How this provision, specifically inserted to allay concerns that refugees would be prevented from landing, was put into practice is discussed further in 3.2.

Measures were also put into place for the control of aliens after landing in the UK. The Home Secretary could also make an expulsion order if it was certified to him by a court that the alien had been convicted in the UK or abroad (where that offence was non-political and there existed an extradition treaty) or if it was certified to him that the alien was receiving such parochial relief that disqualified him from the parliamentary franchise, was found wandering without ostensible means of subsistence, or had been living in unsanitary conditions due to overcrowding.[5] Discrimination on economic grounds was also evident in the fact that only vessels that carried more than 20 alien steerage (as opposed to cabin) passengers were subject to examination.[6] Transmigrants were also excepted from landing restrictions, although they were liable to be examined.[7] Landing in contravention of the

5 Aliens Act 1905, s 3. Section 7(3) provided the power to detain all such persons. Garrard (1971, p 103n) notes that there had been always been considerable bi-partisan agreement relating to the expulsion of criminal and diseased aliens. Sibley and Elias (1906, p 71) were struck by the tenacity of these provisions: 'But neither the receipt of parochial relief disqualifying for the parliamentary franchise, nor living in insanitary conditions due to overcrowding, are acts contrary to law, and the Aliens Act does not make them so even in the alien, since it does not declare either to be a misdemeanour. While there can be no doubt that the proceedings for the expulsion of an alien is an act of administration, it clearly infringes the principles of the common law and Magna Carta, that a person should be sent to prison without being charged with committing a crime.'

6 *Ibid*, s 8(2), defining 'immigrant ship'. The Secretary of State could vary this number. At first, Akers Douglas reduced the number to 12 by regulations (Henriques, 1906, pp 144, 223), but subsequently increased it to 20 again (Landa, 1911, p 195; Garrard, 1971, p 104). One of the reasons cited for the increase to 20 was that, otherwise, the Act would place an 'intolerable burden of work on the immigration officers' (Gainer, 1971, p 203). According to the Memorandum from the Home Office of February 1906, the exception would exclude passengers who travelled first class (see Henriques, 1906, p 223, for text of the Memorandum).

7 *Ibid*, s 8(a) and (b).

Act made an immigrant punishable as a rogue and vagabond, and the master of the ship was liable to a fine not exceeding £100.[8] Obligations were retained upon masters of all ships to provide information on aliens, and failure to make a return or providing false information were made subject to a penalty of imprisonment with hard labour for three months.[9] While these penalties appeared harsh, the Act clearly did not anticipate the control of all migrants, but generally only the poorer ones. Appeals against refusal of leave to land could be made to Immigration Boards which were to consist of three persons selected from a list of those who have 'magisterial, business, or administrative experience'.[10] The refused immigrant had to be informed of his right to appeal and the grounds on which leave had been refused. This was to be under rules for the working of the Board that the Secretary of State was to make.[11] How some of these provisions were actually applied in the case of Jewish refugees, especially after complaints from influential Jewish leaders in Britain, is discussed further below.

3.2 JEWISH REFUGEES UNDER THE ALIENS ACT 1905

The exception for refugees in the 1905 Act did not apply to persons other than those excluded by immigration officers on the ground of want of means or the probability of their becoming a charge on the rates. It seems from the wording of the Act that asylum could not be claimed by other categories of those excluded or selected for expulsion after having landed. But Sibley and Elias (1906, p 130) could still note that, while the 1905 Act was the severest to have found its way into the statute books for 80 years, it contained the 'most comprehensive declaration of the right to asylum that is to be found in the whole range of municipal legislation, not merely in the history of this country, but throughout the civilised world'. The Home Office was placed in a crucial position to influence the operation of the 'roughly drafted' Act. While the Act placed wide discretionary powers in the hands of the Home Secretary to decide whether an immigrant was a refugee, so many cases that had to be decided quickly came up that the officials found it impossible to consult the Home Secretary each time. They had to make decisions themselves according to what became a rough departmental rule for admission on grounds of political asylum (Pellew, 1982, pp 88–89).

8 Aliens Act 1905, ss 1(5) and 7(1).

9 Providing false information also made the immigrant liable to imprisonment with three months' hard labour.

10 Aliens Act 1905, s 2(1). Landa (1911, p 191) states that at the time of his writing no women had been appointed.

11 *Ibid*, s 2(2).

Gladstone had, quite early in the operation of the Act, given special consideration to the problems of the still arriving Jewish refugees. In particular, the Russian Revolution of 1905 had been followed by the wholesale massacres of Jews. Partly in response to that, the Home Secretary moved to send to immigration officers an 'instruction' in the following terms:

> In all cases in which immigrants, coming from parts of the Continent which are at present in a disturbed condition, allege that they are flying from political or religious persecution, the benefit of the doubt, where any doubt exists, as to the truth of the allegation will be allowed, and leave to land will be given [quoted in Landa, 1911, p 223].

A similarly worded circular letter was also sent to the Immigration Boards in March 1906 in which Gladstone expressed the hope that:

> ... having regard to the present disturbed condition of certain parts of the Continent, the benefit of the doubt, where any doubt exists, may be given in favour of immigrants who allege that they are fleeing from religious or political persecution ... and that leave to land may be given.[12]

The circular to the Boards also stated that Parliament had never intended that the Act should be applied without 'considerations as to whether refusal to land would involve great personal hardship or suffering, including women and children and immigrants who were seriously, but not infectiously, ill' (Garrard, 1971, p 105).

Overall, the number of exclusions did show an upward trend while the number of appeals and the number of successful appeals were declining, both in absolute terms and relative to the numbers refused. However, the figures are not specific with respect to the groups involved in terms of nationality or ethnicity (see Figure 3.1).

Figure 3.1

Year	Exclusions	Appeals heard	Appeals successful	Final rejections
1906	935	796	442	493
1907	975	601	173	802
1908	724	321	112	612
1909	1,456	581	109	1,347
1910	1,066	432	144	922

The only grounds of exclusion mentioned are 'want of means' and 'medical grounds'. Medical objections were extremely difficult to reverse. Between 1908

12 Regulations made by the Home Secretary under the Aliens Act, Cd 2879 (1906), p 30 (quoted in Landa, 1911, p 223; Garrard, 1971, p 105).

and 1910, out of 276 appeals against doctors' objections, only 49 succeeded (Landa, 1911, p 228).

Landa's research in London was conducted on charges that the Immigration Board sat in secret and was difficult to access; that pressmen were initially excluded; that relatives of detained immigrants found it extremely difficult to be heard or to learn where the Boards would sit; and complaints that refugees were being cast back.[13] He confirmed many of these suspicions, finding that immigrants who appealed were detained on board ships in unsatisfactory conditions;[14] investigating officers made improper inquiries about aliens and 'added a new terror to the East End'; and that relatives were not told of hearings with the result that there could be no witnesses for the appellant (Landa, 1911, pp 200–03). The Boards were not courts and did not have the power to administer oaths (Sibley and Elias, 1906, p 54), and there was no guarantee that a justice of the peace, who would be legally qualified, would sit as chair.[15] Sibley and Elias (1906, p 57) stated at the outset that:

> The analogy of the inquiry, at all events before the Immigration Board, would appear to be rather to a penal action than to civil proceedings. The difficulty of evidence, on the other hand, would seem to render it almost impossible for the Immigration Board to arrive at certainty in each particular case.

In practice, members of the Board had 'continually shown themselves unacquainted with the rules of evidence and the practice of the courts'. Immigration officers played a dominant role in the proceedings, especially due to the unprecedented nature of the law that the Boards were expected to operate. The officers often led misleading evidence before the Boards and false information collected, and not necessarily assented to by the immigrant, was nevertheless adduced (Landa, 1911, pp 206–09; Gainer, 1972, p 201). Faulty interpretation, misapplication of the Act by some Board members, and the lack of uniformity of procedure were also identified as unfair (Landa, 1911, pp 202–20). The Tribunal was 'often, and avowedly, prejudiced against the entry of aliens' (Landa, 1911, pp 205–06). Further, opinion at the time regarded

---

13 Landa had been commissioned by the Jewish Chronicle to attend the sittings of the Board in London. He later did the same on behalf of the Jewish World.

14 Under r 10 of the Rules made under the 1905 Act, an alien who appealed should have been disembarked for the purpose of being brought before the Immigration Board, and should have been treated as conditionally disembarked until the appeal was disposed of (Henriques, 1906, p 154). But the practice of keeping passengers on the ship may have been influenced by the need for the Secretary of State to be satisfied of the conditions under which disembarkation could be obtained. A shipowner may have been obliged to give security by bond covering all the ships owned by him arriving at the port or ports where conditional disembarkation had been sanctioned (Sibley and Elias, 1906, p 52).

15 Henriques (1906, p 155) notes that 'when any magistrate is a member, he is to act as chairman; otherwise the members may choose their own chairman'.

the Boards as not susceptible to challenge in the High Court since its activities were not treated as 'judicial'. The absence of any check was thought to give too much discretion to the Boards.[16]

On the other hand, lobbying of members of the government by Jewish community leaders showed how, through direct negotiations, alternative arrangements could be humanely worked out without the type of large scale intervention by lawyers and the courts seen in more recent decades. Several of the problems in the procedural aspects of the Boards' functioning were raised with Gladstone in December 1906 by Stuart Samuel, a Jewish Liberal MP, and the former was asked whether a Departmental Committee would look into the matter. Gladstone's reply was dismissive, stating that he had all the information he needed on the Boards and that there were 'obvious [though unstated] objections to establish anything like a court procedure'.[17] Gladstone also resisted the plea to publish the report of the committee that had drafted the regulations to guide the Boards. Landa (1911, pp 222–23) notes that, in the background, Gladstone also had to contend with abuse from those who were agitating for restrictive controls on aliens.

Some reforms were, however, gradually implemented, in partial fulfilment of the representations submitted by the Jewish Board of Deputies to the Home Office in February 1908.[18] The Deputies asked that receiving houses be set up at all immigration ports, where preliminary proceedings could be carried out, and where the potential immigrant could stay pending return or the outcome of an appeal to the Board. At first, Gladstone prevaricated, but receiving houses began to be established towards the end of 1909 and, by May 1910, were extended to London. A second complaint was about the operation of the Boards, including their frequent refusal to give the benefit of the doubt to refugees. The Jewish Deputies proposed the establishment of a proper judicial procedure and the appointment of a legally trained person to each Immigration Board. Twenty-seven Jewish members had already been appointed to the Board, as had been promised during the debates on the Bill, and the Deputies' point was eventually met by adding three of their nominees to the membership of the Board. Thirdly, they had asked that there should be better provision for interpretation and presentation of evidence. Of that there seemed to be no more complaints. Although Gladstone had refused representation by 'legal men', Churchill permitted it in 1910. A Jewish committee had made some arrangements for such representation, but there were so few appeals in London that advantage had not been taken of the new

16 Landa (1911, p 57) was very critical of the discretionary powers of the Boards: 'Punishment by "administrative order" has been established for the system of English rule of law.'

17 The full question and reply are reproduced *ibid*, pp 220–21.

18 The memorial submitted was signed by Lord Rothschild, Lord Swaythling, 11 Jewish members of the House of Commons and other leaders of the Jewish community (*ibid*, p 254).

concession.[19] The Deputies' additional demands that the naturalisation fee of £5 be abolished and that there be an appeal available to the King's Bench Division of the High Court were not met. As to the possibility of an appeal to the High Court, it was said that that would require legislation and could not, therefore, be undertaken. Churchill pointed out that any alien who could afford to pay for such an appeal would obviously be able to enter first class (Landa, 1911, pp 254–58; Garrard, 1971, pp 124–30).

Gainer (1972, p 201), with a more privileged historical perspective, has taken the view that, while the working of the Boards attracted a great deal of public notice, their activities did little to affect the actual working of the 1905 Act. The broad overall figures did not indicate the position of refugees under the 1905 Act, but, on 10 February 1910, Churchill stated that the number of refugees admitted by the Boards under the 'benefit of the doubt' order had been 505 in 1906; 43 in 1907; 20 in 1908; and five in 1910 (Landa, 1911, p 224). Compared to that, in 1906, there were 12,832 Russians and Poles recorded as having arrived and, in the following years until 1914, the number of Russian and Polish Jews arriving was some 5,000 annually (Garrard, 1971, pp 106–07, 109). If anything, the 1905 Act resulted in the avoidance of Britain as a transit point for America which had in any case become a major destination. Indeed, the restrictionists' intention in pushing for the Aliens Act 1905 was partly to deter people from arriving in Britain, although this contention was at the time difficult to rebut or account for and may explain its popularity at the time (Gainer, 1972, p 155). The Royal Commission itself had hoped that legislation that embodied their recommendations (not all of which were eventually adopted), even if ineffective, would frighten off the unfit and make the shipping companies choose their passengers with greater care (Gainer, 1972, pp 155, 160). Gartner's (1973) detailed study of settlement patterns of Jews in England during this period indicates that the Act did indeed have this sort of psychological impact. Discussion of emigration in Eastern Europe seems to have practically excluded England from consideration, while the decade before the outbreak of the Great War was marked by the complete preponderance of America as a destination. Thus, the 'diminution of immigration to England after 1906 was greater than the terms of the Act warranted' (Gartner, 1973, p 279).[20] On the other hand, the psychological

19 Henriques (1906, p 156n) anticipated the problem of legal assistance: 'It may be thought hard that an appellant, who may be wholly ignorant of the procedure and even of the language in which the proceedings are conducted, should have no right to legal or other assistance at the hearing; but it must be assumed that the immigration boards will act reasonably and, in proper cases, give the necessary leave for hearing the agents or representatives of appellants.'

20 Gainer (1972, p 201) also mentions that 'the news of England's immigration law had the psychological effect of encouraging prospective immigrants to bypass it and make at once for the US ...'. Cesarani (1993, p 32) mentions that the volume of transmigrants declined from 110,700 in 1907 to 61,680 in 1908: 'This was the first, and perhaps the most important, discovery for officials and politicians in the new era of State interference in the free movement of populations into the UK.'

impact of the 1905 Act also has to be kept in perspective as, between 1910 and 1914, immigration to Britain reached levels comparable to two decades before the Act was passed (Lipman, 1990, p 73). Further, while the 1905 Act was passed in reaction to the settlement of Eastern European Jewish communities in Britain, its impact was mitigated by its 'light' controls; its provisions to protect refugees; and the influence of the Anglo-Jewish leaders who were allowed concessions by the Government. This type of pluralism in the approach to immigration law and policy was reflected again in the case of Jewish refugees who arrived in Britain in the 1930s (see Chapter 4). However, in the immediate historical context, a counter-example can be seen in the case of the small number of gypsy refugees who arrived in the early 20th century.

3.3 THE GYPSIES FROM GERMANY

The reaction to the few hundred gypsies who arrived in Britain between 1904 and 1906 was vastly out of proportion to their numbers, especially as compared to the size of the other groups that were entering Britain during this period. Also notable is the fact that the three main studies on the background to the passage of the 1905 Act and its aftermath by Garrard (1971), Gainer (1972) and Gartner (1973) do not record the reaction to this group of refugees; they concentrate on Jewish refugees. Only Holmes (1980 and 1988, pp 64–65) has provided some details of that episode which, again, sharply revealed the reaction that could be expected to the migration of refugees of a non-European racial background.

In the early part of the 20th century, gypsies were being expelled from Germany to Holland and a group of some 50, having been expelled in turn from Rotterdam in Holland, arrived in Britain on 1 December 1904. Soon after landing, they were forcibly driven over some county boundaries by police acting for the local authorities. There was some disquiet in central government that the dumping of gypsies might be the first step in the arrival of cargoes from the Continent. It was decided that, under the supervision of charitable organisations, they would be shipped back to Germany, although no information appears of their actual removal (Holmes, 1980, pp 138–42).

Another group of some 80 gypsies came to the attention of the authorities in Scotland in April 1906 when the 1905 Act had already been passed. It became clear to the Scottish and to the Home Offices that the 1905 Act could not be used against the gypsies because they could not be construed as having contravened that Act since they did not fit into any of the excludible categories of migrants. No consideration appears to have been given to treating them as refugees under that Act, however. Instead, they were moved from county to county by the police or were forced away by hostility from the local population. Some MPs asked the Government to get rid of them, whilst others argued for the tightening of the 1905 Act. In May 1906, the Home Office reduced the number of steerage passengers that determined a ship as an 'immigrant ship' from 20 to two in the case of ships of the company that had carried the gypsies to Britain, thereby making them liable to examination under the 1905 Act. This was an early instance of carriers' liability legislation being applied by disadvantaging shippers bringing to Britain immigrants considered undesirable. Then the Government took action to remove the gypsies from Britain, first by instructing the police to hound them to a port town, either Hull or Grimsby. The second phase was attended to by the Society of Friends of Foreigners in Distress, which had helped in 1904, and which managed the actual removal from Britain this time (Holmes, 1980, pp 142–47).

Holmes (1988, pp 149–50) accepts that it was certainly true that the 1904–06 debate over alien immigration was chiefly related to the Jews. The Russian Polish Jews already found a community of established Jews who could help them to adjust to British society and who influenced government policy towards them. However, he points out that the experience of the gypsies differed considerably from that of the Jews in that nobody had attempted to shunt Jewish immigrants across county borders and nobody had arranged for their deportation, even though exclusion had been advocated in some circles. This generally welcoming attitude for European refugees was maintained during and after the First World War, despite the onset of a more comprehensive apparatus for the control of immigration built on a war footing.

CHAPTER 4

INTERNATIONALISATION OF ARRANGEMENTS FOR EUROPEAN REFUGEES

4.1 THE JEWISH REFUGEES FROM EASTERN AND CENTRAL EUROPE

When the Great War broke out, comprehensive restrictions on freedom of movement were applied. The Aliens Restriction Act of 1914 was passed on 5 August, in one day, with four and a half columns of debate dedicated to it in Parliament. There was virtually no opposition to removing the right of asylum, although the Attorney General stated that the Act would not be enforced against political refugees (Morgenstern, 1949, pp 339, 346). One observer has noted that it is in this Act that one can see the level of power granted to the executive right down to his day (Gainer, 1972, p 207). Modelled on the legislation of 1803, the 1914 Act introduced powers for Orders in Council to be made concerning any aliens, not just enemy aliens. Such powers included prohibiting them from landing, prohibiting embarkation for departure, imposing conditions or restrictions on their stay, requiring them to remain in certain areas and prohibiting them from entering certain areas. It gave powers of arrest, detention and search to persons named in an Order in Council. Penalties were imposed upon persons who aided and abetted the contravention of the Act. The Act also stipulated that all aliens register with the police. An Order in Council issued under the 1914 Act gave powers to the Home Secretary to refuse entry and to deport any person whose presence in the UK he deemed not to be conducive to the public good (Dummett and Nicol, 1990, pp 106–07; Fraser, 1940, pp 38–39). Registration of aliens enabled the identification and location of residents thought to be enemy aliens. In September 1914, the Home Office and the War Office decided to intern all Germans between the ages of 17 and 55. Some 20,000–25,000 persons were arrested to the extent that accommodation became scarce and forced the suspension of the policy for some time. Eventually, some 29,000 people were interned in the UK, including Germans, Austro-Hungarians, Turks and some Africans from German colonies (Dummett and Nicol, 1990, p 107; Panayi, 1993).

The 1914 Act, which had been intended to last only for the duration of the national emergency, was extended by the Aliens Restriction (Amendment) Act 1919. Under the 1919 Act, all former enemy aliens could be deported unless an aliens advisory committee deemed them exempt. For a five year period, no former enemy alien was allowed to enter the country. They were barred from acquiring land or a stake in key industries and were not permitted to serve on British ships. It became a criminal offence for any alien to foster disaffection amongst British soldiers or civilians, or to promote industrial unrest. Any alien found guilty of such acts could be deported. All aliens were excluded from employment in the civil service, from serving on juries, as pilots and as senior officers on British merchant vessels (Cesarani, 1993, pp 38–39; Gainer, 1972, pp 208–09; Fraser, 1940, p 39). The Aliens Order of 1920, passed under the 1919 Act, then effected 'the most sweeping changes in the law of aliens that had ever taken place in England' (Fraser, 1940, p 39). That Order provided for regulations for the landing of ships, the supervision of aliens by a system of registration, and their deportation under certain conditions. In fact, it seemed that the 'discretionary power of the Secretary [of State] is made very nearly absolute' (Fraser, 1940, p 40). Thus, an elaborate system of immigration control was erected from 1914 onwards. The war provided the opportunity for the government to assume powers that were hitherto considered to be too authoritarian. Unlike the aftermath of previous emergencies, such as the Napoleonic wars and the mid-19th century crises, the new powers were extended and became a permanent feature of immigration control.

In the period after the Aliens Order 1920 was passed, the executive seemed to possess all authority with regard to questions of immigration and who could claim asylum. Sir William Joynson Hicks, as Home Secretary, denied in 1925 that people were refused admission on the basis that they were political refugees, but stated that they were excluded if considered to be 'undesirable in other respects' (Morgenstern, 1949, p 341). Meanwhile, Fraser asked:

> Has the Aliens Order of 1920 removed from the courts the power to consider whether or not an alien is a political refugee, or has it merely restricted the courts to a consideration of this question in extradition proceedings? [Fraser, 1940, p 45].

But this was not answered by the courts in the period leading up to the Second World War. During that period, a continuous exodus, mainly of Jews, was taking place from Central and Eastern Europe and reaching the shores of Britain, either as a country of transit or as a country of final destination. The absence of the courts in the setting of standards shows that the law in this context provided the framework within which wide discretionary executive powers could be operated without reference to lawyers as has become the usual practice in more recent times.

International organisation to tackle the situation of refugees in Europe was born in an effort to re-organise demographic distribution among the States which emerged when the Austro-Hungarian and Ottoman Empires were defeated as a result of the First World War, and the Russian Revolution of 1917 altered the order in the former Tsarist empire. However, the first of these European efforts were modest in scale. The League of Nations provided only limited administrative expenses to its High Commissioner for Russian and

Armenian Refugees (the 'Nansen Office', so called after the first High Commissioner) under arrangements made in 1922 and 1926 (extended to other, limited groups of refugees in 1928 including Greeks, Turks and Bulgarians). Primarily, the High Commissioner was responsible for ensuring the issuing of identity certificates and could only co-ordinate efforts for relief and settlement made by States and private organisations. The arrangements were not concerned with providing asylum although, in the background, large shifts of population took place between States. Thus, the potential of the Nansen Office was not so great (Zolberg *et al*, 1989, pp 11–19; Holborn, 1956, p 7).

When the flight of refugees from Germany began, the problem was raised in the League of Nations, but Germany objected to that body's direct involvement. The High Commissioner for Refugees (Jewish and Others) coming from Germany was consequently constituted in 1933 as an autonomous organisation, responsible not to the League Council, but to a High Commissioner's Governing Body. An American, James G McDonald, was appointed in 1933 as the High Commissioner (Holborn, 1938, p 692 and 1956, pp 7–8).[1] Between 1933 and the end of 1935, the League of Nations had calculated that 65,000 people fled Germany, including Jews who made up some 40,000–45,000 of that number. Communists, pacifists and Catholics were certainly represented among the rest, although there is virtually no reference to other racial groups such as gypsies and Africans who were also known to be persecuted in Germany. Up to 1935, most emigrants are said to have left for political rather than 'racial' reasons. It was after the passing of the Nuremberg laws, which imposed unbearable legal and economic pressures on Jews, that the number of Jewish emigrants rose significantly. Some 21,000 people left in 1935 and some 25,000 in 1936 (Fox, 1984, p 37). The High Commissioner's Office was then placed more directly under League of Nations auspices in February 1936, with a new, British High Commissioner, Sir Neil Malcolm.[2]

Official British policy in the early phases of flight appeared to be limited in its scope. The British Government was favourably disposed to well known academics or people who had private means and connections, not likely to add to economic problems and who might help to alleviate social problems by establishing new enterprises and factories. Also acceptable were those who would migrate overseas. In 1933, according to the Foreign Secretary, Sir John Simon, the paramount consideration was unemployment and the state of the

1 The High Commissioner's Governing Body was formally set up in December 1933 and was composed of the representatives of the US, Argentina, Belgium, Brazil, Czechoslovakia, Denmark, France, Italy, the Netherlands, Poland, Spain, Sweden, Switzerland, the UK, Uruguay and Yugoslavia. Funds were made available by 'private organisations' (Holborn, 1938, p 692).

2 By that time, Germany had resigned its membership of the League of Nations (Zolberg *et al*, 1989, p 20).

labour market during a period of economic depression. The British delegate to the High Commissioner for Refugees was instructed to say that there were no prospects for those seeking employment in commerce or industry, and that there was little or no possibility of finding openings for more refugees in the professional classes. One reason for the restrictive stance was the fear of an anti-Semitic backlash. There were even suggestions that the German Government wanted to inundate the country with Jews to create a Jewish problem. On the other hand, businessmen and entrepreneurs were sought, especially because of the capital they brought with them which they invested in industries, creating employment, and because of the enhancement of trade and commercial life generally. The issue of the restrictions imposed by the Nazi regime upon Jews to carry their property with them was raised by the High Commissioner with the German Government, although his concern was met with intransigence (Carsten, 1984, pp 11–13, 17–18).

The official position on asylum at that time is reflected in a Home Office memorandum of 1934:

> An individual has no claim as of right to be admitted to this country on the ground that he is a political or religious refugee. The so called right of asylum, as defined both in dictionaries and the legal textbooks, is nothing but the competence of every State, inferred from its territorial supremacy, to allow a political or religious refugee to enter ... The right is not the right of a foreigner to admission. But the right of the State, if it thinks fit, to receive a foreigner fleeing from persecution [quoted in Wasserstein, 1984, pp 69–70].

This document is notable for the manner in which it reflects the new thinking developed in previous years. There is a conflation of the idea of State sovereignty and the right to exclude those seeking asylum in Britain. By a curious logic that had already been developed by judges before the Aliens Act 1905 (see 2.5), political theory disguised as international law came to provide a justification for restrictionism at the domestic level. As will be seen, this view was to continue to influence the framework of the international law of refugees after the Second World War. The memorandum went on to state that the tradition of asylum which had been exercised with a good deal of liberality in the past was to be read together with 'the necessity, which is recognised by the powers given under the Aliens Order, of preventing the admission and securing the removal of aliens whose presence in this country is for any reason undesirable' (quoted in Wasserstein, 1984, p 70). On the other hand, such official statements, which appear to denote a restrictive policy, may occlude the actual pattern of control in Britain.

One reason for the different, though less public, stance on immigration was because of an early indication by the Anglo-Jewish leadership that considerations relating to expenses should not be a factor in favour of restriction. The British Government refused to contribute to the maintenance of the refugees. But, in April 1933, the Cabinet had before it a guarantee from representatives of the Anglo-Jewish community that all expenses for temporary or permanent accommodation, in respect of Jews fleeing Germany, would be met by that community. That did not induce the Government to be more charitable than its narrow criteria for acceptance of the refugees allowed, but it relied on that guarantee for its continued willingness to allow further large numbers of refugees into Britain. Between 1933 and 1939, British Jews collected about £3 million. The priority for the Anglo-Jewish community was not to enable the refugees arriving to be granted the right to work, but only to obtain temporary asylum with a view to transmigration after a short time. A large portion of the funding was used for projects supporting emigration to Palestine, such as the training of individuals for re-emigration and the construction of housing. That was part of a concerted effort, together with Continental and American Jewry (all under the umbrella of the Council for German Jewry from 1936), to enable resettlement to take place successfully. Anglo-Jewish organisations were already involved in redirecting the traffic of Jews from Eastern Europe in the early to mid-1930s, the progress of which had impressed some British officials. Some professional associations, the academic community and charitable organisations also enabled the integration of refugees into British life. The assurance of support in the April 1933 guarantee did not, however, cover non-German Jews. Further, Jews with Polish or Hungarian nationality were already subject to a visa requirement, as were Stateless people, whereas German and Austrian citizens did not require visas under a mutual agreement for the abolition of visas of 1927. There was thus some evidence of a difference of treatment between Eastern European Jews (later, also Austrian Jews) and German Jews. These arrangements reflected both the affinity which the leaders of the older, established Anglo-Jewry felt with refugees from Germany and the influence they had with the British Government (Carsten, 1984, p 15; Wasserstein, 1984, pp 66–69; London, 1990, pp 167–73).

There are still problems in determining the actual pattern of control through the available figures. A League of Nations estimate showed that Britain was not a major absorber of the movement of refugees in the early period of emigration from Germany. By April 1934, France had received 21,000, Poland 8,000, Czechoslovakia 3,500, Holland 2,500 and 'England' 2,000. On the other hand, between 1933 and 1936, British controlled Palestine had absorbed 11,864. Official figures stated that, in 1933, 300–400 refugees were admitted to Britain. These rose to around 100 per month in 1934. There was no marked increase in 1935. On the other hand, despite the increased pressure on Britain from 1935, there were not a significantly larger number of 'undesirable aliens' excluded under the Aliens Order of 1920 – 484 were excluded in 1934, 365 in 1935, and 438 in 1937 (Carsten, 1984, p 11; Wasserstein, 1984, p 69–70). By September 1937, the High Commissioner for Refugees coming from Germany, Sir Neil Malcolm, adopted a cautious stance to the League of

Nations, but also indicated that the problem of resettlement was *more difficult for non-Jews*:

> While there have been no wholesale expatriations from Germany, the placing and final settlement of refugees having already left their country of origin has not made great progress. On the one hand, measures taken by governments in regard to immigration have brought the numbers of departures from Europe for overseas countries down to a very low level. On the other hand, the lack of the funds required to finance refugee emigration – particularly that of non-Jews – has been one of the chief determining factors in that situation. In consequence, and despite the hopes which had been entertained, steps taken during the year with a view to a solution of the problem of refugees coming from Germany have not been numerous [quoted in Wasserstein, 1984, pp 70–71].

By November 1938, Chamberlain claimed that, apart from the 5,000 who had left for other countries, only 11,000 refugees had been allowed to enter Britain; on average, 2,000 a year (Carsten, 1984, p 11). In fact, Chamberlain's version of the figures of those admitted appear not to account for those for whom re-migration had been the main intent. While there were estimated to be some 10,000 Jewish refugees in Britain at the beginning of 1938, thousands more had arrived in the UK as a first port of call and had left mainly for Palestine (London, 1991, pp 486–87). 'Publicly, a cautious and conservative stance was maintained. The Home Office was always reluctant to admit either how many refugees it was letting in, or how high a proportion of entrants were Jews' (London, 1991, p 498). There is evidence to suggest that discretion was exercised in favour of those who may have been thought economically useful and that the strict sounding policy outlined above could have been part of a strategy by the Home Office and the Anglo-Jewish leaders to play down the numbers of people who were actually allowed entry into Britain. Although permission to work had to be obtained in advance from the Ministry of Labour, leave to land was granted usually without conditions, especially if re-migration was the intent and when Jewish voluntary bodies intervened. The flight of refugees did not, it seems, provoke an increase in the number of immigration officers being appointed (London, 1990 and 1991).

The events of 1938 on the Continent were to provoke a change in official policy. Germany occupied Austria and the Sudetenland. A mass flight of Jews and socialists occurred amidst the looting of Jewish property and many thousands were thrown into concentration camps (Carsten, 1984, p 13). The Home Office decided to review whether an uncertain number of refugees who 'may not be individually undesirable, but may create labour and social problems' should be allowed to enter Britain.[3] On 2 May 1938, visas were made obligatory for Austrian passport holders and for German passport

3 The quoted section is from a Home Office Memorandum, 14 March 1938 (Wasserstein, 1984, p 71).

holders from 21 May 1938. This system was supported by the Anglo-Jewish leaders who themselves had a key role in selecting prospective visa applicants who were then ratified by the Home Office. Otto Schiff, founder of the Jewish Refugee Committee, and influential with the Home Office, was concerned to ensure a priority for those who were likely to be transmigrants:

> ... the imposition of the visa was especially necessary in the case of Austrians who were largely of the shopkeeper and small trader class and who would therefore prove more difficult to emigrate than the average German who came to the UK.[4]

London puts it this way:

> The Home Office wished to avoid the worry, extra work and public pressure which would result from an increase in port refusals and was aware that reintroducing visas for holders of Austrian and German passports would increase the control over arrivals. The rationale for making this change was that once refugees had reached British shores it was usually too late to try to get rid of them: 'The proper course is to select our immigrants at leisure and in advance and this means the institution of a visa system for Germans and Austrians ... The real point is to prevent potential refugees from getting here at all.'[5]

The administrative burden that built up forced a relaxation of the scheme later in 1938. On the other hand, the logic of that system as described by London is now applied as a regular measure, with penalties, in order to avert the flight of non-European refugees to the UK, or to criminalise them when entry is sought without required documents.

Meanwhile, a proposal was made by the US Government to establish an international committee for the purpose of facilitating the emigration of refugees from Austria and Germany. The IGCR was thus inaugurated at the Evian conference of 6–15 July 1938. It was supposed to deal only with Jewish refugees from Germany, although that was never admitted publicly by the American Government, nor the American Jewish Committee (Sjoberg, 1991, pp 49–52). The instruction which British representatives carried emphasised that the British refugee policy could only be applied within the narrow limits dictated by demographic and economic considerations. The Colonial Office had blocked attempts by the Foreign Office to resettle refugees in British colonies, claiming that refugees could present security risks as Nazi agents might operate under that cloak. Apart from Palestine, about 3,000 were resettled elsewhere, including 500 in Kenya and some 100 in Northern Rhodesia. The attitude of other Dominions' governments and, indeed, all

4 This statement by Otto Schiff was made during a meeting between a deputation of the Board of Jewish Deputies, in which he took a leading role, and the Home Secretary (quoted in London, 1990, p 176).

5 The quoted section is attributed to Lord McAlpine in a Home Office memorandum of 1 March 1938 (quoted in *ibid*, p 175n).

other governments at the Evian conference was also generally unpromising (Wasserstein, 1984, pp 72–74; Carsten, 1984, pp 18–19; Dummett and Nicol, 1990, p 158).[6]

The threatened occupation of the Sudetenland and the widespread pogroms during the *Kristallnacht* of November 1938 led to a further dramatic increase in refugees arriving from Germany and Czechoslovakia. Further discussion of settlement in British colonies did not reach the level of concrete action. In November 1938, the Jewish community in Palestine offered to absorb 10,000 Jewish children from Germany but was not responded to by the British Government on the basis of a restrictive immigration policy eventually to be set out in the Palestine White Paper of May 1939. That was to limit the immigration of Jews to Palestine to 75,000 during a five year period beginning on 1 April 1939. The strategic British interest there would be compromised by Arab resistance to the planned domination by Jewish settler colonists pursued by Zionists. Instead, British policy for entry to the UK itself was relaxed somewhat and it was decided that 10,000 children should be admitted to Britain as a compensatory measure (Wasserstein, 1984, pp 74–76; Sjoberg, 1991, pp 72–73). Already, in November 1938, a relaxation of the visa scheme had been introduced so that the younger intending migrants, in particular, and those who sought entry only temporarily were not scrutinised in detail. This relaxed approach continued even when it became apparent that, in many cases, re-migration was not an option as other countries were closing that route (London, 1991, pp 507–11). Official figures later revealed that, by the outbreak of the Second World War, an estimated 78,000 refugees from Nazism were in Britain. Adult refugees from Austria and Germany came to about 55,000 and a further 10,000 adult Czechs were counted. Some 13,000 unaccompanied children and an unknown number of children who had come with their parents were also in Britain. About 90% of the total number were estimated to be Jews (London, 1991, p 512).[7]

At the outbreak of the war, the large scale entry of Jewish refugees ceased and all aliens required visas, applications for which were vetted by the security services. However, re-migration for about 13,000 refugees continued between 1939 and 1945, most leaving in 1940 (London, 1991, pp 513–14). All refugees from Germany and Austria who remained, with the exception of all those already naturalised, were classified as 'enemy aliens' and subjected to

6 In the opinion of Thompson (1938), the creation of a United States of Africa should have been pursued, as a land available not only for the resettlement of Jewish refugees but to deal generally with the problem of over-population in Europe. This may not have fitted easily with the British desire to contain local opposition to further European settlement in various colonial territories.

7 The figures do vary according to the source used, as Carsten (1984, pp 7n, 13) and London (1990, p 165n) warn. The Government itself submitted a smaller figure before the war, but the figures used here are based on those released in 1943 by Sir Alexander Maxwell, Permanent Under Secretary of State at the Home Office (London, 1991, pp 487n, 512).

certain restrictions. Initially, 'enemy aliens' were classified into three categories. Category A were cases to be interned forthwith (about 600); category B were doubtful cases (about 7,000); and category C were thought to be genuine refugees from Nazi oppression (about 64,000). Internment was decided by a tribunal headed by a judge, or retired judge, and attended by a police secretary. The second group undoubtedly included many genuine refugees since practice among the approximately 120 tribunals varied greatly. But, starting with the German invasion of the Low Countries in Spring 1940 and ending with the defeat of France by the end of June 1940, the Government in stages interned all male German and Austrian citizens between the ages of 16 and 60.[8] Women in category C were spared internment. Some 30,000 people were interned in makeshift improvised camps, mostly on the Isle of Man, and some 4,200 were shipped to Canada or Australia. This policy went sharply into reverse after a few months as public opinion went strongly in favour of refugees. Internees were screened again and gradually certain groups of refugees who were thought useful for the war effort were released. Those who had been shipped to Canada or Australia were allowed to return. After the internment episode, many refugees took an active part in the British military effort. After the war, many emigrated to America and other continents, but many others remained in Britain and became British citizens, while between 7,000–8,000 orphaned children from concentration camps were also admitted (Carsten, 1984, pp 13, 20–25).[9]

At the domestic level, therefore, the evidence indicates that there was close co-operation between influential Jewish leaders and the Government to underplay the number of refugees and to facilitate their settlement or re-migration. Jews were allowed a qualified welcome by the official system which collaborated in the demand of the Jewish organisations to assist in their migration effort.[10] This record is soured somewhat by the wartime internment episode which indiscriminately targeted those fleeing Nazi policies. On the other hand, British policy at the international level was to understate the possibility of absorption of a large number of refugees from Nazi Europe. However, this was part of a strategy to obtain acceptances from other States for asylum migration and could have also been a means to obtain concessions on the refugees' property rights from the German Government. Palestine, under British domination, was already a special place of interest for Jewish

8 France had at the outset decided to intern in concentration camps all male German refugees up to 50 years of age together with all other German subjects (Sjoberg, 1991, p 64).

9 For critical analyses of the internment episode, see Kushner (1993); Burleston (1993) on press attitudes; and Kochan (1993) on women's experiences of internment.

10 While the present study is not based upon the leading work by Sherman (1995), several other studies cited here do refer extensively to Sherman's work, and his conclusions seem consonant with the view adopted in the present study that the British response to Jewish refugees from the Third Reich was comparatively favourable (see Cohen, 1996).

settler colonialism. When international resettlement efforts were proving more difficult, domestic policy remained flexible enough to accommodate further refugees arriving as a result of Nazi expansionism. After the Second World War, the European refugee situation prompted another effort of internationalisation resulting in the 1951 Refugee Convention, backed up by the promotion of immigration from the refugee camps and from beyond the rising Iron Curtain.

4.2 REFUGEE LAW AND POLICY IN POST-WAR EUROPE

The Second World War had left massive numbers of displaced persons in and outside of camps on the European continent. In 4.2.1, the international arrangements that were made to resettle displaced persons are reviewed, together with the British attitude towards the acceptance of European displaced persons in the UK. It is argued that, at the international level, resettlement was the main aim while, in Britain, the fact that they were European enabled their acceptance. In 4.2.2, an explanation of the main components of a new international regime for refugees, as developed from 1950, is given. There is a discussion of the main treaty instrument, the Refugee Convention of 1951, which remains the key instrument in practice today. It is argued that the subjects of the new international refugee order were European refugees. In 4.2.3, a closer examination is made of how the UK implemented the Convention's obligations in the domestic context. As with earlier regimes for European refugees, the gates tended to be kept open for later arrivals as well, despite the explicit limitation of the Refugee Convention's applicability to those who arrived prior to 1951.

4.2.1 Wartime population displacement in Europe

By 1939, the Nansen Office and the High Commissioner for Refugees coming from Germany had been replaced by the High Commissioner of the League of Nations who took over responsibility for some 600,000 persons coming under the purview of the two previous offices. Another British man, Sir Herbert Emerson, was appointed to the High Commissioner's Office, and he was also to head the IGCR. He was thus responsible for the legal protection of refugees, the co-ordination of material assistance, and extension of aid to governments and private organisations in their endeavours for emigration and settlement.[11] The IGCR was, however, largely inactive between October 1939 and August 1943 due to opposition from the United States and the Americans' wish to see

11 The League of Nations High Commissioner passed on the duty of protection formally to the IGCR at the end of 1946 (Holborn, 1956, p 9).

it act as subsidiary to the League's High Commissioner (Holborn, 1956, pp 8–9, Sjoberg, 1991, pp 59–70, 74). Its mandate was extended significantly at an Anglo-American conference in Bermuda in April 1943 to include 'all persons, wherever they may be, who, as a result of events in Europe, have had to leave, or may have to leave, their countries of residence because of the danger to their lives or liberties on account of their race, religion or political beliefs' (quoted in Sjoberg, 1991, pp 146–47). A number of possible reasons have been given for the desire to extend the IGCR's mandate: refugees were seen in some areas as hampering the war effort; the perceived need for countries other than Britain and America, who were hitherto the sole contributors, to take a portion of the financial cost; and Britain's concerns over immigration into Palestine (Sjoberg, 1991, pp 130–34). Another organisation, UNRRA, was also set up in autumn 1943 as a result of the Bermuda conference (Sjoberg, 1991, p 126). There was an uneasy overlap between the remit of the two organisations – UNRRA's main task was to reconstruct devastated areas, to provide food and medical supplies and the repatriation of so called displaced persons. In practice, however, it was difficult to distinguish clearly between those displaced persons who could be repatriated and those who did not wish to be (Sjoberg, 1991, pp 153–54). Eventually, its mandate was also widened to assisting, 'for a reasonable period', non-repatriable displaced persons, who were also considered to be the IGCR's responsibility.

Towards the end of the Second World War, the Polish displaced persons constituted the largest group in Allied occupied Europe, the overwhelming majority of whom had been in Germany as forced labourers. Many of those who were held by the Allied powers returned to Poland to the extent that, between summer and autumn of 1945, they numbered some 800,000 and, by December 1946, had fallen to 270,000. In September 1945, out of a total of 650,000 displaced persons in the British Occupation Zone in Germany, there were some 510,000 Poles and 51,000 people from the Baltic States. A total of 60,000 persons were also held in the British Occupation Zone in Austria. Although some had political reasons for not returning, most did not seem to be aware of the rapidly changing European political situation (Sjoberg, 1991, pp 175–77; Sword *et al*, 1989, p 34).[12]

At first, the Western powers were agreeable to repatriating large numbers of East European citizens, as agreed at the Yalta Conference in February 1945, and many ended up in Stalin's labour camps upon return.[13] As for Baltic, Polish and Ukrainian nationals, repatriation was harder to manage and ceased by the end of 1946. In the meantime, East European States, which had suffered

12 For a study of the uncertainty of emigration as an option for the Polish displaced persons and demobilised soldiers, see Sword *et al* (1989, pp 357–68).

13 Tolstoy (1977) records the return of over two million Russians to the Soviet Union between 1944 and 1947 by the Western Allies.

massive losses in the war, insisted that all measures should be taken to expedite and encourage repatriation and that, until that programme was completed, the recruitment of displaced persons for labour in Britain or elsewhere should be stopped. The British Government, meanwhile, favoured a broader approach to the problem of displaced persons, primarily with a view to lightening its own share of budgetary commitments that it had had to bear in respect of the IGCR's operational expenditure. In camps holding Polish, Baltic, Ukrainian and Yugoslav displaced persons, a propaganda war was promoted to persuade them not to return to their respective countries of origin, and such activities were supported by the British and Americans. The British and American Governments arrived at a compromise to, first, extend the IGCR's mandate to include the resettlement of non-repatriable displaced persons; secondly, to temporarily extend the funding of UNRRA; and, finally, to mandate the IRO to resettle displaced persons (Sjoberg, 1991, pp 184–93, 197, 213–14; Loescher, 1993, pp 47–48).

The differences between the East European States and the Western countries were hardened with the deepening Cold War, and fed into the new arrangements that were being made. In the United Nations (UN) deliberations on the formation of the IRO, the East European States (Yugoslavia, Byelorussia, Poland, the USSR and the Ukrainian SSR) objected to 'quislings, war criminals, traitors, Fascists, and undemocratic elements who opposed governments of their countries' receiving assistance from an international organisation. Meanwhile, Western States, led by Britain and the United States, argued that only active leaders or political dissidents should be denied assistance; otherwise indiscriminate suppression of all manifestations of political disagreement on the part of refugees would infringe the basic right of freedom of speech (Holborn, 1956, pp 29–46).

Eventually, a compromise formula was reached to enumerate the people of concern to the IRO. If a person wished to be resettled in a country other than a country of origin, it was necessary for him to have sound grounds for his refusal to go home. Such 'valid objections' could be made only after he had received 'adequate information'. That was deemed to consist of full knowledge of the facts regarding conditions in his country of nationality or former habitual residence. Such information was to be communicated to the person concerned by representatives of the governments of those countries who were to be given every facility for visiting camps and assemblies for this purpose. This was a concession to the concerns of East European States. The 'valid objections' had to be well founded, arising from 'persecution or fear, based on reasonable grounds, of persecution because of race, religion, nationality or political opinions, provided these opinions were not in conflict with the principles of the UN ...' from 'compelling family reasons arising out of previous persecution, or compelling reasons of infirmity or illness'; or from 'objections of a political nature judged by the organisation to be "valid"' (Holborn, 1956, p 49).[14]

However, before the IRO came into operation, the passage of the Anglo-American motion in August 1946 to extend the IGCR's mandate led to the withdrawal from that organisation by East European States and their non-participation in all future UN refugee work in the IRO and its successor body, the UNHCR (Sjoberg, 1991, pp 219–20). At the instance of Western governments, and following the communist coup in Czechoslovakia in 1948, the IRO's programme was widened to include escapees from East European communist regimes (Loescher, 1993, pp 49–51). From its official inception in July 1947 to its winding up in December 1951, the IRO did carry out some of the tasks of UNRRA and the IGCR, such as providing aid. But its main task was also to facilitate resettlement. Its health, care and maintenance and vocational training programmes – 'a broad social welfare programme' – were developed with this view in mind (Holborn, 1956, pp 2, 50). The IRO supervised the resettlement of over one million refugees, of whom Britain took some 86,000, mainly as European Volunteer Workers, the vast majority of whom arrived in Britain after the IRO began operations (Stadulis, 1952, p 208).

The British Government had already identified an urgent shortage of labour especially as some 350,000 German prisoners of war, who had contributed a great deal towards British labour needs, were now about to be returned to Germany, while the birth rate was falling and there was a high rate of emigration to the Dominions.[15] The first source of labour to be chosen was General Anders's anti-Soviet Polish army of approximately 200,000 soldiers. They had fought for the Allies under British command and were kept disbanded for some time after the war. They had declared their allegiance to the Polish Government in exile and could not return to Poland under the Communists. As a result of the Yalta Conference of February 1945, the Warsaw Government was recognised from 5 July 1945 in preference to the Polish Government in London. Rather than giving the Polish soldiers the status of displaced persons, the British Government preferred to arrange for their resettlement unilaterally (Sjoberg, 1991, pp 175–77; Kochavi, 1991, p 367).

From 11 September 1946, Polish ex-servicemen, living in camps in Britain, East Africa and the Middle East, were recruited to work in Britain through the

14 These categories of persons were laid down in Section C of Annex I, Pt I of the Constitution of the IRO, 18 UNTS 53. Certain categories of persons were not to be of concern to the IRO, among them, war criminals, quislings and traitors, criminals who were extraditable by treaty, persons of German ethnic origin and sponsors of movements encouraging refugees not to return to their country of origin, Constitution of the IRO, Annex I, Pt II.

15 Stadulis (1952, pp 209–12) and Paul (1997, pp 64–89) provide useful accounts of the population trends and labour needs identified in official circles at the time. Paul (1997, p 25) gives the average annual figure of emigration between 1946 and 1960 from the UK at 125,000 people, about 80% of whom went to Australia, Canada, New Zealand, South Africa and Southern Rhodesia.

agency of the Polish Resettlement Corps. Demobilised soldiers already in Britain did not necessarily give their support to the Corps, some even preferring to emigrate on their own terms. Although the threat of deportation could be used, it was made very unlikely because of the threat of adverse publicity to the Government, the need to show that serious enough criminal offences had been committed to warrant such measures, and the unwillingness of countries of origin to accept persons with an uncertain nationality status, minimised this risk. In 1948, 114,037 ex-soldiers were estimated to have been recruited. Under the 'Pole Jump' Scheme some 30,000 dependants of these men were also admitted to Britain from Europe, East Africa, the Middle East and India.[16] A special measure, the Polish Resettlement Act 1947, was passed through Parliament, but it 'was not as its title may suggest, a piece of immigration legislation' as some 127,000 Polish troops were already in Britain, but it was meant to provide for pensions, unemployment assistance, accommodation, health services and education to Poles and the recognition of foreign medical practitioners' or pharmacists' qualifications (Holborn, 1956, pp 392–93; Holmes, 1988, p 211; Sword *et al*, 1989, pp 298–302, 321–31).[17]

Also, from 1946, a new policy of importing labour from the displaced persons camps was instituted. Several groups of European Volunteer Workers were admitted to Britain. In autumn 1946, some 1,000 women from Latvia, Lithuania and Estonia were recruited under the 'Balt Cygnet' Scheme to supply domestic staff for hospitals and sanatoria in Britain. In March 1947, the 'Westward Ho' scheme was applied in the British Occupation Zone in Germany by the Ministry of Labour with the aim of recruiting 60,000–100,000 displaced persons and their dependants for work in British industries. Initially, men and women of Baltic and Ukrainian nationality were recruited from the British Zones in Germany and Austria, but later displaced persons of Polish, Yugoslav, Hungarian, Czech, Romanian and Bulgarian nationality, from the Western Occupation Zones, were taken. An additional 8,397 Ukrainian prisoners of war were also recruited from camps in Italy, which was at the time under pressure from the Soviet Government for the return of such prisoners. The displaced persons had to be unmarried and they were

16 Holmes (1988, p 211) gives a figure of 33,000 for dependants of the Polish Resettlement Corps group. The total number of family members admitted from these regions is said to be 40,000 (Holborn, 1956, p 393).

17 The figure of 127,000 and the quote is from Sword *et al* (1989, p 326). The difference in recruitment figures and the total number of troops can be to some extent accounted for by the fact that by February 1947, there were about 15,000 men who had not decided to join up with the Corps. Paul (1997, p 68) gives a figure of between 120,000 and 125,500 former members of the Polish armed forces and their dependants as living in Britain by the end of 1949 and who were expected to remain permanently. The Polish Resettlement Act 1947, 10 & 11 Geo 6, c 19 was mainly an enabling act, empowering the various ministries concerned with social welfare and health care to assume powers to provide these services to Poles resettled in Britain. It did not directly deal with who was to be admitted under the various schemes mentioned.

recruited exclusively for work as manual labourers. They had to undertake to only engage in labour selected by the Ministry of Labour and the place of employment could only be changed by the consent of that Ministry. The employment restrictions were considerably lightened by January 1951 by freeing those who had been resident for three years from the most onerous of them (Sjoberg, 1991, pp 193–98; Holmes, 1988, pp 213–14, 230–31; Holborn, 1956, pp 389–92; Sword *et al*, 1989, pp 332–41).[18]

Additionally, from the latter half of 1950, some 2,000 people from Germany and Austria who were thought to have limited prospects of resettlement were admitted to Britain, including widows with children, aged persons, professional people who could not be retrained in a trade, the blind and individuals with relatives they could not leave behind. They were admitted on the condition that friends or relatives would find maintenance and accommodation for them, or that it would be provided by voluntary organisations that would continue to take responsibility for their care. In the aftermath of the war, Britain seems to have been a place where many other people passed through either to return to their countries of origin or to obtain resettlement in other countries. Between the end of the war and 31 March 1952, the Under Secretary of State for the Home Department estimated that 302,396 foreigners who could be regarded as refugees had entered the UK or, having entered the UK during the war, were allowed to remain there. Over 80,000 of these were estimated to have re-migrated or returned to their countries (Holborn, 1956, p 393).

While several commentators have documented the huge recruitment drive by the British Government in the aftermath of the Second World War, few have related the enthusiasm with which the new additions to the British population were thought of in official circles, especially in relation to the migration of other groups in the post-war period. Paul's (1997) study is exceptional in this regard, as she compares the British reaction to the European displaced persons and other potential labour recruits from Europe with the attitudes manifested in the case of migrant workers from South Asia and the West Indies who were not white Europeans. There was a presumption that the European recruits would become potential Britons:

> Like the debates on imperial migration, the vocabulary of foreign labour recruitment resounded with references to blood and stock. The overall image constructed the foreigners, if not quite as family, then at least as potentially acceptable in-laws. It appeared that the external trappings of Britishness could be acquired so long as the basic building blocks of genetic similarity were in place [Paul, 1997, p 84].

18 Paul (1997, p 82) records that both the Ministry of Labour and the Home Office acknowledged that there were limits on the enforcement of the recruits' contracts, and it was believed in the Ministry of Labour that the threat of deportation could only be used in the most extreme cases.

Indeed, Paul (1997, pp 85–89) also reveals that the terms such as 'foreigners' or 'displaced persons' were domestically rejected in favour of 'European Volunteer Workers', and that this was calculated to create a discourse of economic assistance based on European kinship which was backed by the media. The combination of political opposition to the Eastern Bloc and the racial acceptability of European refugees in Britain combined to inform the reactions to further refugee movements, and the institution of a further Western led international agenda for refugees.

4.2.2 Establishing a European framework for refugees: the Refugee Convention of 1951

Since the IRO was envisaged as an agency of limited duration, there were discussions as to what type of organisation should replace it, given that there was still a continuing outflow of refugees from the Eastern Bloc countries. Salomon (1991, p 228) notes that 'the Western powers felt, willingly or unwillingly, obliged to continue in one way or the other the refugee policy introduced during the Second World War'. Within the Western camp, the basic division was between some Western European States on the one hand, and the United States and Britain on the other. The former, led by France, wanted to see an agency that could provide material assistance as well as legal and political protection until a solution was found for the refugees. The United States and the UK, on the other hand, favoured an agency with only a limited budget to provide only legal and political protection, and favoured the integration of refugees in the initial state of asylum. The UNHCR, as the office became known under its statute passed by the UN General Assembly in 1950 (it started operating on 1 January 1951), was therefore left to appeal to governments for material assistance each time an emergency arose. At least initially, it was prevented from organising migration projects as the IRO had been able to do. While no time or geographical limitation appeared in its mandate, the UNHCR only had the facility of using diplomatic pressure that it could bring upon States in order to safeguard the legal rights and interests of refugees (Salomon, 1991, pp 218–21, 229).

When it came to negotiating a UN Convention, the United States, France and Italy, for different reasons, opposed recognising non-European refugees as being eligible for protection thereunder, and also opposed recognising refugees emerging from beyond the immediate post-war context. The UK, on the other hand, took leadership in advocating the broadest possible definition of a 'refugee', both in the UNHCR statute as well as the Convention, arguing that no restrictions of time and place should be included. The British representative, Sir Samuel Hoare (a former Home Secretary), did not believe that the refugee problem in the future would be a serious burden on European countries, even if the definition was extended to embrace non-European refugees. Thus, at this point, the possibility of flight to Europe of Asian and African refugees was perceived as negligible. Sir Samuel Hoare also considered that it was of the utmost importance that a convention negotiated under the auspices of the UN should provide minimum guarantees for all refugees, wherever they came from. In this, the UK was supported by non-European States such as China, Iraq and Pakistan. India, in a similar position to Pakistan, with millions of refugees on its territory, did not, however, advocate a broad definition (Salomon, 1991, pp 221–32; Hathaway, 1990, pp 151–57).[19] Eventually, the Convention relating to the Status of Refugees was adopted unanimously by a Conference of Plenipotentiaries in 1951, and came into force three years later with the sixth ratification. The Convention was, first, extended to those recognised as refugees under the previous international arrangements (both pre- and post-war).[20] Secondly, a new refugee was defined in Art 1A(2) of the Convention as someone who:

> ... As a result of events occurring before 1 January 1951 and owing to a well founded fear of being persecuted for reasons of race, religion, nationality, membership of a particular social group or political opinion, is outside the country of his nationality and is unable, or owing to such fear, is unwilling to avail himself of the protection of that country; or who, not having a nationality and being outside the country of his former habitual residence as a result of such events, is unable or, owing to such fear, is unwilling to return to it.

The States which had advocated a narrow approach had won; the Convention was limited in its application to individuals who were refugees as 'a result of events occurring before 1 January 1951', and governments were given the discretion to apply it to those who were refugees 'owing to events in Europe or owing to events in Europe and elsewhere'.[21]

Perhaps as a magnanimous gesture from other States, the Conference of Plenipotentiaries included in the Final Act appended to the Convention a paragraph on a proposal by the UK. It was stated in the Final Act that the Conference:

> ... Expresses the hope that the Convention relating to the Status of Refugees will have value as an example exceeding its contractual scope and that all nations will be guided by it in granting so far as possible to persons in their

19 UN discussions on this topic are reproduced in Takkenberg and Tahbaz (1989, vol 3, pp 391–93, 400–03, 408–13, 544–48, 553). India's opposition to a broad definition was due to the inability to predict in advance exactly what categories of refugees would be covered (vol 2, p 15).

20 Refugee Convention 1951, Art 1A(1). Article 10 recognised any residence in a contracting State as being lawful if the refugee concerned had been forcibly displaced during the Second World War.

21 *Ibid*, Art 1B.

territory as refugees, and who would not be covered by the terms of the Convention, the treatment for which it provides.[22]

When the UK ratified the Convention on 11 March 1954, it was accepted that refugees displaced as a result of events from 'elsewhere' and 'in Europe' were to be recognised.[23] The new arrangements were largely influenced by the interests of Western governments, as they perceived them, particularly as driven by the United States.[24] The formula of 'persecution' was seen as condemning the policies of the countries of the Eastern Bloc towards their citizens, while a steady outflow of people occurred, until those countries took measures to stop people from leaving (Hathaway, 1990, pp 148–51). A large number of refugees were received in the United States and in Germany during the 1950s and 1960s. Of these movements there is a good deal of recorded information (Loescher, 1993, pp 58–61). What is not clear is the extent to which the UK played a part in this scenario, a question that is addressed below in 4.2.3. In sum, a dual protection system for refugees was established – a conventional, legalistic focus for European refugees who were mainly already in countries of asylum, and a material assistance paradigm which the UNHCR was to eventually, but not immediately, pursue in containing situations of large scale displacement in the so called 'Third World' (Hathaway, 1990, pp 151–62).

Some explanation of the provisions of the 1951 Convention itself is necessary, bearing in mind that several important works have already been dedicated to analysing them in detail (for example, Robinson, 1953; Weis, 1953; Grahl-Madsen, 1972; Goodwin-Gill, 1983, 1996; Hathaway, 1991).[25] The question of defining eligibility under the Convention gave rise to a difference of opinion among States, as has been noted above. Apart from deciding who would benefit from its provisions, it also laid down what benefits would be granted. These included a promise of non-discriminatory treatment of refugees as far as considerations of race, religion and country of origin were concerned.[26] Other provisions deal with juridical status; rights to gainful employment, self-employment or professional activity; welfare including housing, public education and public relief; and administrative measures such

22 The UK's original proposal to the conference read: 'Expresses the hope that this Convention will have value as an example exceeding its contractual scope and that all nations will be guided by it in granting so far as possible to persons present in their territory as refugees and who would not be covered by the terms of para A of Art 1 the treatment for which this Convention provides.' UN Doc A/CONF2/107, 25 July 1951.

23 *Molefi v Principal Legal Adviser* [1971] AC 182, p 190, PC.

24 The US in fact stayed out of the arrangement that it had bargained for hard, preferring instead to adopt an independent refugee policy which could favour its own interests centring around Cold War considerations (Loescher, 1993, pp 58–63).

25 Takkenberg and Tahbaz (1989) provide an accessible compilation of the Convention's *travaux preparatoires*, while Weis (1995) analyses the *travaux* relevant to some, but not all, provisions of the Convention.

26 Refugee Convention 1951, Art 3. Article 4 also provides for the freedom to practise religion and freedom of religious education for children.

as the provision of travel documents.[27] These rights were to be enjoyed on the basis of a mixture of treatment equal to that of nationals, most-favoured-nationals treatment or treatment accorded to aliens generally.

Most important for practice today, and certainly more than they were at the time, are the provisions in the Convention that are pertinent to asylum, although 'a right to asylum' as such is not guaranteed by the Convention. Such a lack reflects the reluctance of States to give away their freedom of action in this field, and was also reflected in the earlier discussions on the Universal Declaration on Human Rights of 1948. Article 14 of the Universal Declaration declared that: 'Everyone has the right to seek and to enjoy in other countries asylum from persecution.' However, in the debates leading up to its adoption by the UN General Assembly, the UK successfully proposed an amendment to substitute 'to enjoy' for 'to be granted'. Mrs Corbet, for the UK, declared that 'the right of asylum was the right of every State to offer refuge and to resist all demands for extradition. This was the meaning of the expression "to enjoy asylum" contained in the amendment' (quoted in Morgenstern, 1949, pp 336–37).[28] Hersch Lauterpacht, a leading international lawyer (and later a judge of the International Court of Justice), severely criticised this provision in the Declaration as being:

> ... couched in a language which is calculated to mislead ... concealing the determination of States to maintain full freedom of action. Thus, few persons – and perhaps few lawyers – reading Art 14 of the Declaration relating to asylum will appreciate the fact that there was no intention to assume even a moral obligation to grant asylum [Lauterpacht, 1948, p 373].[29]

On the other hand, some Articles of the 1951 Convention are considered to have developed further the international law relating to admission, expulsion and refoulement of refugees, thereby certainly affecting conditions under which asylum may be enjoyed (Plender, 1988, pp 397–98). Article 33 of the Convention contained a prohibition on States to 'expel or return (*"refouler"*) a refugee in any manner whatsoever to the frontiers of territories where his life or freedom would be threatened ...'. Its benefit could not be claimed by a person whom there were reasonable grounds for regarding as a danger to the security of the country or who had been convicted by a final judgment of a particularly serious crime.[30] Article 32 further provided that States shall not expel a refugee 'lawfully in their territory save on grounds of national security or public order', and then only after the due process of law was undergone (except in danger to national security cases).[31] The Convention further

27 See Refugee Convention 1951, Arts 10–30.

28 The amendment was carried by 30 votes for, one against, with 12 abstentions (Morgenstern, 1949, p 337).

29 See, also, Plender (1988, p 397) for a discussion of this point.

30 Refugee Convention 1951, Art 33(2).

31 *Ibid*, Art 32(1) and (2).

provided that a reasonable time must be given for the refugee to seek legal admission into another country, although any 'internal measures' could be applied.[32] Under Art 31, States were prohibited from imposing penalties on account of refugees' illegal entry or presence if they came directly to their territory, provided they presented themselves to the authorities without delay and showed good cause for their illegal entry or presence.[33] Only necessary restrictions were allowed to be imposed on the movements of refugees under that Article, and reasonable time and 'all the necessary facilities' to obtain admission into another country had to be given.[34] These provisions could certainly involve problems of interpretation (Plender, 1988, pp 425–33; Goodwin-Gill, 1983, pp 74–81). However, these ambiguities have come to the fore in legal debates only in more recent decades as States have sought to minimise the Convention's applicability in the case of non-European refugees. At the time, however, as both Coles (1989) and Hathaway (1990, p 160) have remarked, the Convention carried an 'exilic bias', implying that the (European) refugees who had found places of resettlement would not be asked to return.

Meanwhile, European movements towards harmonisation in various legal fields have had some relevance for immigration matters for nationals of States which are members of the variety of organisations established in the post-Second World War period. The Council of Europe, towards which the UK had some scepticism as a mere 'talking shop' and because of possible dilution of relations with the United States and the Commonwealth (Robertson, 1973, pp 4–15), developed several instruments on migration. The European Convention on Establishment of 1955[35] which regulates, on the basis of reciprocity, the rights of nationals of Member States residing in another such State, was not acceded to by the UK until the passage of the Immigration Appeals Act 1969. That Convention has been seen, in particular, as relevant to the strict regulation of expulsion of Member State nationals in the European Economic Community context which guarantees free movement of persons in a wide variety of situations (Plender, 1988, pp 236–40). The European Convention on Extradition of 1957 specifically excludes its application where a crime is of a political character or where there are substantial grounds for believing that an extradition request is based on a crime the prosecution of which or the punishment for which is intended against a person for his race, religion, nationality or political opinion.[36] The UK did not accede to that Convention until February 1991.

32 Refugee Convention 1951, Art 32(3).

33 *Ibid*, Art 31(1).

34 *Ibid*, Art 31(2).

35 529 UNTS 141.

36 European Convention on Extradition 1957, 359 UNTS 276, Art 3.

The most relevant Council of Europe instrument, especially in more recent years, has been the European Convention on Human Rights of 1950 ratified by the UK on 8 March 1951.[37] That Convention guarantees a number of rights to each person within the jurisdiction of a State Party that have been pleaded by asylum seekers before the European Commission and the European Court of Human Rights set up under it, although its legislative recognition within British domestic law takes place only from October 2000, with the coming into force of the Human Rights Act 1998. Nevertheless, no right to asylum is guaranteed in the European Convention on Human Rights and a recommendation of the Parliamentary Assembly of the Council of Europe of 1961 that such a right be included in the Second Protocol to the Convention was not accepted by the Member States (Plender, 1988, pp 256–57). Further, the Court and Commission (as well as the Committee of Ministers), while upholding certain of the Convention's norms in asylum cases, have failed to ensure their full protection, in particular where cases have arisen against the UK.[38] It is relevant to note that the European Convention on Human Rights, as with the Refugee Convention of 1951, was not tested until the British authorities began to prevent the settlement of non-European refugees especially from the 1960s. While European refugees continued to be the main subjects of the right of asylum, the domestic legal system continued to remain unobtrusive.

4.2.3 The UK's refugee policy in the Cold War context

As for the articles of the Refugee Convention of 1951 which dealt with civil, economic and social rights of refugees, the UK maintained the position that the law in the UK was not dependent on reciprocity with other States and that, in general, it applied to aliens and British subjects alike, except with respect to the franchise (reserved for British subjects) the requirement of leave to enter for aliens and their liability to deportation (Takkenberg and Tahbaz, 1989, vol 2, p 32).[39] When the Aliens Order 1953 was issued,[40] a prayer to have it annulled was moved in the House of Commons by Leslie Hale. Those who opposed the Order concentrated on the fact that it was issued under the Aliens Restriction Acts of 1914 and 1919 which had been passed into law during a period of war with virtually no parliamentary debate (although that system had been kept alive by continual yearly renewals by Parliament).

---

37 213 UNTS 221.

38 For a fuller appraisal of the Council of Europe's work in the asylum field, see Plender (1988, pp 256–63).

39 Weis (1953, p 485) noted in the context of of the 1951 Refugee Convention, Art 12 (question of resolving a refugee's domicilary law) that the common law position was moving towards acceptance of the possibility of loss of the domicile of birth.

40 Aliens Order 1953, SI 1953/1671.

However, the Order was also objected to on the basis that there was no recognition in it of the historic right of asylum. The prayer for annulment was unsuccessful.[41] The UK's policy on refugees therefore remained relatively unpublicised except for some ministerial statements given in Parliamentary answers. In 1949, there was an assurance from the Government, in a discussion of refugees from Franco's Spain, that regard would be had to what could happen to them if they were returned because of their political or religious beliefs, although no general assurance was given (Morgenstern, 1949, p 346). In 1954, Sir David Maxwell Fyfe assured the House of Commons in a written answer that, if a person's life or liberty was in danger because of his political opinion were he to be required to leave the UK, he would normally be regarded as a political refugee. Reference was also made to the possibility of recognising a person as either Stateless or as deserving leave to enter on 'compassionate grounds', implying that all such cases would lead to a person being granted permanent residence.[42] Although the tests enumerated for refugee status in such public statements were narrower than those provided for in the 1951 Convention, there was little scope, or it seems need, to test the Government's interpretation in the courts.

To those refugees considered to have entered 'lawfully', Art 32 of the Refugee Convention provided an obligation of due process before effecting expulsion. The suggestion that any right of appeal was imported by Art 32 was eagerly dismissed by the UK during the discussions leading up to the adoption of the Convention. The UK proposed the inclusion of the words 'or a person or persons specially designated by the competent authority' in Art 32. According to Sir Samuel Hoare, the UK representative, that was done because otherwise:

> ... The second sentence of para 2 appeared to suggest some kind of procedure for appeal. A person served with a deportation order in the UK had wide facilities for presenting his case to the Home Office either personally or through a solicitor. However, it was a matter on which public opinion was very vigilant and which often gave rise to interventions by Members of Parliament or to questions in the House of Commons. There was, however, no appeal tribunal, nor did the UK Government wish to be obliged to institute one [quoted in Takkenberg and Tahbaz, 1989, vol 3, p 333].

Few other references to the legal position of refugees in the 1950s and 1960s can be found. The 1967 Wilson Committee Report examined the possibility of establishing an appeal system within the context of immigration control. That Committee also made some findings as to the procedure which had been applied to claims for asylum. Where there was a question regarding the risk of deportation against the provisions of the Conventions on Refugees and

41 For the relevant debate, see House of Commons Debates, vol 522, cols 1881–1924, 27 January 1954.

42 House of Commons Debates, vol 550, written answers, cols 4–5, 21 June 1954.

Stateless Persons, aliens did not always have the possibility of making representations to the Chief Magistrate (who only could hear pleas against a recommendation to deport if the alien had been in the UK for two years).[43] On the other hand, a decision to make a deportation order could be made by the Secretary of State without a court recommendation. In such cases, aliens were given the chance to make representations to an officer of the Immigration and Nationality Department of the Home Office who could visit the applicant and bring his report to the notice of the Home Secretary.[44] No mention was made by the Wilson Committee about how a claim for asylum was treated if made at a port of entry. Grahl-Madsen (1966, p 366) found, however, that claims for asylum submitted at the port of entry were passed on to the Home Office by the immigration officer concerned, although the primary investigation of the claimant's *bona fides* would be carried out by the latter. 'It makes no difference whether the person concerned is a Convention "refugee" or a refugee in a wider sense. The same applies in the case of a person who requests asylum while he is allowed to stay in the country.' The Home Office had 'lately' also made it a practice to ask the opinion of the UNHCR before a decision was made. There was thus a minimalistic incorporation of the Refugee Convention's norms in the UK legal system. It appeared rather that the Home Office was content to retain a large amount of discretionary power to admit aliens, including any refugees among them, while the powers under the Aliens Order were retained until 1 January 1973 when the Immigration Act 1971 came into force.[45]

The actual *practice* of control in the early decades after the Second World War showed that wide powers of immigration control were seldom utilised against European refugees. 170,000 nationals of countries under Communist rule were declared as registered in the UK by the end of 1955.[46] As a result of the Hungarian crisis of 1956, about 180,000 refugees left for Austria and 20,000 for Yugoslavia. The question of an international mandate for UNHCR action came up. The then High Commissioner, Auguste R Lindt, a Swiss lawyer, reasoned that it was reasonable to relate the departure of the Hungarian refugees to the fundamental political changes during the Second World War, not merely to the events which took place in November 1956. Thus, he argued that refugees ought to be considered as coming within the scope of the Convention despite the fact that flight took place after 1 January 1951. There was little doubt that resettlement rather than repatriation was the preferred

43 Grahl-Madsen (1966, p 366) also notes this point, although he could be read to imply that a deportation order would be made against a person only if there was a criminal conviction which, in theory at least, was not the case under the Aliens Order.

44 *Report of the Committee on Immigration Appeals* (the Wilson Committee), Cmnd 3387, Parliamentary Papers, vol XXXVI, p 457, para 54 (1966–67).

45 The subsequent amendments to the Aliens Order 1953 made no reference to asylum.

46 House of Commons Debates, vol 550, written answers, col 68, 21 June 1954.

solution to the plight of the Hungarian refugees (Holborn, 1975, vol 1, pp 391–97). A media campaign was mounted in many countries for the refugees. Both France and Britain announced their intention to take an unlimited number of refugees. The British response to an appeal from Austria for international assistance was immediate, and was led by the Red Cross. Possibly upwards of 20,000 Hungarians found asylum in the UK within a few days, the highest of any European country.[47] Tabori (1972, p 340) recounts that, had the UK Government not been so generous, 'there would have been something of a revolution, for there was a tidal wave of sympathy and compassion for the men, women and children who were stumbling across the minefields and barbed wire into Austria'. A rescue type operation was mounted, with independent charter aviation companies and the BOAC lending aircraft for the purpose of conveying refugees to the UK (Oliver, 1966, pp 527–32). No qualifications were demanded from the refugees; 'the fact that they were refugees and wanted to come was enough' (Oliver, 1966, p 529). In her study of the British Red Cross, Oliver recounts the type of treatment received by the arriving refugees:

> ... The most dramatic incident was when an aircraft was bringing a party scheduled to leave Euston at midnight. The plane was late. British Railways were persuaded to hold the express. When the refugees landed they were passed through Customs and Immigration as if by magic and then with a police motor escort at nose and tail the convoy of three coaches roared through London in half an hour and the train steamed out only a few minutes behind time [Oliver, 1966, p 529].

Apart from the Hungarians admitted in large numbers, there were cases of individual asylum seekers rather than a mass flight out of any Eastern Bloc country since exit barriers constituted a significant hurdle to movement.[48] There was also a trickle of younger Poles arriving to settle in Britain since the late 1950s, the overwhelming majority of whom were women for whom the intention to stay in Britain has been linked to marriage to a British citizen (Sword, 1996, p 81). According to the 1971 census, some 13,470 persons who had arrived in Britain between 1950 and 1971 had been born in Poland. Patterson (1978) estimated that between 1971 and 1975 the number of new arrivals from Poland was about 2,600. Among them were noted to be 'small but significant contingents of active political exiles from Communist Poland' (Patterson, 1978, p 216). Sword (1996) estimates that from 1976 to 1990 7,060 Poles arrived giving a total of some 23,130 since 1950. For the present

47 Figures do vary according to the source. Loescher and Scanlan (1986, p 52) put the figure at 21,100 for the UK. Tabori (1972, p 339) puts the figure of those admitted at about 30,000 and those who eventually remained at about 20,000. Holborn (1975, vol 1, p 418) gives a total of 20,690. Holmes (1988, p 210), noticing the scarcity of information on Hungarian exiles of 1956, states that only about 14,000 came to Britain.

48 Dummett and Nicol (1990, p 188) noted only a 'trickle' of individual asylum seekers from Eastern Europe

discussion, it is notable that, while the primary refugee movements to Britain remained those of Europeans, a generally favourable reaction was evident from British officialdom. This picture changed, however, when the migration of non-European refugees began to take place, which has led to perceptions of a crisis of asylum law and policy in recent decades.

CHAPTER 5

REFUGEES FROM THE BRITISH COMMONWEALTH

5.1 NATIONALITY IN THE BRITISH EMPIRE

There was a generally accepted notion, at least in a rhetorical sense, that those who were 'British subjects' had a common status throughout the British dominions.[1] In theory, British subject status was extended by the feudal rule of the common law to persons born within the Crown's dominions,[2] which by the 20th century was applied to all Crown colonies as well as the UK. However, the concept of a rigid code of citizenship demarcating the British and the non-British did not arise during the period of imperial expansion (Deakin, 1969, p 77). In 1907, Sir Francis Piggott wrote that, 'There must be a multitude of persons who cannot say with certainty whether they are British subjects' (quoted in Dummett and Nicol, 1990, p 113).[3] The development of more definite nationality or citizenship statuses, for which documentary proof came to be demanded, is thus a relatively recent phenomenon.

The Old Commonwealth or 'Dominion' countries (Australia, Canada, New Zealand and South Africa) were free in the 19th century to control their own immigration policies, and they had begun to restrict the free immigration of Chinese and other 'Asiatic' peoples to their territories, including that of nominally British subjects from Hong Kong and India. This freedom to control the make up of their population was recognised by Britain in successive Imperial conferences. The imposition of passport controls in the early years of the 20th century against Indians migrating to Canada may have been one manifestation of race-based discrimination at this time (Mongia, 1999). Their right to grant or to withhold local naturalisation on the basis of race was also recognised in the British Nationality and Status of Aliens Act 1914. However, the official British position had been not to restrict immigration to Britain on the basis of race and the legislation in the Dominions was framed so as to look neutral on its face, although it was clearly understood that racial

1 Dummett and Nicol (1990, p 115) point out that the word 'Dominion' with a capital 'D' was by the early 20th century used to denote the white settler colonies, to be distinguished from the general term 'dominions' with a small 'd' which was used to refer to the Crown's possessions at common law.

2 *Calvin's Case* (1608) 7 Co Rep 1 is usually cited as authority for this proposition (see, eg, Dummett and Nicol, 1990, pp 59–63).

3 The reference for the quote is given as Piggott, F (1907), *Nationality Including Naturalisation*, London: William Clowes, Preface.

discrimination was the intended outcome (Dummett and Nicol, 1990, pp 115–27).[4] Meanwhile, Britain itself asserted by the British Nationality Act of 1914 that 'any person born within His Majesty's dominions and allegiance' was a British subject.[5] Jones (1948, p 178) suggests that the main purpose of this definition, apart from the tradition behind the word 'allegiance', was to exclude from British nationality persons born within the dominions who were children of heads of State, ambassadors and other persons with manifest allegiance to another authority.

In fact, it was not the case that Britain itself had recognised the right of all British subjects to come and go without hindrance. The Aliens Act of 1905 exempted someone who was born in the UK, 'his father being a British subject'.[6] Thus, according to Sibley and Elias (1906, p 35), an alien was defined, implicitly, as someone who either was not born in the UK, or who was born in the UK, but whose father was not a British subject. In so doing, it designated as aliens persons who could claim British subjecthood under the common law or under earlier statutes.[7] The idea that British subject status freed one from any disability under English law was persistent, however. Dicey, for example, claimed that a:

> British subject, whatever be the place of his birth, or the race he belongs to, or I may now add the religion which he professes, has, with the rarest possible exceptions, the same right to settle and trade in England which is possessed by a natural born Englishman [Dicey, 1915, p xxxvii].

But the reality was often in contradiction to the claim of legal equality made by Dicey. Although the non-white population in Britain was not very large in the 19th century, various attempts had been made to remove Lascars, Indian seamen who worked in the British merchant navy (Visram, 1986). In 1903, a third of British merchant seamen were either foreign or non-white British, including West Indians, Africans, Indians and Chinese. The Merchant Shipping Act of 1906 introduced a language test for those signing onto British ships in the UK, and was intended to discriminate against all non-white sailors. In 1919, after rioting by white people in almost every major seaport city, a gratuity was offered to West Indian and African veterans and seamen to leave Britain, and the wholesale repatriation of Chinese living in Liverpool

4 Southern Rhodesia was in an anomalous position, in that it was not a Dominion and was not represented at Imperial conferences, but could define its own local citizenship. India, on the other hand, was not a Dominion, but was represented at the Imperial conferences. Its representations regarding the rights of Indians in other parts of the Empire were generally ignored by the British, however (Dummett and Nicol, 1990, pp 130–31; Ghai and Ghai, 1971, p 13 on Indian representations).

5 British Nationality and Status of Aliens Act 1914, s 1(1)(a).

6 Aliens Act 1905, s 1(3).

7 These were 4 Geo II, c 21, s 1 and 13 Geo III, c 21. Henriques (1906) also has a large section on establishing British subjecthood, indicating the further concretisation of nationality as decisive of status.

was considered (Dummett and Nicol, 1990, pp 163–66).[8] The Coloured Aliens Seamen Order 1925, made under the Aliens Restriction (Amendment) Act 1919, stipulated that all 'coloured' alien seamen should register with the police. In practice, all non-white seamen were affected by the Order, as even those who held British status were also forced to prove it, which was not generally possible due to the lack of documents demanded. The 1925 Order was revoked just before the Second World War when Britain again needed extra seamen (Dummett and Nicol, 1990, pp 167–68; Lane, 1994).

British nationality was also being divided as between British subjects and British protected persons (BPPs), although it was not always possible to make a neat differentiation between the two categories. In India, for example, there were several hundred princely States that lay outside the territory of British India. Persons born in those States were regarded as BPPs although, in practical terms, their position under British domination could hardly be distinguished from that of subjects under direct British rule: '... often, administrators seem to have described people without regard to birthplace, and it can be difficult today to establish with certainty the status of a person born in the days of the Raj' (Dummett and Nicol, 1990, p 114). The problem of tracing the status, and therefore the rights, of people originating in the subcontinent can today depend on these classifications. In Africa, British colonial domination was divided between colonies and protectorates although, in practice, there may not have been much difference in their treatment because of such a classification. Nigeria was composed of both a protectorate and a colony; Uganda was a protectorate; Kenya was a colony after 1920; Zanzibar was a protected State under its own Sultan. After the First World War, other territories, such as Palestine, Tanganyika (East Africa) and Iraq, were mandated to Britain and the inhabitants, and those subsequently born there, became BPPs (Dummett and Nicol, 1990, p 125). This complex picture was overlapped by successive statutes altering the position of various groups. The British Nationality Act of 1943 provided that children of British subjects born in a protectorate, protected State or a mandated territory were deemed to have been born within the Crown's allegiance and were therefore British subjects. Although the 1943 Act was a response to the concern of white British colonists about their children's nationality status, a considerable number of people who had migrated from the Indian subcontinent to East Africa could claim the status of British subjects under it (Dummett and Nicol, 1990, p 126). These distinctions therefore emerged as constitutional niceties during the colonial period, but eventually British immigration laws began to

8 Starkey (1997) records hostile attitudes towards African and West Indian settlement in Liverpool through the 19th and 20th centuries, particularly by the law enforcement agencies. See Ramdin (1999, pp 119–28) on Cardiff and Liverpool in the aftermath of the First World War.

draw the line according to them as a means of denying entry to refugees from East Africa who wished to move or even flee to the UK.

5.2 DECOLONISATION AND THE NEED TO RETAIN LABOUR SUPPLIES

In 1948, Britain had to enact another law on nationality because of a Canadian move to enact its own citizenship legislation in 1946 without reference to London. This meant the potential compromise for Britain of the ideal of imperial unity enunciated in the British Nationality and Status of Aliens Act 1914. As Dummett and Nicol (1990, p 135) point out, 'within Britain the term "British subject" stood for Britain's own national identity as well as her Imperial supremacy'. British nationality law had now to be altered in order to reconcile the ideal imperial mould of citizenship with the new realities of independence for various territories (Paul, 1997, pp 14–20). The new scheme, as set out in the British Nationality Act 1948, was to arrange for British subject status to be acquired as a consequence of having a citizenship of an independent Commonwealth country or citizenship of the UK and colonies (CUKC), a new British nationality status. Both categories fell under the umbrella term 'British subject' or 'Commonwealth citizen', as would those persons who were thereafter known as 'British subjects without citizenship', a category specifically designed for people who failed to acquire the citizenship of a newly independent country. Newly independent countries were originally listed in s 1(3) of the Act as Canada, Australia, New Zealand, the Union of South Africa, Newfoundland, India, Pakistan, Southern Rhodesia and Ceylon, only three out of which (Canada, Ceylon, and New Zealand) had already enacted citizenship laws, while the rest, it was intended, would enact them in due course. Other States were added to this list as moves towards decolonisation advanced. In the UK, civil and political rights, including freedom of movement, attached to British subject status rather than CUKC status, thus continuing the common law regime (for details, see Fransman, 1989, pp 57–77; Dummett and Nicol, 1990, pp 133–40).

There was some disquiet about the new categories that the 1948 Act set out, especially from those parliamentarians who were concerned that CUKC status lumped together the white British and citizens under colonial domination, while the Dominions were seen as having been inappropriately consigned to another status that did not recognise their closer relationship with the white British. Such concerns were met with the prophetic response by Lord Jowitt, the Lord Chancellor, that the issue of colour was separate from the issue of citizenship statuses and that, even though CUKCs of all colours were united in one citizenship, if one wished to discriminate one could do so whether one called them 'subjects' or 'citizens' (Dummett and Nicol, 1990, pp 140–41; Deakin, 1969; Paul, 1997, pp 20–24). However, as things stood, he declared that:

> We can say that people who come from one part of the British Empire should not be allowed in and people from another part shall be allowed in, but in this great metropolitan centre of the Empire, I hope we shall never say such a thing [quoted in Deakin, 1969, p 79].

Dicey's bold claim of equality among all British subjects was beginning to metamorphose into a mere hope.

During the debate on the 1948 Act, the *Empire Windrush* arrived, carrying West Indian workers to Britain. This event marked the beginning of a period during which debates on the effects of non-white migration to Britain intensified, and eventually culminated in the enactment of statutory controls against immigrant workers from the West Indies, South Asia and other parts of the Commonwealth and still existing Dominions. This period of post-war migration and the gradual settlement of communities from various Commonwealth and colonial territories has been researched widely by writers from different perspectives.[9] Especially since most groups enjoyed the status of British subjects who were, at least nominally, free from immigration control, until 1962 the extremely complex nature of migratory processes, which included persons who were refugees, has tended to be obscured, especially in the legal literature. This perception has probably been compounded by the fact that refugees from the British Commonwealth were not treated as coming under a separate 'refugee' or 'asylum seeker' category until the late 1970s.[10]

However, there were worries quite early on in Britain about the potential resort that could be had to British nationality laws that were drafted so widely, and distancing strategies were being developed. Upon partition in the Indian subcontinent, there began a huge exchange of population between India and Pakistan of up to 10 million people, of whom perhaps a million did not survive. Hundreds of thousands were left without citizenship of either country as both erected barriers in their respective laws. The British Nationality Act of 1948 provided that 'potential citizens' of Commonwealth

---

9 For examples, see Ballard (1994) on South Asians; Hiro (1991) and Ramdin (1999) on South Asians and West Indians; Anwar (1979) on Pakistanis; Cottle (1978) on West Indians; Helweg (1979) on Sikhs; Desai (1963) on Indians; Adams (1987) on Sylhettis; Ng (1968) on Chinese; and Holmes (1988), whose book is a historical study of the major groups, including non-Commonwealth migrants up to 1971. Specifically on legal questions on these new 'ethnic minorities', see Pearl and Menski (1998) on Muslims; and Jones and Welhengama (2000) generally.

10 Some studies do indicate the presence of refugees during this period of Commonwealth migration: see Weil (1974) on 'Bene Israel', Jews from India; Jeffery (1976) on Pakistani Christians; Al-Rasheed (1994) on Assyrians in Iraq; and Khan (1977) on Mirpuri Pakistanis partly displaced as a result of dam building projects.

countries, who were left out when new citizenship laws 'took effect', could become CUKCs. However, Indian and Pakistani citizenship laws were never given such effect under the 1948 Act, and thus such people were classified as 'British subjects without citizenship', a category that could not be transmitted to the descendants of the holders (Fransman, 1989, p 68; Dummett and Nicol, 1990, p 136). It may be that the Indian and Pakistani laws were not given effect under the 1948 Act as, by the time they had been enacted, agitation in Britain for immigration control of non-white British subjects was becoming more pronounced although, when the line was eventually drawn in 1962, it cut across all categories of British nationality of the 1948 Act.[11] Paul (1997) provides some evidence of reluctance to enhance the status of people caught in between the citizenship laws in the Indian subcontinent. The 1948 Act was amended by the British Nationality Act 1957 in order to provide for the registration of the children of white British expatriates as CUKCs, as many had failed to do so already. Although by this time both the Indian and Pakistani Governments had enacted citizenship laws, the 1957 Act did not act to pick up the other formally Stateless citizens. The Home Office 'explained this lapse by reference to the three million Hindu and Muslim refugees with "not the slightest connection with this country" who would have qualified' for CUKC status had Britain so acted (Paul, 1997, p 151).

Since the end of the Second World War, there was a continued hostility demonstrated by the public in Britain towards non-whites, through acts of violence, discrimination in employment opportunities and in housing. These local tensions were also expressed in official circles which had their own brand of racism.[12] Two recent studies (Paul, 1997, pp 111–69; Spencer, 1996) have pointed out that official disquiet had been expressed in top government circles since before the arrival of the *Empire Windrush*. A Cabinet committee was instituted in the summer of 1950 to examine whether the time had come to restrict the existing right of any British subject to enter the UK. Official statistics to measure non-white Commonwealth immigration, largely inaccurate, were kept since 1955. In the meantime, the Government tried to reconcile Commonwealth and colonial interests by applying extra-legal controls on people from the Indian subcontinent, the West Indies, Cyprus and

11 Dummett and Nicol (1990) do not speculate on this point, simply stating that the result was not anticipated in 1948. Fransman (1989, p 68) only mentions that, while Pakistan's Citizenship Act of 1951 was fairly comprehensive, India's citizenship provisions in the Constitution were 'hopelessly inadequate', perhaps implying official reluctance to pick up any Stateless people. The citizenship provisions in the Indian Constitution came into effect on 26 January 1950, although those provisions merely declared who was a citizen at the time, and did not encompass those who may *acquire* citizenship after its effect. That was done in the Citizenship Act 1955 (Fransman 1989, pp 68–69).

12 Steel (1969, pp 30–42) gives an account of the political debate prior to the 1962 Act.

West Africa, for example, by limiting the issue of passports.[13] However, the stream of settlers and sojourners, mainly from the West Indies, the Indian subcontinent, Cyprus, various parts of Africa, Aden and Hong Kong, who sought opportunities in Britain continued. Disquiet about free movement for these 'coloured' British subjects continued to be voiced in official circles, although publicly the need for control was linked to employment. Entry into the European Economic Community, it was felt, should be preceded by the imposition of controls on the Commonwealth front, early evidence that further linkages with Europe would involve trading off the rights of non-white people, a trend which has intensified more recently. In the autumn of 1961, a Bill was finally introduced in Parliament that sought to provide statutory authority for controls over non-white British subjects, by then politely coming to be known as 'Commonwealth citizens', although both terms were analogous in the British Nationality Act 1948 (Holmes, 1988, pp 255–63; Dean, 1993; Dummett and Nicol, 1990, pp 177–83; Paul, 1997, pp 111–69; Spencer, 1996).[14]

Neutrality as regards Commonwealth citizens of different races was kept up on the face of the resulting Commonwealth Immigrants Act of 1962, although ministers were privately confident that immigration officers vested with discretion would be able to distinguish between white and non-white Commonwealth citizens. All Commonwealth citizens formally came under control, except those who had been born in the UK or Ireland, or those who had a passport issued either by the UK or Irish Governments.[15] Colonial subjects who were issued with passports by the colonial authorities and citizens of independent Commonwealth countries who were issued with passports by their own governments thus came under control. The issue of passports had already been used as an administrative mechanism of regulating entry into Britain, as Spencer's (1996) research on recently declassified documents confirms. The formula adopted in the 1962 Act shows a striking continuity in this approach through the use of finer distinctions among passports, and the requirement of documentary proof as a condition of

13 In Cyprus there had been controls applied since the 1930s which required intending migrants to be sponsored by a guarantor who was obliged to provide employment or maintenance and accommodation (George and Millerson, 1967, p 278). Dean (1993, pp 58–59) writes of dubious administrative means to 'weed out' criminal elements, stowaways and 'undesirables', and of the ceaseless attempts by the Commonwealth Office after 1955 to secure agreements with India and Pakistan to restrict the numbers of people leaving their shores. Paul (1997, pp 151–55) records the pressure applied to India, Pakistan and governments in the West Indies, while Spencer (1996) provides details on the same countries as well as Cyprus and West Africa.

14 For details of the Bill's reception in and outside Parliament, see Steel (1969, pp 43–56).

15 Commonwealth Immigrants Act 1962, s 1(2).

issue.[16] CUKCs born overseas and who were not colonial citizens remained free from control, thus still enabling CUKC Asians living in East Africa to claim the right to live in Britain. This gap was cut off during the exodus of Asians from Kenya by the Commonwealth Immigrants Act 1968. The 1962 Act, however, already brought in powers to control BPPs. That would affect BPPs among the Asian population in East Africa as the process of Africanisation took place after independence, although it appears that it was hardly noticed, nor enforced, at the time.

Under the 1962 Act, a person under control had to satisfy an immigration officer that he or she was a returning resident, or the wife or a child under 16 of a resident man (or a man being admitted at the same time), or was in possession of an employment voucher, or intended to study, or had enough funds to support himself and his dependants without taking any paid work. Persons under control could also be refused on medical grounds, if they were subject to deportation orders, or if the Secretary of State decided that their admission would be contrary to national security. The subjective discretion of immigration officers was wide enough for them to admit or refuse according to instructions issued by the Home Office. Some instructions were published but they were supplemented by secret instructions to immigration officers. Immigration officers were empowered to search baggage and examine documents in the possession of a Commonwealth citizen and keep such documents for seven days. Immigration officers could also detain Commonwealth citizens pending further examination or pending removal from the country. A police constable or an immigration officer could arrest without warrant any person required or authorised by the Act to be detained, deeming that to be legal custody. Certain immigration offences were also introduced, including knowingly making false statements or producing false documents, exceeding the time limit, or breaking conditions of stay. These offences carried a fine and/or a term of six months imprisonment. A power to deport any Commonwealth citizen was given, if that citizen, being 17 years of age, had been convicted by a court of an offence punishable with imprisonment and recommended by a court to be deported. That power could not apply to a person who was born or whose father was born in the UK, or both of whose parents had been residents of the UK at the time of birth, or who was the wife of any such person, or to someone who had been continuously resident in the UK for at least five years (Dummett and Nicol, 1990, pp 183–85).

16 The distinction made by the 1962 Act between 'UK' British subjects and 'colonial' British subjects received the endorsement of the courts in *R v Secretary of State for the Home Department ex p Bhurosah* [1968] 1 QB 266, which concerned a planeload of Mauritians. In this case, the Home Office revealed some of its policies as to the type of passports which brought holders under control (see Shah, 1995b, pp 68–70 for comment).

Alongside the 1962 Act was introduced a system of labour vouchers, issue of which was phased out for work seekers, and reduced drastically for the skilled and professionals by 1965. Notably, there had been a high rate of applications for them in the Indian subcontinent. On the other hand, instead of decreasing, immigration from the West Indies and the subcontinent actually increased in the years immediately prior to and after the Act (Dummett and Nicol, 1990, pp 185–86). It is evident that many decided to settle in Britain and therefore to be reunited with their families as a result of the fear caused by the restrictions. The 1962 Act thus indirectly established the trend towards family reunification and formation which also came under attack by the State in the forthcoming years (see Sachdeva, 1993, pp 44–50 for the early developments). The continuing influx also meant the perpetuation of agitation against further immigration, especially from the Indian subcontinent, which was now featuring prominently in government statistics (Holmes, 1988, p 263).

No mention of the possibility to apply for asylum was made in the instructions to immigration officers issued under the Commonwealth Immigrants Act 1962, and the later Act of 1968, although the published instructions were supplemented by unpublished instructions.[17] Even after the ratification by Britain of the 1967 Protocol to the 1951 Convention, when immigration rules on asylum applicable to both aliens and British subjects/Commonwealth citizens alike were introduced (see Chapter 6), there was no sign that the East African Asians were treated as refugees coming under these instruments. Besides, the protection of the 1951 Refugee Convention was, on its face, available only to those who were outside the country of nationality; British subjects (or Commonwealth citizens), even though mostly now subject to immigration control, could still be considered as 'nationals' under the British Nationality Act 1948. Arguments about the status of the East African Asians, who emerged as the primary stream of non-European refugees from the Commonwealth, were focused rather on the duty, under international law, of a State to receive its own nationals and the compatibility of the UK's policies under the European Convention on Human Rights, than on issues of asylum law. Regardless of the legal framework in which questions about further non-white Commonwealth migration were dealt with, the reaction of the British authorities was, in line with precedents already set, decidedly hostile.

17 See Instructions to Immigration Officers, Cmnd 3465, Parliamentary Papers, vol XXXVIII, p 219 (1967–68). For the instructions amended after the 1968 Act, see Cmnd 3566, p 225.

5.3 THE EAST AFRICAN ASIANS

Links between India and Africa long predated the onset of European colonialism (Chaudhuri, 1990). When European influence in the Indian Ocean became pronounced, it began to determine the terms of the interaction between Africa and the Indian subcontinent. Indian labour, mostly from Punjab, was vital in the construction of railways in East and Central Africa, although that did not contribute significantly to a settled Indian population of Africa, as most workers returned. However, in their wake followed small traders, artisans, craftsmen, and administrative staff, mostly from Gujarat (Mattausch, 1998). Hostility between Africans and Indians was then promoted by the British who berated the 'Asian' for exploiting the 'African' (Humphry and Ward, 1974, pp 9–11), thus laying the foundations for antagonism between the two groups.

East and Central African territories also became subject to immigration controls introduced through colonial laws similar in nature to those in other parts of the Empire (see 2.5). As in other European settler colonies, there was opposition to Asian settlement from the white settlers in Nyasaland and Northern and Southern Rhodesia. A European language test was imposed in Southern Rhodesia in an Ordinance of 1904, and a complete ban on Asian immigration was imposed in 1924, immediately after the introduction of self-government for the white settlers. By 1904, the same test was introduced administratively in Northern Rhodesia. After the Second World War, the rate of immigration quickened until the formation of the Federation of the two Rhodesias and Nyasaland in 1954, when the 1924 legislation was extended to that whole territory. In Kenya, Uganda and Tanganyika, considerable Asian settlement had already taken place, and a move by white settlers in Kenya to achieve self-government was successfully blocked by resistance from Indian settlers. During the Second World War, white settlers enjoyed considerable freedom to restrict immigration in all the British East and Central African territories, but after the War the pace of Asian settlement, mostly from the Punjab (in part augmented by partition) and Gujarat, quickened in all these territories, with most going to Kenya, Uganda and Tanganyika.[18] In Kenya and Uganda in particular, 80–90% of commercial trade and a fair slice of industrial investment was in their hands (Ghai and Ghai, 1971, pp 5–8; Humphry and Ward, 1974, pp 11–12). In anticipation of the independence

18 By 1970, there were estimated to be the following numbers of Asians in East and Central African countries: Kenya – 140,000; Uganda – 80,000; Tanzania – 100,000; Malawi – 12,000; Zambia – 12,000; Rhodesia – 10,000 (Humphry and Ward, 1974, p 11). Aga Khan III (1954, pp 163–68) mentions his role in mediating between the British settlers, who were agitating in the 1920s for the imposition of racial 'white' supremacy and the Indians' exclusion politically and socially, and the British Government in London. These issues remained live until the early 1950s as he saw them. His own followers of Indian origin numbered some 17,000 in Kenya; 27,000 in Tanganyika; and 6,000 in Uganda.

arrangements for those territories, a scheme for premature retirement and for compensation was introduced for European civil servants and a land purchase fund to the tune of £50 million (a further £7 million was added in 1973) for any farmers who wanted to sell their farms at generous 1959 prices was arranged. A campaign for the adoption of a similar scheme for Asian civil servants, or a compensation scheme for Asian traders, was rejected (Ghai and Ghai, 1971, p 13; Humphry and Ward, 1974, p 13).

After independence in East and Central Africa, the Indian Government kept aloof and advised Asians to identify with the new countries, advocating that they should take out local citizenship (Ghai and Ghai, 1971, p 13). Indian law conditioned acquisition of citizenship upon domicile in India, although it did permit the acquisition of Indian citizenship to those born extra-territorially of parents or grandparents who themselves had been born in undivided India through the registration of such persons. Most Asians living in East Africa had not so registered and did not therefore benefit from these provisions. However, Indian law did not at first require Commonwealth citizens to obtain prior permission before immigrating there (Plender, 1972, pp 424–25).

In East Africa and Malawi, automatic citizenship was granted only to those who were born in the country if one of their parents had also been born there. In Zambia, automatic citizenship was conferred if a person was born there. A period of two years was prescribed in all the countries for the registration of those who did not acquire citizenship automatically, although the range of qualifying persons was differently enunciated. In East Africa and Malawi, those who were born on the territory, but neither of whose parents was born there, were included in this category. Another method of qualifying for registration was where a person had acquired CUKC status by naturalisation or registration in that country. In Kenya, an additional category for registration was included for those who were CUKCs or citizens of the Republic of Ireland at independence and were ordinarily and lawfully resident in Kenya. Additionally, there were rights to naturalise as citizens. The constitutions of East and Central African countries also provided that, save for the offspring of diplomats and enemy aliens, those born after independence were automatically citizens. The safeguard was that no person would lose his or her British status without acquiring the citizenship of the newly independent countries (Ghai and Ghai, 1971, pp 14–15; Plender, 1971, pp 293–94). For the 90,000 British settlers a choice was available: those who had taken up African citizenship could revert to being CUKCs under the British Nationality Act 1964, but no similar offer was held out for Asians (Dummett and Nicol, 1990, p 198; Humphry and Ward, 1974, p 14). Applications for citizenship made in the two years after independence were marred by uncertainty on the part of Asians about their future, bureaucratic delays by the British Home Office (which had to grant a certificate upon the relinquishing of citizenship within three months) as well as the local governments, with the consequence that most Asians remained without

African citizenship (Humphry and Ward, 1974, p 16). The politics of citizenship began to go sharply against the Asians in the post-independence phase, first in Kenya and then in Uganda, forcing many Asians to leave those countries.

5.3.1 Kenyan Asians and the Commonwealth Immigrants Act 1968

There appears to have been an assumption that all British passport holders were to remain free from immigration control in the UK, although the 1962 Act had silently brought in powers to control BPPs and British subjects without citizenship. It is only later with increasing restrictionism that the distinctions in status appear to have more direct consequences.[19] There also seemed to be an ambiguity about East African CUKCs' exemption from immigration control in the UK. It seems more likely, however, that this ambiguity was created later on in the 1960s as, in the meantime, a small number of Asians continued to be issued with passports indicating that they were free from immigration control (Steel, 1969, pp 57–64).[20] During the negotiations for Kenyan independence, it was agreed that residents of Asian and European origin retained an option for Kenyan citizenship and that was reflected in the Kenya Independence Act of 1963. However, as in other East and Central African countries, many chose to retain British status as CUKCs, BSWCs or BPPs (Fransman, 1989, pp 475–87). That created the impression in Kenya that Asians were not willing to participate as full citizens. Meanwhile, in all countries of former British rule in East and Central Africa, Asians began to experience discriminatory policies. Kenya, where the Asian presence was the largest, was a pioneer in this respect with its policy of 'Africanisation', under which legislation favouring African interests in employment and business and discriminating against Asians was enacted (Dummett and Nicol, 1990, pp 198–99; Steel, 1969, pp 122–31).

A trickle of movement before 1967 intensified later that year when more restrictive legislation against non-citizens was passed in Kenya. Reports that the UK Government threatened to legislate against the East African Asians also caused considerable panic in Kenya. As families started to develop

19 Commonwealth Immigrants Act 1962, s 1(4). Apart from Plender (1971), other writers appear to assume that the freedom from immigration control was applicable to all British passport holders from East Africa. For example, Yash P Ghai (1973) states that: 'The 1962 British legislation restricting the rights of entry into Britain of Commonwealth citizens did not apply to British passport holders and thus exempted the East African Asians.' See, also, Steel (1969).

20 Certainly the wording of the Commonwealth Immigrants Act 1962, s 1(2), explicitly premised liability to control upon the type of passport held. A CUKC passport issued by a British High Commission in an independent country such as Kenya thus exempted the holder from control. See, also, Steel (1969, p 140).

strategies to send some members, often younger males, to Britain, Asians started to arrive in the UK in larger numbers by early 1968. This in turn led to further pressure within the Government to stem the flow. Another Commonwealth Immigrants Bill was introduced in Parliament on 27 February 1968 and was passed on 1 March 1968 within three days, with heavy majorities in the House of Commons from both the Labour Government and the Conservative Opposition. The reasoning of James Callaghan, Home Secretary since the end of 1967, was that, were legislation given more time in Parliament, it would have the effect of more refugees travelling to Britain to beat the impending controls (Steel, 1969, pp 132–45; Dummett and Nicol, 1990, pp 200–02; Shah, 1995b, p 76).[21]

The Commonwealth Immigrants Act of 1968 had far reaching effects. It took away the rights of any CUKCs who did not have a specified connection with the UK to travel freely to Britain. The 'connection' was made applicable by s 1(2) to those who themselves had been born, adopted, registered or naturalised in the UK, or to those whose parents or grandparents had been. Its effect was to curtail the right of entry of more than a million CUKCs worldwide, including those in Malaysia, Singapore, South Yemen and the Caribbean, although its immediate targets were the Asians coming from East and Central Africa. The International Commission of Jurists estimated that a total of some 350,000 CUKCs would remain without the citizenship of another country. While some West Indians and the Chinese, in particular, in Malaysia had already obtained the citizenship of their home countries, the British passport holders among the East African Asians did not have the security of another citizenship (Steel, 1969, pp 148–52). However, 'for the purposes of inflating the problem and giving the appearance that a massive influx of immigrants was possible, it was necessary to include the million more who were dual citizens' (Steel, 1969, p 152).[22] Such fictitious presentations of the prospects of further migration from the Commonwealth continued to be echoed most recently in the case of British passport holders from Hong Kong who were assumed to want to migrate to Britain en masse (Shah, 1995b).

Meanwhile, the assumption that a flood of Asians from East Africa would wish to migrate to Britain was also contradicted by the evidence which showed that India was still a favoured destination. When the 1968 Act came into force, an estimated 67,000 British passport holders were still resident in

21 For estimates on the numbers of Asian British nationals who left Kenya before the 1968 Act came into force, see Steel (1969, p 252). The estimates do not distinguish clearly between CUKCs and non-CUKCs.

22 See, also, Steel (1969, pp 251–53) for more detailed figures. The effect of cutting off the right of abode of a far wider pool of CUKCs was not lost on Lord Brooke who asked in the House of Lords whether the argument of discrimination could be maintained, 'if Malaysia were to force one million Chinese fellow citizens of ours to exercise their present right to come here – a right equal in all respects to the right of an Asian in East Africa' (Steel, 1969, p 199).

Kenya. Some 20,000 people from Kenya had already travelled to India in the previous seven years, and an estimated 67% of those who remained would have preferred to go to India. On the other hand, some 50,000 Asians had also moved to Britain since 1963. The enactment in Britain of the 1968 Act caused a reaction in other countries of potential migration. Uganda, Tanzania, Zambia, Ethiopia and, significantly, India and Pakistan – tightened up their laws. On 3 March 1968, India curtailed its facility for Commonwealth citizens in the case of CUKCs whose passports showed their place of residence as Kenya, by requiring of them that permission should be obtained before settlement. Thereafter, Zambia and India came to an agreement with the UK whereby this group would be permitted to relocate only if they bore passports endorsed by the British High Commission with a statement to the effect that they also had a right of entry to the UK. Such assurances were not always stated in clear terms by the British High Commission in Nairobi, with the result that individuals faced further problems in relocating (Steel, 1969, pp 221–27, 252–54; Shah, 1995b, p 77, Plender, 1972, p 424).[23] Neither were such assurances by the British Government observed, as queues at British High Commissions in other countries continued to build up in succeeding years.

The UK Government argued that it was not denying entry to UK citizens with nowhere else to go. Callaghan had announced that a system of non-statutory vouchers for 'heads of households' would be issued at the rate of 1,500 a year (Dummett and Nicol, 1990, p 292). These vouchers were generally issued to male British passport holders, whether CUKCs or BPPs.[24] In practice, the manner in which applications were handled in East Africa elicited many complaints. Documents, such as birth certificates from India, which were known to be unlikely to exist, were demanded from applicants (Moore and Wallace, 1975, pp 36–41). Evidence of accommodation or bank balances in the UK was also demanded. Students were also denied the possibility to come to Britain to attend schools and colleges at which they had been accepted (Steel, 1969, pp 219–20). Eligibility was restricted to heads of households who had already become unemployed and were not legally permitted to work again. With the long wait ahead thereafter (between 14 months and two years), and the short notice before actual issue, families could not plan ahead for resettlement and many became destitute in the process (Moore and Wallace, 1975, pp 30–36).

The definition of 'head of household' was normally applied only to men, and vouchers were issued to women only in cases where they were widowed,

---

23 Steel (1969, pp 253–54) provides a text of the agreement between India and the UK.

24 This can be concluded from the reasons for refusal given to CUKCs as well as British protected persons arriving in Britain in early 1970, some of whom then complained to the European Commission on Human Rights about their treatment, see *East African Asians: Twenty-Five Applications Against the UK*, Decision of 10 October 1970 (1970) 13 Yearbook of the European Convention on Human Rights, pp 928–50, where the facts of the cases are detailed.

divorced or single, 'preventing British women married to non-British men from ever settling in Britain' (Bhabha and Shutter, 1994, p 41).[25] Such a practice would inevitably impact on the strategy of many Asian families, where a husband may register as a citizen of the country of residence, while a wife may retain her British nationality as 'insurance' (Zolberg *et al*, 1989, p 299). The criteria for dependency were applied rigidly and excluded daughters and sons over the age of 18 and dependants over the age of 65, thereby splitting up family units (Moore and Wallace, 1975, pp 42–47). In particular, those criteria were criticised for denying the 'realities of the Muslim and Hindu responsibility to their unmarried daughters' (Moore and Wallace, 1975, p 44).

It was clear that pressures on Asians to emigrate were being intensified in Tanzania and Uganda as well.[26] The quota voucher queue could take 10 years to clear for all the Asians in East Africa, including those who had gone to India. By 1970, the British High Commission in Kampala was besieged by applications for entry vouchers to Britain. The Reverend David Mason who was sent by the British Council of Churches to Uganda, reported that the queue for quota vouchers involved a wait of two to three years, which led to poverty, family separation, homelessness and despair. The British High Commission excused itself for the delays, stating that it already had 2,000 applications in hand in 1970. By the time that Idi Amin made his expulsion order, the official queue was up to 3,000. Some 12,000 people had already come to Britain, while the rest had gone to India, either temporarily or permanently, and had been admitted on the condition that Britain guaranteed their right to move to the UK. Usually, it was the younger or poorer people who were forced to exercise this escape route (Humphry and Ward, 1974, p 18). After the declaration of its view that Britain was potentially in breach of the European Convention, a friendly settlement was attempted by the European Commission on Human Rights and, in June 1971, the Government raised the allocation of vouchers from 1,500 to 3,000 a year. For that year only, there would be a special allocation of 1,500 vouchers to clear the most deserving cases. Reginald Maulding, the Home Secretary, announced later in that year an extra allocation of 500 vouchers to UK passport holders in India where there were already 2,200 people on the waiting list (Humphry and Ward, 1974, pp 19–20; Drzemczewski, 1978, p 340).[27]

25 Such gender discrimination also implied racial discrimination that was already a part of the Immigration Rules on the re-unification of spouses (Sachdeva, 1993, pp 47–50).

26 For instance, in Uganda, an Immigration Act and a Trade Licensing Act had been passed in 1970 making it impossible for British passport holding Asians to have a livelihood (Dummett and Nicol, 1990, p 203).

27 Humphry and Ward (1974) are slightly misleading on the point as they state that the European Commission of Human Rights had decided in 1970 that the UK was in breach of the Convention by passing the 1968 Act. Technically, that was not the final decision in the cases, as Drzemczewski (1978) shows, although the moral pressure is of course evident from the Government's reaction.

Those who did not go to India and could not wait for a voucher tried to establish a foothold in other countries, although many could not establish their 'returnability' anywhere, and thus found it difficult to gain admission even temporarily. Airlines were pressured into rejecting people who tried to leave East Africa while the Government justified such tactics on the basis of the Commonwealth Immigrants Act 1962.[28] Those who arrived in the UK without quota vouchers were refused admission, even though there was no other country bound to admit them. They were thus shuttled back and forth between Britain and other countries. If admitted, they were placed in prisons, before eventually being allowed to remain. Such policies were being used deliberately to discourage others from coming (Dummett and Nicol, 1990, p 203; Humphry and Ward, 1974, p 20).[29] One plea for help received by the JCWI came from a group of 18 Ugandan Asians 'of British nationality' who had waited in the quota voucher queue for 18 months; without 'any proper reply' from the British High Commission in Kampala, they faced no other choice but to push their way to England (Dummett and Nicol, 1990, p 203). Some such individuals complained to the English courts and the human rights institutions in Strasbourg. Their reactions are discussed below in 5.3.3. Meanwhile, in Uganda, the pressure to leave became especially manifest when Idi Amin decided in 1972 to expel all Asians there.

5.3.2 The Ugandan Asians crisis

In 1971, the Obote regime in Uganda, which increasingly opposed Western capital interests there, was overthrown by Idi Amin, a former British military officer, with the support of Israel and with the knowledge by Edward Heath that one of the leaders at the Commonwealth Prime Ministers Conference in Singapore would not be able to return home. Amin, however, began to realign Uganda's international relations towards Muslim countries and the Soviet Union and nationalised British and American economic interests (Mamdani, 1983, pp 29–32, 61–67). By January 1972, Amin announced that all Asians would have to go. In August, that announcement turned into a deadline; Asians were to leave Uganda by mid-November 1972. Initially, it seemed that only the UK passport holders would be affected by Amin's decree, but within a fortnight it became clear that every Asian was included (Shah, 1995b, p 79; Humphry and Ward, 1974, p 29).[30]

28 House of Lords Debates, vol 312, cols 798–800, 12 November 1970. In particular, Lord Windlesham, the Minister of State in the Home Office, confirmed this when he stated (col 797): '... all possible steps are taken, in co-operation with airlines and foreign governments, to prevent UK passport holders who are subject to immigration control from coming to this country for settlement without the proper documents.'

29 See, also, the facts stated in *East African Asians* (1970), at fn 24.

30 Amin also forced out some 30,000 Kenyans so that their jobs could be given to Ugandans, and Tanzanians were deprived of employment (Humphry and Ward, 1974, p 19).

Britain's response was to move slowly in order to buy time, partly in order to see what sort of diplomatic pressure could be applied to Amin, by Britain directly, and through Kenyan, Tanzanian, Indian and Pakistani leaders. Amin's action was condemned, but Britain's announcement of a Commonwealth Prime Ministers Conference was not followed up, while Amin was still defiant. The UK Government also attempted to secure the assistance of the UN, which was eventually forthcoming as other countries agreed to receive a proportion of the expellees. Meanwhile, Robert Carr, Home Secretary since June 1972, saw representatives of the airline and shipping firms with business in East Africa and asked them not to accept UK passport holders as passengers to Britain unless they had entry certificates or special vouchers, the issue of which was controlled by the British High Commissions. In the first month, only 3,000 people were cleared, mainly consisting of those who had already been waiting in the queue. By 11 September 1972, only 50 people were being processed per day. The High Commission was slowing down the process of sifting through the applications on orders from London, although some 25,000–30,000 people had, in principle, been accepted as being eligible for entry. Behind these were the Stateless persons, those of indeterminate status, and those whose Ugandan passports were being torn up by officials.[31] Robert Carr admitted that the delay was deliberate in order to search for international assistance (Humphry and Ward, 1974, pp 28–40).

On 15 September, permission was given to issue clearance documentation. But, again, there were impossible demands for proof, such as the production of birth certificates for people born in India who had never been issued them in the first place, while evidence from leading doctors or lawyers as a substitute for these certificates was rejected under instructions to the High Commission officials.[32] The High Commission also refused to issue entry vouchers for wives and children of men who were either citizens of Kenya, Uganda or Tanzania or who were Stateless. The Co-ordinating Committee for the Welfare of Asians leaving Uganda (composed of Asian community leaders and whites in Uganda) came to the conclusion that such treatment was intended to discourage women from coming to Britain at all or, once they had realised that their position could not be improved by going to Britain, they would be encouraged to leave Britain and join their husbands wherever they went (Humphry and Ward, 1974, pp 40–42; Moore and Wallace, 1975, pp 47–51).

31 Zolberg *et al* (1989, p 66) state that between 12,000 and 14,000 persons were rendered Stateless after having had their papers confiscated.

32 The policy at the British High Commission during the Ugandan crisis is found wanting by Moore and Wallace (1975, pp 54–55), who mention that the opening hours remained unchanged and that, while Asians were not freely allowed to enter the High Commission causing days of queuing, Europeans could enter without restrictions.

When the House of Commons debated the matter of the Ugandan Asians in October 1972, Robert Carr, the Home Secretary, was at pains to emphasise that the UK had accepted legal and moral responsibility because, had it not done so, assistance from other countries would not have been forthcoming.[33] He relied on the government law officers' opinions to declare:

> I believe there is a legal responsibility. I feel sure that when we gave the opportunity to these people who had been either citizens of the UK and colonies [or] British protected persons to apply for our passports, we must have intended – speaking for myself, I did intend – that one of the rights they acquired, but not the only right, would be the right to come to this country if they were expelled and had nowhere else to go.[34]

This pronouncement was echoed in other ministerial statements,[35] but with respect to BPPs, it was later contradicted by the Court of Appeal. Meanwhile, Carr prevaricated on specific matters: 'Those who we genuinely believe had not renounced and who therefore retained our citizenship will be given papers.'[36] Families of UK nationals, where the head of household (usually male) was not a passport holder, would be expected to reunite in third countries. No clear indication was given about the criteria for establishing dependency so that families would not be separated.[37]

The 'delay and disperse' strategy meant that, out of some 50,000 Asians in Uganda by the time of the expulsion decree, Britain received some 27,000. India admitted its own citizens and some 6,000 British passport holders, reaching a total figure possibly similar to that of Britain. Over 6,000 went to Canada and over 1,000 to the US and Pakistan each. Some 4,000 people were sent to UN refugee camps. Canada stuck to rigid criteria for immigration, operating a points system by which only those with the most skills qualified, and it rarely took aged or sick relatives who were left to UK or UN care: 'All the countries' selection procedures showed insensitivity to the networks of financial support in the "extended family" pattern of Asian family life'

33 House of Commons Official Report, 5th series, vol 843, cols 261–63, 18 October 1972.

34 *Ibid*, col 270.

35 The Attorney General, Peter Rawlinson, said in a radio interview that, under international law, 'a person with nowhere to go should be permitted to come to the country where he is a citizen' (Humphry and Ward, 1974, p 37). Lord Hailsham, the Lord Chancellor, stated: 'In international law, a State is under a duty, as between other States, to accept in its territories those of its nationals who have nowhere else to go. If a citizen of the UK is expelled, as I think illegally from Uganda, and is not accepted for settlement elsewhere, we could be required by any State where he then was to accept him.' House of Lords Debates, vol 335, col 497, 14 September 1972. Plender (1988, p 137) records statements to similar effect by the Foreign and Home Secretaries.

36 House of Commons Official Report, 5th series, vol 843, col 266, 18 October 1972.

37 *Ibid*.

(Humphry and Ward, 1974, p 43).[38] Among those dispersed across many other countries, some 4,000 members of immediate families coming to the UK had been refused permission to travel with them. They were mainly sons over 21 who were automatically considered citizens of Uganda or Stateless, or Ugandan husbands of UK passport holding wives who were admitted to Britain with their young children (Dines, 1973, p 382).[39]

How the refugees should be dealt with, once in the UK, also became a matter of controversy. Mary Dines, joint secretary with Vishnu Sharma of the JCWI, had suggested that £2,000 be given to each family and that they be told to make their own way, a strategy that had been adopted by the Egyptian Resettlement Board.[40] The intention behind this suggestion was that the existing structures of support within the Asian communities should be the main factor in the resettlement process. That was not accepted by the Government, and neither was the question of cash grants to help establish businesses. The Uganda Resettlement Board set up by the Government had, on the other hand, instructions to disperse the new arrivals as widely as possible throughout the country, although ministers and civil servants were later agreed that such proposals would not have more than a negligible chance of success. The refugees arriving at Stansted airport were at first accommodated in reception centres where they were persuaded not to go to areas designated as 'red'. These were assumed to be areas where there were already considerable numbers of non-white people living. For example, the London boroughs of Ealing, Brent, Tower Hamlets and Lambeth were placed on the list, as well as Leicester, Birmingham, Wolverhampton and Bradford –

38 The figures and their base levels do vary widely among the sources. Humphry and Ward (1974, p 43) state that 10,000 Asians went to India, including 3,000 UK passport holders, in the period since the expulsion decree when 50,000 Asians were still in Uganda. Zolberg *et al* (1989, p 66) start their figures from the date of the international airlift from mid-September 1972, citing that a total of 41,000 persons were airlifted.

39 Despite the official stance, in January 1973, 300 Stateless Asian men were allowed to enter Britain as their wives were holders of British passports (Drzemczewski, 1978, p 340). Dines (1973, p 382) also reported that, by October 1973, about 300 husbands who had initially been refused permission to come to the UK were allowed under a 'concession' to do so, and a further 63 'dependants' had also been admitted, bringing the total of dispersed family members to 3,600.

40 During the Suez Crisis in 1956, the Egyptian Resettlement Board had been set up to welcome about 8,000 evacuees who held British passports. They received £50 clothing grants on arrival, a £1,000 rehousing grant for each family, and every local authority that granted a house was given £300. The Government also paid all private school fees. The files of the Egyptian Resettlement Board were consulted, but the generous treatment that they had received was dismissed as not worthy of emulation in the Ugandan case (Humphry and Ward, 1974, pp 29–30).

at first the suggested name for these areas was 'black areas' (Humphry and Ward, 1974, pp 47, 50–51, 55–58).[41]

Dipak Nandy, Director of the Runnymede Trust, breaking ranks with his colleagues on the Trust, castigated the policy as conceding the entire racist case and 'as near to harassment as you can get' (Humphry and Ward, 1974, p 58). By May 1973, it was reported that most of the Asians had in fact made their own arrangements and, despite official discouragement, they did settle in areas where there were already Asian communities (Bristow, 1976, p 272).[42] The dispersal policy was clearly motivated by racial considerations, and contested by the Asians themselves as they chose to settle among existing South Asian communities. However, the precedent of a dispersal scheme was applied again later in the 1970s in the case of Vietnamese refugees in disregard of the social and psychological cost to the refugees. While they were regarded as acceptable on the basis of the political capital which they brought for Western countries at the international level, they were not regarded as culturally acceptable. The concept of dispersal has now been legislatively incorporated in UK law under the Immigration and Asylum Act 1999.

Acknowledgment by Britain of its obligation to receive at least British nationals or British passport holders from Uganda was, in practice, balanced with a delay and disperse strategy which was implemented through 1972 in order that frustrated prospective entrants would decide to go elsewhere, as many in fact did. In part, this flow to other countries added to official queues in British diplomatic posts that had already begun to develop since the 1968 Act. Some frustrated applicants even attempted to make it to Britain regardless of the administratively imposed criteria for entry. This shifted complaints about the operation of the voucher queues, or treatment once in Britain, to the courts.

41 At the non-governmental level, political campaigning and immediate welfare work were brought under the Co-ordinating Committee for the Welfare of Evacuees from Uganda – which brought together a variety of organisations including the repatriation agency the International Social Service, the JCWI and the statutory bodies – the Race Relations Board and the Community Relations Commission. The Women's Volunteer Service, the Red Cross and St John's Ambulance Brigade worked directly with the Home Office (Humphry and Ward, 1974, p 38). Bristow (1976, pp 268–70) mentions the fact that in Leicester and Birmingham, among other areas, local campaigns had been mounted to lobby the Government to ensure that the refugees did not settle there. There was reported to be a welcoming response when it was revealed that these areas had been designated as 'red'.

42 Bristow here cites (1973) *The Guardian*, 4 May, but actually disagrees with that assessment arguing that it was the nationwide lack of housing, combined with racial discrimination experienced in obtaining it, that was responsible for the Asians' patterns of settlement, and that the Uganda Resettlement Board could have done more to find accommodation for the refugees. However, this view has the risk of perpetuating a dependency hypothesis linked to State welfare provision.

5.3.3 Continuing exclusion

In 1973, the year following the Ugandan expulsions, the Immigration Act 1971 came into force. The 1971 Act was intended to be a permanent code of immigration control, and it extended the exclusionary tendencies against non-white British nationals already established under the earlier legislation *inter alia* through the new formula of 'patriality' which added to the complexity of the overlapping British nationality and immigration laws (Fransman, 1989, pp 115–31; Dummett and Nicol, 1990, pp 216–19). The 'racist undertones' of the 1971 Act have already been noted by writers such as Sachdeva (1993, pp 27–29) and Humphry and Ward (1974, pp 139, 143). Although administrative discretion meant that few, if any, citizens of the old Commonwealth countries had a problem retaining a connection with the UK, an attempt to enshrine that practice in statute by extending a right of abode to those with a grandparental connection in the UK was defeated by a coalition of interest between Labour MPs, who did not favour the preferences for the Old Commonwealth countries' citizens, and the Powellite faction which did not wish to extend such rights to Anglo-Indians, the descendants of British servicemen in India. The Immigration Rules made under the 1971 Act were at first defeated, and a second attempt was accepted by Parliament, after the insertion of a 'Grandfather Clause' which allowed men and women who had a grandparent born in the UK to obtain entry and work opportunities.[43]

The parallel extension of free movement rights to nationals of the then eight other Member States of the European Economic Community was also made with effect from 1 January 1973 without, it appears, very much debate about the consequences of immigration from Europe (Dummett and Nicol, 1990, p 215). It had been considered since the 1960s that membership of the European Community would first have to entail curtailment of free movement of Commonwealth citizens, which perhaps suggested that other Member States would also not accept free movement of non-white British subjects. Certainly, at the time of accession to the Treaty of Rome, 'UK nationals' for Community purposes included only 'patrial' British subjects as well as Gibraltarians (Fransman, 1989, p 134), effectively excluding any British passport holders who could not demonstrate that they had a right of abode in the UK. Dummett and Nicol (1990, p 227) point out that 'concern had been expressed by certain continental politicians lest large numbers of colonial and Commonwealth citizens gain freedom of movement in Europe'. Whether any further pressure from European countries was imposed upon the UK not to recognise such British passport holders, whose freedom to enter the UK had

43 The privileges that this group of people enjoyed over European Community nationals were emphasised: the latter could not vote in the UK, had to complete landing or embarkation cards and had to register with the police (Humphry and Ward, 1974, p 143).

already been curtailed, or whether it was a result of the unilateral policy of the UK, is an open question which needs further research.[44]

The issue of Kenyan Asians was kept alive by the press, although the Kenyan President, Jomo Kenyatta, did not pander to the anti-Asian lobby so long as the UK continued to receive a regular number of Asians made rootless as a result of Africanisation programmes. Reportedly, a secret agreement between Britain and Kenya had been made for an orderly transfer over seven years while the aid package to Kenya was increased. Robert Carr made it clear at the time of the introduction of the new Immigration Rules that, apart from those qualifying through the voucher system, no more East African Asians would be accepted so that 'community relations' in Britain could be maintained (Humphry and Ward, 1974, pp 142–47; Zolberg *et al*, 1989, p 300).

As already noted in 5.3.1, married women were not considered as heads of households under the extra-statutory voucher scheme introduced after the 1968 Act, save in particularly compelling circumstances, which were interpreted virtually out of existence. A British woman married to, for example, a Kenyan citizen could thus be rendered 'even more nearly Stateless than the British men in East Africa' (Bhabha and Shutter, 1994, p 114). Divorced women were suspected of disingenuously attempting to improve their chances while young unmarried women were investigated to ensure that they were really unmarried. Even when women were eligible in their own right, efforts were made to delay processing of applications. Those women who applied for vouchers were subsequently not granted visas to Britain for family visits upon suspicion that they would seek to remain. For women who did find their way to Britain, the Home Office adopted a policy of yearly renewals of leave to remain, that could only be made indefinite after four years. Such problems were complicated by the fact that the Government in India, where many individuals and families waited, could make return travel difficult unless assurances were given by the UK authorities that a person had a right to remain in Britain. Moore and Wallace (1975, pp 47–51) and, more recently, Shah (1992a) and Bhabha and Shutter (1994, pp 113–17) describe some harrowing stories of East African Asian women who were caught up in a conflict between their fight for survival for their families, which could range across three continents, and the exclusionary orientation of British immigration laws right up to the 1990s.

Criticism was voiced about the behaviour and attitude of officials in British High Commissions when dealing with voucher applications, in particular, about the entry clearance officer, 'who does not have to explain

44 CUKCs not attached to an existing British dependent territory and without the right of abode in Britain were reclassified by the British Nationality Act 1981 as British overseas citizens (5.3.4). A decision by the European Court of Justice is now awaited to test whether British overseas citizens are entitled to rights of free movement under European Community law (McGrory, 1998).

himself at all' (Moore and Wallace, 1975, p 55). Yet, possible further challenges on judicial review were also frustrated. In one case, the Court of Appeal said that neither the administrative criteria of the special voucher scheme nor their application were justiciable. Lawton LJ argued that the Secretary of State:

> ... was exercising prerogative powers of the Crown and that constituted part of the power to decide who should be allowed into the country ... This court has no jurisdiction to interfere with the terms of the ... scheme made by the Secretary of State or how it is administered by High Commissions overseas.[45]

It will be recalled that the prerogative power was used first against so called 'aliens'. Although the application of that power to British subjects (or Commonwealth citizens) had still been denied at times,[46] no such reservations appeared to be evident in the case under discussion.

After the passage of the Sex Discrimination Act 1975, a number of women complained to the Equal Opportunities Commission (EOC) that they were suffering sex discrimination under the voucher scheme, but the EOC could not investigate the scheme on the basis that it predated the 1975 Act. As the applicant in *Amin v Entry Clearance Officer, Bombay* found out, neither were the courts willing to construe the scheme as a violation of the 1975 Act as they adopted a restrictive interpretation.[47] The applicant in the *Amin* case was a woman living in India whose husband was an Indian citizen. Her father had been issued with a voucher in Tanzania for himself, his wife and the applicant's unmarried siblings, although she, being married, fell outside the conditions of issue. She applied to the British High Commission in Bombay for a voucher in her own right but was refused, being told that she was not a 'head of household'. Her application for judicial review was dismissed by the High Court, the Court of Appeal and the House of Lords on the sex discrimination issue. Before the House of Lords it was also argued that there should be a right of appeal in cases refused under the voucher scheme. A majority of the Lords held, however, that there was no possibility of appealing the refusal of vouchers as it was wholly discretionary and outside the framework of the appeals structure set up under the 1971 Act. Lord Fraser added: 'In my opinion ... a right of appeal would be unworkable in practice.'[48] Thus, a succession of judicial decisions endorsed the discretionary aspects of

45 *Re Javeed Iqbal Bhatti* (1981) unreported, 7 September, cited by Harlow and Rawlings (1984, p 562).

46 Macdonald and Blake (1991, p 90) point to the case of *DPP v Bhagwan* [1972] AC 60; [1970] 3 All ER 97, HL as recognising the common law right of abode for British subjects, albeit subject to statutory control in recent times.

47 [1980] 2 All ER 837, DC; [1983] 2 All ER 864, CA and HL.

48 [1983] 2 All ER 864, p 868a–b. The only judges who found in favour of the applicant were Lords Scarman and Brandon in the House of Lords. Harlow and Rawlings (1984, pp 562–63) and Shah (1992a) point out that the competence of the Parliamentary Commissioner for Administration (the Ombudsman) was drafted so that it excluded examination of the special voucher scheme.

the quota voucher scheme allowing officials a free rein to reject Asian applicants, affecting women in particular.

On the other hand, attempts to make arrangements to travel without vouchers were not considered favourably. In an early case, the Immigration Appeal Tribunal held that it had no jurisdiction to hear an appeal against a refusal to issue a special voucher while an applicant, who had first entered as a visitor, was still in the UK.[49] In September 1973, a Mr Thakrar, claiming BPP status, arrived in Britain after having lived in a UN camp and worked on a farm in Austria since fleeing from Uganda in October 1972. He had attempted to obtain a British passport in order to leave due to the Amin decree, but was told after reaching the front of a mile long queue that confirmation was needed from the Ugandan authorities that he had not acquired Ugandan citizenship. The local authorities confirmed this, but on the way to the British High Commission he was attacked by soldiers and robbed of all his papers, including an expired BPP passport. He only managed to leave the country after obtaining a Red Cross permit that was being issued to the expellees. He was refused leave to enter the UK by an immigration officer. Thakrar then applied to the High Court, *inter alia*, for an order of certiorari to have that decision quashed. The case was reported widely and provided an opportunity for judges to pronounce on a number of issues, although it was not necessary to spell them out as it was made clear that BPPs could not be admitted as 'patrials' under the Immigration Act 1971.[50]

Lord Widgery already decided in the High Court that, although an international law duty was imposed upon a State to admit its own nationals who have nowhere else to go, that could not override the express words of the 1971 Act. At the conclusion of the High Court proceedings, the Home Office challenged whether Thakrar had a British nationality at all, claiming that he had obtained Ugandan citizenship and thus lost BPP status![51] That contention was upheld by Lord Denning in the Court of Appeal, without any compelling evidence in its support, and against evidence that Thakrar had not been recognised as a Ugandan citizen and could not, therefore, have lost his British

49 *Shah v Secretary of State for the Home Department* [1972] Imm AR 56.

50 *R v Immigration Officer ex p Thakrar* [1974] QB 684, QBD and CA; *Thakrar v Secretary of State* [1974] 2 All ER 261, CA, affirming the Divisional Court of the Queen's Bench Division *sub nom R v An Immigration Officer at Heathrow Airport ex p Thakrar* [1974] 1 All ER 415. For the High Court's judgment, the *All England Law Reports* are referred to here as they record the Home Office's motion after the hearing to question the authenticity of the applicant's BPP status. See, also, White (1974) for a critical comment on the case.

51 BPPs apparently lost that status automatically upon becoming Ugandan citizens under the Ugandan Independence Act, proviso to s 2(1). CUKCs, on the other hand, had to renounce that status before being accepted as Ugandan citizens. In practice, there may not have been a difference so far as the Ugandan authorities were concerned. Further, renunciations of British nationality were not always effective (Fransman, 1989, pp 800–01).

status. All three judges took the opportunity to pronounce on the international law position, reversing Lord Widgery's admittance of some duties under international law, if not in domestic UK law. Lord Denning MR and Orr LJ stuck to the view that any rule of international law to admit nationals was an obligation as between States and could not be raised by an individual. Lawton LJ took the view that BPPs did not derive their status from allegiance, but through statute and that therefore any such rule could not apply to them.

The perspective adopted by Lord Denning MR and Lawton LJ on the position of BPPs under UK law is reminiscent of the rewriting of law done at the end of the 19th century with respect to aliens (2.5). In the High Court, the Home Office had decided not to raise the position of BPPs' right to enter the UK as distinct from that of 'British subjects'.[52] In the Court of Appeal, both judges sought to distance 'BPPs' from 'British subjects' and sought to assimilate the former's status to that of aliens, with Lord Denning claiming that BPPs never had a right of abode in Britain.[53] Lord Denning utilised a creative reading of the statutory history of BPPs, while Lawton LJ deployed the concept of allegiance. Neither judge sought assistance from the fact that BPPs were included in the quota voucher scheme, and neither addressed the explicit statement of the Home Secretary that both CUKCs and BPPs fleeing from Uganda would engage a British obligation to admit them (see 5.3.2). Lord Denning, adapting Shakespeare, instead cast a terrifying picture of BPPs from East Africa:

> They are said to be British nationals but they are not British subjects. These number, or used to number, many millions. They were not born here. They have never lived here. They live thousands of miles away in countries which have no connection with England except that they were once British protectorates. Is it to be said that by international law every one of them has a right if expelled to come into these small islands? Surely not. This country would not have room for them. It is not as if it was only one or two coming. They come not in single files 'but in battalions'.[54]

---

52 [1974] 1 All ER 415, pp 417j–18b.

53 Lord Denning found that British protected persons 'never had, so far as I can discover, the right of entry, without leave, into the UK' [1974] QB 684, p 702G–H. But he also found: '[In] the Aliens Restrictions Acts 1914 and 1919, the expression "alien" shall not include British protected persons. *But those Acts did not deal with the right of entry into the UK.*' [1974] QB 684, p 703A–B, emphasis added. Parry (1957, pp 89–91) suggests the status of British protected persons was never very clear. Certainly they had not been referred to by any UK immigration or aliens law before the Commonwealth Immigrants Act 1962. The logical step would have been to adopt the more generous common law perspective that did not permit restrictions unless Parliament had authorised them (see Chapter 2). Fransman's (1989, p 60) leading text on British nationality law uncritically accepts the Court of Appeal's view of the position of British protected persons, however.

54 [1974] QB 684, p 702B–D.

Thus, the judicial response to the challenges made against refusal of vouchers, or against refusal to admit individual Asians without vouchers, was itself hostile: the first signs that judges too would adopt a hostile attitude towards non-European refugees in the post-Second World War period.

By the late 1970s, it was obvious that holding British nationality status did not correspond with obtaining a right of abode in Britain. Another revision of nationality law was considered since the 1970s, but enacted under the new Conservative Government. The ensuing British Nationality Act 1981, in force since 1 January 1983, was also framed primarily around immigration considerations (Dummett and Nicol, 1990, pp 241–48). Under the 1981 Act, CUKCs who derived their British status from a former colony were reclassified as 'British overseas citizens' (BOCs). This was really only a change of wording and BOCs remained without a right of abode in the UK.[55] The Government relied once more on lumping all potential beneficiaries of the status together to inflate the image of the consequences were a right of abode to be granted: '... if this group, of which the UK passport holders from East Africa form only a part, were to have [full] British citizenship, the potential immigration commitment would be so large as to be quite unacceptable.'[56] Instead, it was advocated that they should remain in the special voucher queue.[57] Further, the status of a BOC was not to be transmissible: '... it is generally understood that the country of birth should be responsible for remedying the situation.'[58] By the 1980s, therefore, the law indicated that there was no more interest in providing protection for the *de facto* Stateless people created as a result of earlier laws. In the meantime, the European human rights organs looked as if they may provide some guarantees, but even there the mood was largely disinterested.

---

55 Another distancing strategy with significant implications in the British Nationality Act 1981 related to the Hong Kong British nationals, mostly CUKCs, who were reclassified as British Dependent Territories citizens (Shah 1995b, pp 84–88).

56 *British Nationality Law: Outline of the Proposed Legislation*, Cmnd 7987 (July 1980), para 26. Fransman (1989, p 144) draws on official statistics to estimate that one and a half million people became British overseas citizens on 1 January 1983, out of which one and a third million were dual citizens (Malaysians/British overseas citizens). The total number of British overseas citizens with no other citizenship could have been up to 216,000 (pp 1104–05). However, see Dummett and Nicol (1990, pp 243–44) on the inflation of statistics indicating the potential beneficiaries of BOC and BBP status, and on the unrealistic immigration prognoses made by the Government.

57 *British Nationality Law: Outline of the Proposed Legislation*, Cmnd 7987 (July 1980), para 27.

58 *Ibid*, para 103. The Home Office view concerning UK passport holders in India was that they 'may also consolidate their position by seeking citizenship in India', *First Report from the Select Committee on Race Relations and Immigration*, HC 303-II, p 417 (1977–78).

5.3.4 Little relief from Europe

From February 1970 onwards, there were some 300 applications lodged with the European Commission of Human Rights. Most of them were either adjourned pending the outcome of the case of 31 BPPs and CUKCs who had been refused entry, or they were struck off the Commission's list. The Commission's decision, given on 14 December 1973, also made a distinction between the status of BPPs and CUKCs. In the case of six BPPs, it found that they could claim a violation neither of Art 3 (prohibition on inhuman and degrading treatment) nor of Art 5 (security of the person) either by itself or in combination with Art 14 (freedom to enjoy Convention rights without discrimination). That view was motivated by the fact that BPPs had already lost the right of abode in the UK under the 1962 Act.[59] In the case of the remaining 25 CUKCs, a majority of the Commission found that a violation could be claimed of Arts 3 and 8 (right to family life) together with Art 14, although not of Art 5. The Commission took into account that the UK had given a pledge of unhindered entry to CUKCs who were not 'aliens' and retained the same duties towards them as towards other CUKCs; that they found themselves deprived of livelihood, suffered continuation of their illegal presence in East Africa having nowhere else to go; and that their situation had been aggravated by the practice of 'shuttlecocking' between countries. In a bold report, it concluded that the UK had discriminated against the CUKCs on the ground of race, which was not only prohibited discrimination but could amount to inhuman and degrading treatment under Art 3.[60]

However, that was not the end of the process under the European Convention, as the Commission could not finally establish a juridical violation; only the European Court of Human Rights or the Committee of Ministers could make such a finding. The 25 CUKC cases, together with 10 others, were not referred to the Court by either the Commission or the UK Government,[61] but were dealt with by the Committee of Ministers after the Commission forwarded its report on 5 March 1974. However, the report of the Commission remained confidential and some of the applicants had to wait

59 *East African Asians v UK* (1981) 3 EHRR 76, p 87.

60 *Ibid*, p 82. There was a majority of 8:3 for a violation of Art 3 and a majority of 9:2 for a violation of Arts 8 and 14 combined. It is significant that such a bold finding of race discrimination has seldom been repeated by either the Commission or the Court in subsequent cases involving immigration and ethnic minorities in Britain, providing a useful topic for the discussion about 'colour blindness' at the European level. Sachdeva (1993, pp 91–93) discusses the case of *Abdulaziz, Cabales and Balkandali v UK* (1985) 7 EHRR 471, where a race discrimination argument was rejected.

61 Anthony Lester QC, counsel for the applicants in this case, reported that the UK Government chose not to refer the matter to the Court, *First Report from the Home Affairs Select Committee*, HC 434, p 38 (1979–80).

seven years to find out what the views of the Commission were. Neither were the applicants informed of deliberations in the Committee which were held *in camera*. In the event, the Committee of Ministers decided that, since all the applicants concerned had been allowed to remain in the UK and the annual quota of vouchers had been augmented to 5,000, it could not reach the required two-thirds majority to find a violation and removed the case from its agenda. The Committee's decision was given more than eight years after the lodging of the first applications with the Commission (Drzemczewski, 1978).[62] The Commission's report, of at least some jurisprudential value to other applicants, was only made partly public during the January 1980 sitting of the Home Affairs Select Committee,[63] and a leaked extract of the Commission's report was eventually only published in the *European Human Rights Reports* in their 1981 edition, some eight years after it had been issued.[64]

In the meantime, people remained in voucher queues in East African countries or in the Indian subcontinent. The quota voucher scheme had been extended to India in 1972, but during the course of the 1970s, complaints were increasingly heard by individuals and representative organisations such as the JCWI that those who had left for India were experiencing a long wait in the voucher queue, while their economic position declined.[65] The waiting time in India, where the quota had finally been declared by the Government to be 600, had increased from three years in 1977 to six years in 1982, although by then the East African queue was down to a trickle (Harlow and Rawlings, 1984, pp 559–60).[66] The bias against applicants from India was to be seen in decisions of the European Commission issued after the major East African Asians litigation already discussed. In one admissibility decision it was held that the applicants had not been subject to inhuman and degrading treatment by being obliged to remain in the voucher queue in India.[67] In another case,

62 The final proceedings in the matter are noted at 35 *East African Asians (Citizens of the UK and Colonies) v UK* (1979) 13 Decisions and Reports 5.

63 *First Report from the Home Affairs Select Committee*, HC 434, p 49 (1979–80). Anthony Lester QC, who had been counsel for the applicants, stated in a memorandum to the Home Affairs Select Committee that 'the Committee of Ministers cannot be regarded as having overruled the Commission's findings of violation of Art 3 and of Art 8 read together with Art 14', p 38.

64 *East African Asians v UK* (1981) 3 EHRR 76.

65 For details of how the scheme was being operated in India and its effect on individuals and families, see *First Report from the Select Committee on Race Relations and Immigration, Immigration*, HC 303-II (1977–78), pp 226–32 (memorandum by JCWI), pp 412–15 (letter and memorandum from the British Passport Holders Association in Jamnagar, Gujarat), pp 416–18 (memorandum from the Home Office).

66 In 1978, the Home Office still resisted the Select Committee on Race Relations and Immigration's suggestion that the Indian quota should be made public on the basis that that would make the position of the UK passport holders 'more difficult' and that the result would 'mean a loss of flexibility' for the Government, *Immigration: Observations on the Report of the Select Committee on Race Relations and Immigration*, Cmnd 7287, p 20 (July 1978). Finally, in a written parliamentary answer on 18 March 1982, the 600 figure was announced (Commission for Racial Equality, 1985, p 67).

67 *X and Y v UK*, Appl no 5302/71, CD 44, p 29 (extracted in Stevens, 1992, p 23).

the individual concerned had attempted to enter Britain 'illegally' upon being required to leave Kenya and then was to be removed to India. The application was declared inadmissible although the Indian authorities had already indicated that he would be refused admission there if sent against his will.[68]

An application to the European Commission from a (now reclassified) BOC, in *Lalljee v UK*, could now take advantage of the Commission's views in the earlier *East African Asians* case.[69] But the Commission was at pains to distance itself from its previous views in this case of a man who had had to live in Pakistan since 1964:

> The Commission considers that the subjection of British overseas citizens to immigration control for entry to the UK, by way of limited quotas, or otherwise, does not as such, constitute racial discrimination or degrading treatment contrary to Art. 3 of the Convention ... notes that there is no indication that the applicant has been refused permission for racist motives. There do not appear to be serious difficulties in the applicant remaining in Pakistan.[70]

The application was declared manifestly ill founded, indicating that the European human rights institutions had also lost interest in the problem of the East African Asians, and were anxious to close off the argument that the UK's distancing policies were motivated by the race of the British passport holders.

While the European human rights bodies looked on, the situation for applicants in East Africa and India did not improve, however. Further cases of restrictions by the several governments concerned arose through the 1980s and 1990s. The Indian Government introduced a visa requirement for return travel to India as well as the need for a residence permit for British passport holders residing there (JCWI, 1985, p 6). By 1987, the voucher queue in India involved a wait of some eight years, according to the findings of a field investigation carried out by JCWI (1987a, p 7). In July 1985, a constitutional amendment was passed in Kenya which retrospectively removed Kenyan citizenship from those born there after independence, if neither parent was a Kenyan citizen at the time (Shah, 1992b). Cases emerged of people whose passport renewals were refused on the basis of that amendment, leaving them Stateless even where their parents held the non-transmissible statuses of BPPs or BOCs (JCWI, 1985, p 6).[71] The British Home Office's reaction towards the Kenyan Stateless minors was to insist that no issue arose from the UK's obligations under the Convention on the Reduction of Statelessness, and that responsibility fell on the Kenyan Government. Where individuals entered the

68 *X v UK*, Appl no 9505/81, np, DS supplement to vol 1 (3.0.3.4), p 9 (extracted in Stevens, 1992, p 36).

69 *Lalljee v UK*, Appl no 10556/83 (1986) 8 EHRR 84.

70 *Ibid*, p 85.

71 Shah (1992a, 1992b) records some examples of difficulties imposed by the Kenyan authorities on Asian travellers.

UK on a temporary basis, Home Office policy was usually to agree to consider cases exceptionally outside the Immigration Rules but, even here, decisions were delayed for months making travel impossible (JCWI, 1989, p 9). When leave to remain was granted, it was normally renewed yearly and made indefinite only after four years.

During the early 1990s several cases of BOCs arose, mainly involving women, where the Home Office refused to grant leave to remain and made decisions to deport them instead. In 1992, five such decisions were made (JCWI, 1993, pp 17–18). In one such reported case, *Patel*, leave to move for judicial review was applied for, but the High Court and Court of Appeal rejected the claim. Mrs Patel refused to apply for an Indian visa and Schiemann J, in the High Court, held that fact against her and denied judicial review.[72] The Court of Appeal was not convinced by an affidavit from JCWI that, in all their experience, there had been no case of a BOC being refused a variation of leave in the UK, and refused leave on the basis that there was no legitimate expectation to be followed in this case.[73] Sixteen months later, Ognall J, in the High Court, refused leave to move for judicial review on the basis that the female applicant, a BOC (who was also mysteriously considered to be an 'Indian subject') with five children, was considered to be deportable although there was no indication that the Indian authorities would consider an application for a visa except in the normal way.[74]

While there is overwhelming evidence that Asian British nationals have found constant difficulties in being accepted in Britain, the immigration of various groups of white British people in the phases of decolonisation were hardly problematised. Instead, specific legislative enactments recognised their linkages with the UK, as in the case of whites from Kenya already discussed. Even after the enactment of general controls, it was clear that through discretion, officials could ensure that white people from other parts of the Commonwealth or Empire would not be harassed. The conferral of 'patrial' status to many under the Immigration Act 1971 has ensured that they have simply disappeared from statistics. Dummett and Nicol (1990, p 221) reflect on another such instance: 'Many of the settlers in Rhodesia who left for Britain

---

72 *R v Secretary of State for the Home Department ex p Pushpaben Kiritbhai Patel* [1993] Imm AR 257, QBD.

73 *R v Secretary of State for the Home Department ex p Pushpaben Kiritbhai Patel* [1993] Imm AR 392, CA, Balcombe, Kennedy and Evans LJJ.

74 *R v Immigration Appeal Tribunal ex p Nargis Sunsara and Others* [1995] Imm AR 15. Applying *Mahli* [1990] 2 WLR 932, CA, Ognall J held that it was outside an adjudicator's 'power in law' to consider the Secretary of State's decision to make a deportation order requiring the applicant to go to a place where she could not go, the adjudicator being restricted to considering whether she remained in the UK without authority. *Mahli* itself was a decision interpreting restrictively the truncated right of appeal introduced by the Immigration Act 1988 in certain cases of deportation (see Macdonald and Blake, 1991, pp 373–74)

after 1973, particularly around the time of Zimbabwe's independence in 1979, were patrials but their immigration passed unrecorded and scarcely noticed.'

Through the 1980s and 1990s legislative developments have shown further evidence of distancing from non-white British nationals, while whites have been absorbed without question. The Rhodesian example has been followed in the case of whites arriving from post-apartheid South Africa, and most recently again from Zimbabwe. On the other hand, the transition of Hong Kong to full Chinese rule in 1997 was met with a response which was again evidently based on a paranoiac appreciation of the cultural impact on Britain upon decolonisation. In closing off the prospect of immigration avenues through the retention of British nationality, the British response overstated the attachment of the Hong Kong people to Britain after successive negative indications had been given to them, and also overstated the potential Asian refugee outflow from Hong Kong (Menski, 1995). As the East African Asians debacle unfolded, significant developments took place at the international and domestic level which appeared to enhance legal rights for refugees, notably as a result of the extension of the Refugee Convention of 1951 by the Protocol of 1967. On the other hand, the increasing visibility of non-European refugees, especially from the 1970s, has led to a legal regime designed to curtail their movement, and these developments have intensified further in the 1980s and 1990s whereby a high level of arbitrary State power is exercised upon Asian and African refugees.

CHAPTER 6

TURNING AGAINST NON-EUROPEAN REFUGEES

6.1 THE 1967 PROTOCOL RELATING TO THE STATUS OF REFUGEES

The Refugee Convention of 1951 was limited to refugees emerging as a result of events occurring before 1 January 1951. However, during the Hungarian crisis in 1956, the UNHCR adopted the view, without objection from Western States, that refugees from Hungary could be recognised under the Convention despite the time limitation since the crisis at hand had its origins in events before 1951.[1] The adoption of a Protocol Relating to the Status of Refugees in 1967 enabled recognition of refugees without reference to this dateline. The geographical limitation that also appeared in the 1951 Convention could, under the Protocol, be retained by a State only if it had held that position upon its adoption of the 1951 Convention (Weis, 1967).

Why exactly Western governments were keen to support the Protocol has not been made very clear. Certainly, discussions took place in the UNHCR's Executive Committee at its second session in 1964 and at its 12th session in 1965, while in the background, independence wars and European decolonisation of certain territories was also accompanied by the movement of thousands of refugees. The Executive Committee reached the conclusion that the dateline in the 1951 Convention should be deleted (Qureshi, 1988, p 86). The US, which ultimately had not accepted the 1951 Convention, ratified the Protocol in October 1968. But a detailed study of US refugee policy has noted the 'sparse legislative history' associated with it (Loescher and Scanlan, 1986, p 83), suggesting that behind the US' support was a manifestation of solidarity with the UN's humanitarian mission timed to coincide with the 'International Year for Human Rights', a wish to back the UNHCR and pressure from voluntary bodies. Although ratification of the Protocol involved a broadening of the existing legal categories of refugees then accepted in the US, it is significant that that was not the view held by some authorities in the US at the time (Qureshi, 1988, p 87).[2]

1 A similar interpretation was rejected by the Privy Council in *Molefi v Principal Legal Adviser* [1971] AC 182, where the applicant had been released on bail in 1961 pending a prosecution under the South African Suppression of Communism Act 1950, had escaped to Lesotho, and sought to resist removal to South Africa.

2 Frank (1977) discusses the possibility of invoking the Protocol in US law, although legislation implementing the 1951 Convention and the 1967 Protocol was deferred until 1980 (Tang, 1994, pp 583–84).

For the UK there is also no contemporary 'legislative history' to speak of. Two questions were asked in the House of Commons regarding the UK's adherence to the 1967 Protocol.[3] In one of them, the questioner, Mr Archer, referred to the problem of refugees in camps abroad, wishing to know when ratification would be carried out.[4] In one sense, that question betrayed the perceived foreign policy importance of the Protocol for the mainly Western governments which financed the UNHCR. The mandate in that organisation's governing statute[5] was not adequate for direct intervention in refugee movements, although the General Assembly of the United Nations had moved in the 1960s to give sanction to *ad hoc* interventions and contributed to the development of a 'good offices' function, particularly for intervention in Africa (Goodwin-Gill, 1983, pp 7–8; Zolberg *et al*, 1989, pp 27–29; Aga Khan, 1976, pp 302–07). Yet it was not made very clear that adherence to the Protocol would have placed on a treaty footing the 1951 Convention's obligation to co-operate with the UNHCR for the now expanded categories of refugees.[6] Paul Weis, who was special adviser to the High Commissioner in 1967, obliquely points to this aspect when he states:

> The dateline of 1 January 1951 excluded from the application of the Convention persons who had become refugees owing to political events that occurred after that date (and that were not the after effects of earlier events in Hungary in 1956 and the occupation of Czechoslovakia in 1968) – particularly large numbers of refugees in Africa [Weis, 1982, p 31].[7]

Louise Holborn, in her 'official' history of the UNHCR, also points to the situation of refugee groups in Africa by the 1960s for whom Convention type treatment could not be assured by the High Commissioner's limited mandate. She states that the High Commissioner, Sadruddin Aga Khan, personally exercised control over the contents of the Protocol, vigorously promoted it, and it was adopted within a time frame that is unusual for an international treaty (Holborn, 1975, vol 1, pp 178–81).[8] She further explained that:

3 House of Commons Debates, vol 754, col 311, 21 November 1967 and vol 765, col 6, 20 May 1968. Both questions from Mr Archer were directed to ascertaining when ratification would be undertaken, and the main reason for the delay, given by two Ministers of State in the Foreign Office, was that the discussions on the impact on British overseas territories were still being undertaken.

4 House of Commons Debates, vol 765, col 6, 20 May 1968. Mr Mulley, Foreign Office Minister, stated that the Protocol was not connected with the question of people in camps abroad.

5 Statute of the Office of the UNHCR, GA Res 428(V), 14 December 1950.

6 The obligation to co-operate with the UNHCR arose under the Refugee Convention 1951, Art 35.

7 Earlier, Weis (1967, p 40) had noted that 'the limitative nature of this dateline became increasingly apparent as time went on and as new refugee situations arose, particularly in Africa, involving hundreds of thousands of persons'.

8 Sadruddin Aga Khan was Deputy High Commissioner from 1962–65 and elected High Commissioner by the General Assembly from 1965. He was elected again, each time for five years, in 1965 and 1973. He points to Art 35 of the Convention but without elaboration (Aga Khan, 1976, p 330).

> While the Protocol does not directly expand the scope of the HC's [High Commissioner's] authority since it applies to obligations undertaken by States, indirectly it has strengthened his position substantially ... the authority of the HC is now broader because the obligations of States are broader [Holborn, 1975, vol 1, p 182].

The UK ratified the Protocol on 4 September 1968 while the East African Asians refugee crisis was at a high point, despite the fact that ratification would bind the UK internationally to undertake specific obligations to post-1951 refugees. In any case, its consequences for immigration policy were not discussed in depth and, while Commonwealth citizens were still the primary focus of control, the Convention and Protocol were not applied to them. Indeed, it may be argued that the main intention behind the Protocol was to facilitate the retention of post-colonial influence in Africa through the agency of the UNHCR.[9] These developments mark a splitting of the functions of the UNHCR, from an agency concerned to supervise the application to European refugees of the 1951 Convention, to one concerned to pursue the aims of Western governments outside the West through 'aid' missions to contain refugee movements.[10] Since the 1970s, advocates of refugees' rights have used the fact of the UK's adherence to the Protocol to insist that explicit legal provisions and specific procedures should be enacted into domestic UK law. In response, the UK has selectively, and in stages, chosen to 'incorporate' relevant provisions into the legal system, notably as part of its immigration law, while retaining as much discretion in the Home Office as possible. These developments have taken place in the background of an increasing shift in the origin of refugees from Europe to the non-European world and an officially declared stop on the recruitment of labour from outside Europe.

6.2 RECOGNITION OF REFUGEES IN UK LAW

As evident from the discussion in Chapter 5, the main targets of control from the 1960s were Commonwealth citizens. This emphasis continued to drive legal developments in the immigration field. As discussed further in 6.3, the immigration law system had begun increasingly to deal with cases of non-

9 A more recent study of the UNHCR's activities by the Lawyers Committee for Human Rights (1991, p 32) echoes the view of Weis and Holborn that, in the 1950s and 1960s, expanding the scope of refugee law instruments provided one way of increasing the influence of the UNHCR. The other method adopted was to expand the UNHCR's mandate less formally through the UN General Assembly.

10 The possibility of intervention over African refugee crises was reinforced by the adoption by the Organisation of African Unity of the Convention on Refugee Problems in Africa of 1969 which significantly widened the refugee definition, but which also carried a commitment to co-operate with the UNHCR. This argument needs further study, however, particularly in the light of further developments and the expansion of the role of the UNHCR. For a critical analysis of the phenomenon of refugee camps and associated aid distribution programmes, see Voutira and Harrell-Bond (1995).

European refugees at the same time, and further refugee specific legal developments were based on legislation which was already largely in place in the 1970s. In this section, the main aspects of control of refugees as they appeared from the 1970s are described. The immigration laws, by this time, dictated the use of formal statements of policy in the form of Immigration Rules which supplemented the powers under the main statute, the Immigration Act 1971. Also present, however, were the extra-statutory powers which allowed the Home Office a wide element of discretion as to how to treat refugees, as well as other categories of migrants. These aspects are considered in 6.2.1. A description of the formal administrative practice in dealing with claims for asylum is given in 6.2.2. Administrative appeals against decisions made by the immigration authorities were only made available from 1969. Recourse to the appeals system was allowed for some refugees, while others were subject only to the powers of the entry clearance officers, immigration officers or the Home Office. A discussion of the appeals framework follows in 6.2.3.

6.2.1 In and outside the Immigration Rules

The combined effect of legislation controlling the movement of aliens since 1905 and controlling that of British subjects (or Commonwealth citizens as they were now generally referred to) since 1962 was to place the power of regulation mainly with the Home Office. The Aliens Orders under the 1914–19 Aliens Restriction Acts gave broad powers to immigration officers, while leaving the Home Office to supplement those Orders by instructions to immigration officers which were not public. After 1962, a similar situation had arisen for Commonwealth citizens. More detailed regulation was then achieved by issuing instructions to immigration officers as to how their discretion 'on entry' should be exercised. These were a mixture of published and unpublished material. There were also some public, but obviously quite incomplete, statements about how 'after entry' regulation would be carried out. Since the passage of the Immigration Appeals Act 1969, a more detailed public statement was issued of the conditions under which the claims to enter or remain in the UK would be processed and the conditions under which deportation powers would be exercised or, importantly for refugees, withheld. Four separate statements were made for control on entry, applicable to immigration officers at ports, and control after entry, for which the Home Office was directly responsible; these were further divided as between aliens and Commonwealth citizens.[11] The first appearance of recognition of the new

11 These were: Aliens. Control after Entry: Immigration Rules, Cmnd 4297, Parliamentary Papers, vol 15, p 1 (1969–70); Aliens. Instructions to Immigration Officers, Cmnd 4296, p 13; Commonwealth Citizens. Control after Entry: Immigration Rules, Cmnd 4295, p 33, Commonwealth Immigrants Acts 1962 and 1968. Instructions to Immigration Officers, Cmnd 4298, p 49. Each of these statements was placed before Parliament in February 1970.

obligations under the 1967 Protocol was made in the Instructions and Rules issued in February 1970.[12] For example, the Instructions to Immigration Officers on aliens stated that:

> An alien who does not otherwise qualify for admission should not be sent away if the result would be his going to a country to which he is unwilling to go owing to a well founded fear of being persecuted for reasons of race, religion, nationality, membership of a particular social group or political opinion. If an alien claims to be in such a position, *the case should be reported immediately to the Home Office*.[13]

The statement was repeated *mutatis mutandis* for Commonwealth citizens.[14] Similarly, it was stated that a revocation or variation of landing conditions would not be refused by the Home Office, nor a deportation order made, if the result would be that a person would have to go to a country in the above mentioned condition.[15] It is clear that, at this stage, the Home Office could keep monitoring the number of such qualifying persons by having the provision to directly refer a potential refugee case to the Home Office.[16]

The Immigration Act 1971, the main statute applicable to immigration law generally, made provision, in s 3(2), for 'Immigration Rules' which the Secretary of State should lay before Parliament 'from time to time' for 'regulating the entry into and stay' of those who require leave to enter the UK, including any period for which leave is to be given and any conditions which may be attached to that leave. It further provided that such Rules could discriminate on the basis of nationality or citizenship. The Rules can be dismissed by either House of Parliament upon a resolution passed within 40 days of their being laid. The 1970 provisions for refugees were repeated in Rules laid before Parliament on 23 October 1972[17] and were reiterated in new

12 Macdonald (1987a, p 277) has stated that: 'During the 1960s, the first Immigration Rules were published. As a result of correspondence with the [UNHCR] the Home Office inserted references to political asylum and refugees.' The findings in the present study suggest that 1970 was, in fact, the first year that the Immigration Rules carried explicit reference to asylum.

13 Aliens. Instructions to Immigration Officers, Cmnd 4296, Parliamentary Papers, vol 15, p 13 (1969–70), para 53. Emphasis added.

14 Commonwealth Immigrants Acts 1962 and 1968. Instructions to Immigration Officers, Cmnd 4298, Parliamentary Papers, vol 15, p 49 (1969–70), para 52.

15 Aliens. Control after Entry: Immigration Rules, Cmnd 4297, Parliamentary Papers, vol 15, p 1 (1969–70), paras 26 and 44 respectively; Commonwealth Citizens. Control after Entry: Immigration Rules, Cmnd 4295, p 33, paras 26 and 42 respectively.

16 Later events suggest that statistical information on asylum claims was not kept by the Home Office until 1979.

17 Statement of Immigration Rules for Control on Entry, Parliamentary Papers, no 509, vol 35, p 567 (1971–72), para 58 (leave to enter); Statement of Immigration Rules for Control after Entry, Parliamentary Papers, no 510, vol 35, p 547 (1971–72), paras 30 (extension) and 61 (deportation).

Rules laid before Parliament on 25 January 1973.[18] Notably, however, the need for immigration officers to refer 'on entry' refugee cases to the Home Office was omitted. Further, a reference to the need for full account to be taken in asylum cases of the 'relevant international instruments' to which the UK was a party was inserted in the 'Control After Entry' Rules.[19]

The new provisions for the enactment of Rules under the 1971 Act gave the impression that the use of more or less secret policies outside the Rules would not have a place in immigration practice. Indeed, Vincenzi (1992) has argued, after almost two decades of the operation of the 1971 Act, that it was no intention of the Wilson Committee, which recommended a revised system of control including appeals, to see the use of 'extra-statutory discretion' in the exercise of immigration control because, among other reasons, that would leave the new appellate system unable to supervise the authorities' powers. Nevertheless, it is the case that a considerable flexibility remains within the Home Office to implement policies 'outside the rules' with virtually no appellate scrutiny (Macdonald and Blake, 1991, pp 34–37). One aspect of such flexibility was seen in the continuation of the special voucher scheme for East African Asians after 1969. Another is the policy on granting leave to enter or remain on compassionate grounds, now more frequently referred to as 'exceptional leave to remain'. On the other hand, Harlow and Rawlings (1984, p 504) have noted that the Rules themselves 'often appear to leave officials with considerable freedom of manoeuvre'. They even distinguish between 'outside the Rules' policies and 'rules within Rules' which include administrative schemes and instructions to immigration officials by their superiors with varying levels of secrecy (Harlow and Rawlings, 1984, pp 503–04). In any case, the scope of the Rules was realised only in the actual practice of control.

6.2.2 The formal practice on claims for asylum

As seen, the Immigration Rules carried specific provisions on asylum from the early 1970s. On the other hand, there is very little information about the practice surrounding the treatment of people who claimed asylum, as most

18 Statement of Immigration Rules for Control After Entry. Commonwealth Citizens, HC 80, Parliamentary Papers, vol 31, p 498 (1972–73), paras 30 (variation of leave) and 50 (withholding deportation); Statement of Immigration Rules for Control After Entry. EEC and Other Non-Commonwealth Nationals, HC 82, p 515, paras 28 (variation of leave) and 57 (withholding deportation); Statement of Immigration Rules for Control on Entry. Commonwealth Citizens, HC 79, p 535, para 54 (leave to enter); Statement of Immigration Rules for Control on Entry. EEC and Other Non-Commonwealth Nationals, HC 81, p 555, para 55 (leave to enter).

19 Statement of Immigration Rules for Control After Entry. Commonwealth Citizens, HC 80, Parliamentary Papers, vol 31, p 498 (1972–73), para 49; Statement of Immigration Rules for Control After Entry. EEC and Other Non-Commonwealth Nationals, HC 82, p 515, para 56.

textbooks took their cue from the Rule changes from 1980 to include a discussion on asylum (see 6.3.1). Most of the following description of actual practice is based on the account by Fortin (1978) of a conference convened in December 1977 by the Institute of Development Studies and the World University Service, with participants from various organisations involved with refugee advocacy including the UNHCR and the UK Immigrants Advisory Service (UKIAS). That this discussion was taking place may already indicate that the issue of refugees was moving to a more prominent place in public debates.

A grant of asylum under the Refugee Convention 1951, would entail admission for one year at a time, and was convertible into leave to remain with no time restriction after four years. No employment restrictions were imposed, however, and full access to social security was formally given. A travel document was issued in line with the period of leave given. In practice, however, the Convention status was seen as a subsidiary part of the scheme in that a grant of asylum was seen as a last resort. If a student refugee, for example, expressed an intention to remain in the UK, he or she would be granted student status. A grant of asylum was even seen as subsidiary to a grant of leave on compassionate grounds, which was not necessarily given free of employment restrictions, while access to social security was at the discretion of local officials. Such cases could give rise to the problem of adjustment of status at a later point in time.

The procedure for determination of status also varied depending on the point at which a claim for asylum was made. The least problematic category here was claims for asylum that were made when the applicant was already legally in the UK. Such an applicant was 'normally' in a position to receive guidance from agencies such as UKIAS, the British Council for Aid to Refugees (BCAR) or the JCWI and would apply directly to the Home Office. An interview would follow with a Home Office official or, less commonly, by a local immigration officer or even the local police. The interviewing officer would add a comment on the credibility of the applicant's story, which could often be decisive in the first instance and also at appeal. The interview was structured around a form used for all immigration categories and the interviewing officer had no expertise in refugee problems and often no knowledge of the political situation in the applicant's country of origin.[20]

Where an individual made an application to enter at a port of entry, an immigration officer would conduct an interview if the terms 'asylum' or 'refugee' were used, after which it was likely that the case would be referred to the Home Office. As will be recalled, the reference in the Rules for

20 Problems in the attitude and the lack of training of immigration officers continued to be identified as found by the Home Affairs Select Committee in 1985, despite intervening legal changes. *Third Report from the Home Affairs Committee, Refugees and Asylum, with Special Reference to the Vietnamese*, HC 72-I (1984–85), para 106.

mandatory referral to the Home Office had been dropped, and it was not always the case that details reached the Home Office. In an unknown number of cases a decision would be made on the spot after reference to the Chief Immigration Officer on site. Advice agencies did not hear of applications where there had been a summary refusal except in cases where they had been alerted by friends or relatives meaning that a person may have no idea about how to go about framing an application that had less chance of being refused outright. Especially where asylum was referred to, detention would be likely to follow, although temporary admission could be granted pending a decision by the Home Office. Passports were retained in the latter case and an obligation to report periodically to the officials at the port of entry was imposed.

If a person had entered illegally or overstayed a legal entry, he or she would be tried in a magistrates' court which could recommend a deportation. In such cases, imprisonment by the police pending deportation would result, which would take some five or six months due to other more pressing matters. Where a person claimed asylum at any point during this process the case would be considered by the Home Office in a manner similar to the procedure on 'after entry' cases.

Where someone was abroad at the time of making an application, he or she would normally have to go to a British Embassy to be interviewed by an Embassy official. Above all, a test of personal acceptability, which took into account security considerations, was important. The granting of asylum in this manner was purely a matter of executive discretion. On the other hand, the Rules were read by the Immigration Appeal Tribunal as only being applicable to persons who were to be removed from the UK, thus denying a right of appeal to a person whose application from abroad was rejected.[21] Although the Immigration Appeal Tribunal had not examined the 1951 Refugee Convention, its interpretation of the Rules was later ratified by commentators as being consistent with the Convention's provisions which could not be extended to an individual who is within the territorial jurisdiction of his 'own country' (Grant and Martin, 1982, p 326; Macdonald, 1983, p 239).

Within the Home Office's Immigration and Nationality Department sections for 'aliens' and 'Commonwealth citizens' were set up, and each was subdivided into 'case working groups'. These groups would decide whether a case should be dealt with as an asylum claim. If asylum was not formally requested, then a case would be dealt with under other criteria, even if it disclosed the substance of an asylum claim, underlining the 'last resort' nature of asylum under international obligations.[22] If it was decided that the case

21 *Secretary of State for the Home Department v X (A Chilean Citizen)* [1978] Imm AR 73.

22 The 'last resort' nature of the Rules on asylum was also mentioned by a Home Office official, Mr JA Chilcot, in evidence to the Select Committee on Race Relations and Immigration in November 1977, *First Report from the Select Committee on Race Relations and Immigration, Immigration*, HC 303-II (1977–78), p 355.

was one to merit consideration as an asylum claim, it would go to a 'special group' in either section. Asylum cases were considered under the criteria of Arts 1 and 33 of the Refugee Convention 1951. It was also taken into account whether an applicant had already obtained asylum in a third country or had arrived from a third country considered to be 'safe', that is, one which would afford political asylum in line with the Convention provisions and where he would be able to return. Applications from such persons to remain on other grounds, however, continued to be considered.[23]

The division between Commonwealth citizens and aliens went beyond separate treatment in the Rules or administratively within the Immigration and Nationality Department. In practice, too, refugees from Commonwealth countries were treated differently. It was thought that refugees from the Commonwealth were treated less favourably than 'aliens'. Fortin's (1978, p 5) report recorded that:

> As the main source of immigrants to Britain are the former colonies, there is always the suspicion that Commonwealth citizens claiming refugee status may be simply prospective immigrants trying to circumvent the various obstacles to entering and settling in Britain. They tend, therefore, to be subject to particularly rigorous checking and vetting procedures; if accepted in Britain, it is normally under some category other than political asylum, thereby denying them refugee status and the rights this entails.

In Chapter 5, it was seen that Ugandan or other East African Asians were not considered as coming under the Refugee Convention, and the same treatment was also to be noted for other groups, for example, refugees coming from Zimbabwe.[24] Any leave given to this group was under the other (that is, non-asylum) Immigration Rules categories or outside the formal Rules altogether as seen in the extra-statutory special voucher scheme devised from 1968 for East African Asians. Commonwealth citizens would be granted a Certificate of Identity which had much less international acceptability than a Convention Travel Document.

6.2.3 Appeals

The institution of an appeals system against refusals under the immigration legislation was the recommendation of the Wilson Committee on Immigration

23 This information was submitted by the Home Office in a memorandum appended to the *First Report from the Select Committee on Race Relations and Immigration*, HC 303-II (1977–78), p 338.

24 For complaints of the lack of protection for Zimbabweans in the UK, as a result of an 'understanding' made between the UNHCR and the UK Government in 1970, excluding them from the UNHCR's mandate, see JCWI (1979, p 11). The difference in treatment of Commonwealth citizens was also confirmed by Chilcot, in evidence in the *First Report from the Select Committee on Race Relations and Immigration*, HC 303-II (1977–78), p 355.

Appeals which reported in August 1967. It was thought necessary to have decisions subjected to an impartial review to dispel the widely held belief that the Immigration Service dealt with claims of Commonwealth citizens seeking admission in an arbitrary and prejudiced way.[25] Juss (1993, p 128) observes that it was thought that the system of immigration control was just and that immigration officers acted fairly, only that it was not apparent that this was so. Therefore, the appeals system was designed to provide legitimacy to a system of immigration control which deliberately targeted non-whites, mainly Commonwealth citizens, at this time. It is interesting to note that it is this appeals framework which has been deployed to defuse grievances against massive refusals of asylum claims by non-European refugees, especially from the 1990s.

The Wilson Committee recommended the institution of a two-tier appeals structure. It was clearly contemplated that appeals against any exclusion should be allowed, and leave granted where a person was making a bona fide claim to asylum.[26] The UNHCR also made representations to the Wilson Committee and the Committee was satisfied that asylum claims could be dealt with suitably under the system of appeals that it was recommending. However, asylum cases were seen by the Committee as 'special cases'.[27] Not much thought was given to how the mechanics of asylum appeals would work in practice, as distinct from appeals involving other immigration issues. The two exceptions in this regard were the Committee's recommendations that provision should be made for *in camera* proceedings and that the UNHCR should be informed and have the opportunity to make its views known in all asylum proceedings.[28]

The ensuing Immigration Appeals Act 1969 (governing Commonwealth citizens) and the Aliens (Appeals) Order 1970 (governing aliens) were not strictly brought into force, because of a failure to make an instrument for commencement, but an extra-statutory appeals mechanism system was run from 1 July 1970 (Dummett and Nicol, 1990, p 207). Those instruments served as a model to be followed in the Immigration Act of 1971. Broadly speaking, upon a negative decision by an entry clearance officer, immigration officer or the Home Office, a first appeal could be made to an adjudicator and, with leave, to the Immigration Appeal Tribunal (a three person chamber with a legally qualified chairman) in the second instance. Where a deportation order

25 *Report of the Committee on Immigration Appeals* (the Wilson Committee), Cmnd 3387, Parliamentary Papers, vol 36, p 457 (1966–67), para 84. See, also, Commission for Racial Equality (1985, p 115).

26 *Ibid*, vol 36, p 457 (1966–67), para 115.

27 *Ibid*, p 49.

28 *Ibid*, para 145.

was made on the basis that a person's presence in the UK was not conducive to the public good an appeal lay direct to the Immigration Appeal Tribunal. But gaps in this system began to appear soon, showing that not all powers to expel an individual from the UK could be tested by it.

The Wilson Committee of 1967 had recommended that an appeals system be instituted for both 'deportation' and 'exclusion' (that is, for a refusal at port).[29] But the system of appeals instituted after 1969 failed to provide for an in-country (or suspensive) appeal right where a person who did not already hold an entry clearance or visa was served with a notice of refusal at port.[30] Instead, an individual was expected to mount an appeal from abroad. While the Wilson Committee approved the principle of entry clearances as a means of ensuring smoother processing once an individual was in the UK, the post-1969 Rule scheme made entry clearances for dependants of Commonwealth citizens compulsory, thus shifting decision making overseas (Harlow and Rawlings, 1984, p 509; Bevan, 1986, pp 164–65). Denying a right of appeal to a person who arrived without an entry clearance may have been thought as a way of securing that system by enabling his or her summary removal from the UK. The imposition of compulsory entry clearances or visas has subsequently been widened to include other categories, especially targeting citizens of those countries which are seen as producing a significant number of refugees.

The second gap in the appeals system began to appear in cases where a deportation order was made pursuant to a recommendation of a court as part of the sentence for a criminal offence. Here, the appeals system did not provide a remedy, but it was assumed that such a recommendation could be appealed in the courts dealing with criminal appeals. Two early asylum cases in the tribunal dismissed the idea that the appellate authorities would hear pleas based on asylum grounds where a deportation order by the Secretary of State had been made pursuant to a court recommendation.[31] In one of the cases which reached the Court of Appeal, Lord Denning stated that the proper person to deal with an asylum claim was the Secretary of State and not the court recommending the deportation, as the Immigration Appeal Tribunal had thought.[32]

---

29 *Report of the Committee on Immigration Appeals* (the Wilson Committee), Cmnd 3387, Parliamentary Papers, vol 36, p 457 (1966–67), para 145.

30 That bar was replicated in the Immigration Act 1971, s 13.

31 *Secretary of State for the Home Department v Fardy* [1972] Imm AR 192, IAT and *Ali (DM) v Secretary of State for the Home Department* [1973] Imm AR 19. The latter case was confirmed in its outcome by the Court of Appeal [1973] Imm AR 33.

32 *Ali (DM) v Secretary of State for the Home Department* [1973] Imm AR 33, CA.

Thirdly, although in the 1970s there was still an assumption that those people who had entered 'illegally' or who had overstayed would normally be dealt with by the criminal court system (Fortin, 1978, pp 5–6), the system of summary removal for 'illegal entrants' was already being pioneered by the Home Office and sanctioned as lawful by the courts (Lloyd Jones 1979; Grant and Martin, 1982, pp 262–63, 277; Bevan, 1986, pp 345–56; Macdonald and Blake, 1991, pp 6–7). In the 1980s, asylum seekers were being declared 'illegal entrants' with increased frequency and thus subject to summary removal, whilst at the same time being deprived of any appeal.[33] Judicial review in the High Court was still available, and came to be used much more, creating pressures which the courts then sought to resist.

Further, as already seen in the case of the East African Asians, a class of cases was totally immune from the appeals system (5.3.3). Partly, this was the result of the manner in which the jurisdictional powers of the appellate authorities were written in the Immigration Act 1971 which permitted re-examination of only that aspect of discretion already expressed or implied in the Rules. The 'outside the Rules' powers which the Home Office was exercising in operating the East African Asians' voucher scheme or by granting exceptional leave to a person outside of the Refugee Convention, are both examples of situations which neither adjudicators nor the Tribunal could re-examine, precisely because they could be seen as being 'outside the Rules'.[34] As already seen in 5.3.3, the courts were also reluctant to interfere with decisions made under such powers.

Most adjudicators, who, until 1987, were appointed by the Home Office, had some legal experience, although they were not required to be legally qualified. Many had experience of administration or law in former colonies at the time the appeals system was set up (Commission for Racial Equality, 1985, p 123). General critiques of the appeals system were dismal. Adjudicators have been criticised for their incompetence, their lack of familiarity with the legal issues involved, including the question of ethnic minority laws, and their racial bias (Juss, 1993, pp 132–35). Progressive tightening of the Rules by Government amendments and tribunal interpretation took place and the procedures themselves were thought to stack the cards in favour of exclusion. The UKIAS was set up in 1970, along with the appeals system, to advise individuals who were in difficulty with immigration matters and to assist them in presenting their case to the Home Office and the appellate authorities (Commission for Racial Equality, 1985, p 122). Some critics viewed it as supporting this system through its maintenance of cosy relationships with

33 Macdonald and Blake (1995, p 586) point out that, in *Khawaja v Secretary of State for the Home Department* [1984] AC 74, the House of Lords held that a person only became an illegal entrant by deception when the Home Office declared them to be such, and thus adjudicators should not act to usurp this function.

34 See Immigration Act 1971, ss 19 and 20. This problem remains a live issue in immigration law (see Macdonald and Blake, 1995, pp 576–84).

immigration officers, the appellate authorities and the Home Office (which funded it) (Harlow and Rawlings, 1984, pp 504, 517–30).[35]

The appeals system also became more legalistic than anticipated by the Wilson Committee with complex primary legislation, 'awesome' subordinate legislation and a mounting pile of case law (Juss, 1993, pp 130–31). On the other hand, there was widespread ignorance of immigration law, with few practitioners apart from the UKIAS and JCWI having the relevant expertise, and with few books synthesising the relevant precedents (Harlow and Rawlings, 1984, p 530). In his leading textbook, which first appeared in 1983 and included many unreported decisions, Macdonald (1983, p v) stated that 'even now I cannot be sure that I have not missed something important either at Tribunal or High Court level'. Noting the mushrooming of judicial activity in the immigration field, Macdonald (1983, pp v–vi) fired an opening shot about the problem of discerning the attitude of the appellate authorities and especially the higher courts:

> Precedent plays an important part in [the Home Office's] decision making process. It plays an important part in adjudication before the appellate authorities. And they have access to all the precedents. We do not, although clearly the news of a new trend setting case travels round the unofficial grapevine pretty quickly. That does not help the public. There is only one set of Immigration Appeal Reports published by HMSO. They are very fine reports. But they only deal with cases that have been through the immigration appellate system. They do not cover habeas corpus and many judicial review applications in the High Court, criminal cases, EEC cases affecting free movement rights, or relevant decisions on the European Convention on Human Rights.

The process was also criticised for not carrying basic legal safeguards. For example, the Home Office's 'explanatory statements' were automatically admitted as evidence, although they could be written months after a decision was taken. The statements are described by Dummett and Nicol (1990, p 210) as 'an extraordinary mixture of primary facts, hearsay, inference, and argument which are sometimes difficult to tease apart'. The Home Office, to which notice of appeal had first to be sent, could also determine the manner in which appeals were run, for example, by delaying hearings indefinitely (Juss, 1993, pp 137–40). Such observations were part of a growing chorus of criticism directed towards the appeals process which was designed to be user friendly, but which demanded the expertise of, and dependence upon, lawyers who had to generally work ill equipped.

35 Juss (1993, pp 130–31) maintains that the UKIAS did not always follow their internal instructions and often failed to draw the attention of the tribunals to an important case. Staff varied in competence and quality and most were underpaid. Dummett and Nicol (1990, p 209), while asserting that the UKIAS was impartial, write: 'Some immigrants were suspicious that, because the Home Office appointed its chairman and funded it, it was not impartial.' They also recount the background to its formation after the JCWI's bid to act as the representative organisation was rejected by the Government.

Similar criticisms were heard about claims involving asylum. Before the Home Affairs Select Committee which reported in 1985, JCWI and UKIAS were less concerned about interviews at the Home Office in Lunar House, Croydon, but interviews by immigration officers at ports were subject to criticism involving the attitudes of immigration officers, who breached confidentiality, and who had little knowledge of the background of the countries of origin.[36] Only brief reasons for refusing an asylum claim were given, making it difficult to know whether to mount an appeal.[37] The UKIAS told the Committee that appellants commonly protested that comments in the explanatory statements represented either incorrect or partial records of their comments at interview which surfaced at appeal. On the other hand, discrepancies in the appellants' evidence were cited as a reason for distrusting them, while adjudicators were prone to using them to dismiss an appeal.[38]

From the late 1960s, therefore, a legalised approach to dealing with questions of immigration was created, primarily as a response to the need to control immigration from the Commonwealth. It was thought that legal guarantees could provide satisfaction that persons had been dealt with fairly under the new controls. Asylum was viewed as a relatively minor part of this control framework, and had hardly been considered in its formulation. Yet some cases did emerge where the framework of legal protection was seen as wanting. These cases showed that the Rules could not be relied upon by all prospective entrants and informal policies continued. Gaps also appeared in the appeals system, partly as a result of a wish to keep some entrants outside it altogether, as in the case of the East African Asians, or through declaring arrivals as 'illegal entrants' due for summary expulsion. Further, the model of administrative justice needed the assistance of legally qualified personnel whose work could be made difficult by the above mentioned constraints. Yet, it is this general framework which, after further fine tuning, has more recently been deployed to control the entry of non-European refugees.

6.3 RE-ORIENTING ASYLUM LAW

While a general contraction in the demand for immigration has been noticed throughout Western Europe, there has, at the same time, been an intensification of asylum law as a field of State control during the last 20 years. At first sight, it appears as if the emergence of an asylum law represents a

36 *Third Report from the Home Affairs Committee, Refugees and Asylum, with Special Reference to the Vietnamese*, HC 72-I (1984–85), para 106.

37 *Ibid*, para 110.

38 *Ibid*, para 107.

commitment to accept the presence of refugees, under Britain's international obligations. On the other hand, and perhaps precisely because of its coincidence with timing of the recruitment stop, holding up the possibility of asylum can be viewed as an 'under the counter' means of recruiting new labour into the economy. As such, it can be seen as part of the means by which the State retains control over a pliable source of labour, although the stigma of economic migrants is frequently applied to asylum seekers at the same time.[39] Some explanations for the increasing controls on worker migration from the 1970s point out that Western European countries switched their strategy from being importers of labour to become exporters of capital (for example, Castles *et al*, 1984, pp 11–39). This would appear to be at odds with the idea that recruitment is still taking place under a different legal form. However, Collinson (1993, pp 134–35) argues that 'demand for immigrant labour not only persists in Western Europe (despite high levels of unemployment), but may well increase in years to come'. In his more recent work on the legal position of Turkish settlers in Germany, the Netherlands and Britain, Çiçekli (1998, p 259) argues to similar effect:

> Empirical studies clearly show that immigration has been and is also likely to be further beneficial for the receiving countries, as long as it is under control. However, there seems to be immense political pressure against immigration which may influence policy makers to give more attention to political rather than economic rationality.

Çiçekli (1998, pp 260–61) also notes the widespread tendency among Turkish citizens towards taking up self-employment which is itself impeded by legal barriers.[40] That such considerations substantially qualify a labour import/capital export trade-off should be obvious. In any case, analyses based upon solely economic premises would miss an important dimension, especially since public debates on the economic implications of immigration on receiving countries have seldom taken into account the contributions made by migrants or settlers, who have generally been portrayed as liabilities to State budgets.

In fact, the experience of recruiting beyond the borders of Europe had left most Western European countries in a state of tension due to the presence of non-Europeans in their territories, and an official halt to recruitment was called by the early 1970s across Western Europe. The parallel application of immigration policies across several Western European States is quite striking even as the EEC expanded in 1973, and it preceded the discussions in various

39 McDowell (1996, pp 54–55) highlights this economic view of asylum migration in Switzerland.

40 Indeed, in the case of various groups from the Indian sub-continent, including East African Asians, there is growing evidence about the preference for self-employment and professionalisation, the latter especially for the second generation (see Tambs-Lyche, 1980; Modood, 1992, pp 27–43; Mattausch, 1998).

international fora on the workings of a possible common European immigration policy (Hammar, 1985; Collinson, 1993, pp 53–63). Findlay (1996, p 47) perceives that restrictions on immigration in Western Europe, particularly from countries of the south, 'were primarily initiated in the early 1970s in response to political and social pressures relating to the size of certain visible immigrant groups rather than as a direct function of economic forces'. Collinson (1993, pp 53–54) also points out that, whereas the economic recession was often given as a reason for the immigration 'stop' of 1973–74, the underlying reason was the presence of larger non-European populations. While this merely shifted the emphasis of migrants to family re-unification and formation, States also undertook commitments to allow no further (non-white) immigration. At this point, the possibility of prospective settlers from outside Europe claiming asylum was also not likely to be welcome from a racially calculated demographic point of view.

Writers have tended to agree that, while the general patterns across Britain, France, Germany, the Netherlands, Sweden, Switzerland and Belgium may have been similar, for Britain, the racial aspect of control was already obvious from the Commonwealth Immigrants Act 1962 and the manner in which further migration routes were cut off, as in the East African Asians case (Collinson, 1993, pp 54–55; Castles *et al*, 1984, pp 92–93). The UK legal system then became more generally occupied with attempts to further reduce migration from the Commonwealth and several innovations in policy and practice were made. The Immigration Act 1971 provided the structure, and policy changes were effected through the Immigration Rules or other administrative rules as already noted. Increased use was made of the powers of deportation, and summary administrative removal became more commonplace; scrutiny at missions overseas was tightened, in particular, by making the use of entry clearance or visas compulsory in several categories; internal controls were geared to detection of overstaying and illegal immigration as well as being linked to access to social welfare rights; nationality law changes with immigration implications were introduced (see Sachdeva, 1993, pp 31–39). Very prominently, from the late 1970s, the legal system began to attack rights of family reunion and family formation. That was achieved, for example, through the application of the 'primary purpose rule' directed at mainly South Asian spouses and the 'sole responsibility rule' directed mainly at West Indian and Filipino children (see Sachdeva, 1993 on spouses; Cheney, 1993 on the sole responsibility rule; Bhabha and Shutter, 1994, pp 55–61; Dummett and Nicol, 1990, pp 231–34 generally).

It was also clear that further refugee movements outside Europe would not bypass the West. The Independent Commission on International Humanitarian Issues (ICIHI) quite sensitively pointed out that it was the fact that the new refugees were culturally distinct which provoked a crisis of conscience and of the laws in the 'north':

> In the early 1970s, a new phenomenon emerged. Refugees from the crisis areas of Africa, Asia and Latin America began to move in increasing numbers to the industrialised countries ... the arrival of many refugees from geographically and culturally distant areas constituted an unprecedented challenge to the legal machinery and conscience of the receiving countries. The refugee problem, previously regarded as a factor in east-west relations, now had a north-south dimension added to it [ICIHI, 1986, p 33].

For Britain, too, a marked change in the origin of refugees before and after the 1960s could be noted since the arrival of the Ugandan Asians. Other groups were now coming from newly independent African and Asian countries and, by the mid-1970s, from Latin America (Fortin, 1978, p 1). Admissions from Chile after the fall of Allende were agreed to by the UK as part of an international request from the UNHCR.[41] To the list can be added some 12,000 Cypriot refugees who arrived in the last three months of 1974 and the first half of 1975, and Asians from Malawi arriving in 1976 (Fortin, 1978, p 15). The British Council for Aid to Refugees reported that:

> Ten years ago it was the exception to have a refugee referred to us who had not come from Europe. In 1974–75 we were called on for help to refugees from Latin America (mainly Chileans), from Africa (Ethiopians, Rhodesians, Ugandans and South Africans), from Indochina (Vietnamese, Cambodians and Laotians) as well as Kurds [quoted in Fortin, 1978, p 1].

Thus, there was a notable shift in the origin of refugees coming to Britain, and a parallel hostility was already developing against these new refugees in practice which was directly linked to their racial background.

While there is little public information about rates of refusal by the Home Office of asylum claims in the 1970s, individuals appealing refusals of asylum were experiencing difficulties, although they constituted less than 1% of the total number of appellants during the 1970s. It has been noted (6.2.2) that interviewing officers could make findings of credibility, although the decision to grant or withhold asylum could rest in another office. The appeal statements would be written by a group in the Home Office separate from the decision making groups. The onus was on the applicant to establish the truth of his or her claim and broad credibility in itself was not enough to win. The Home Office representative would cross-examine an appellant rigorously to throw doubt on his or her credibility and not much allowance was made for the possibly different requirements for refugees. Although the appellate authorities were intended to function as relatively informal bodies, they soon became more like courts of law, adopting an adversarial system (Fortin, 1978, p 7). A UNHCR survey showed that all appeals lodged between 1 January 1974 and 30 April 1977 had failed. Since then, three had been allowed by

41 This was stated in evidence by a Home Office official, Mr JA Chilcot, to the Select Committee on Race Relations and Immigration in November 1977, *First Report from the Select Committee on Race Relations and Immigration*, HC 303-II (1977–78), p 356.

adjudicators, two of which had been reversed by the Immigration Appeal Tribunal. The UNHCR representative, who had intervened to provide evidence about the likelihood of persecution, decided to discontinue participation in appeal proceedings as a consequence (Fortin, 1978, p 10). A definite change of practices, directly linked to the racial origin of refugees, was noted:

> In recent years there has been a noticeable toughening up of the criteria to deal with appeals in refugee cases ... With the change in the origin of refugees has come a change in attitude toward refugee appeals [Fortin, 1978, p 9].

Despite the relatively small number of refugee appeals at this time, the legal position was already moving against non-European refugees. At the parliamentary level, the House of Commons Select Committee on Race Relations and Immigration recommended in 1978 that the Government should make it clear that there would, in the foreseeable future, be no further primary immigration (to be understood as not including the immigration of dependants). It recommended also that, if events compelled an exception to this norm on the grounds of political asylum, then that should be done under the UK's responsibilities within agreed international arrangements, under the type of burden sharing scheme organised in the case of the East African Asians, where other countries such as India and Canada had also assisted.[42] Yet, also by the late 1970s, the possibility of new regulations for refugees were being discussed, and Rule changes were introduced in 1980, which appeared to recognise more clearly the obligations undertaken by the UK under the Refugee Convention of 1951 and its Protocol of 1967. How can these seemingly contradictory developments be reconciled?

6.3.1 New rules and procedures for asylum seekers

The need to introduce new procedures for determination of refugee status was linked to discussions about the protection of refugees at the UN level where the issue of refugees had gained momentum. The Lawyers Committee for Human Rights, in their study of the role of the UNHCR, stated that Sadruddin Aga Khan's tenure as High Commissioner (from 1965–78) was in part helped by the fact that: 'It could be assumed that those fleeing conflict in Africa had no wish to settle abroad in Europe or North America. Instead, most simply moved across the border to stay with relatives in the same tribe until

42 HC 303-I (1977-78), paras 90 and 99. The report of the Select Committee has been noted as 'preoccupied with the need to "batten down the hatches" more securely against Commonwealth immigration. Commentators have detected an almost obsessive concern to find further ways of tightening immigration controls ... Most of the Report's suggestions have in fact subsequently been implemented by changes in the Immigration Rules' (Sachdeva, 1993, p 33). Lord Wells-Pestel, endorsed the Committee's views on behalf of the Government, House of Lords Debates, vol 393, cols 813–14, 22 May 1978.

they could go home' (Lawyers Committee for Human Rights, 1991, p 33). The changes which were put into place during this period – the Protocol of 1967, the 1969 OAU Convention on refugees, as well as *ad hoc* changes in the High Commissioner's mandate – were directed towards interventions in refugee situations outside of Europe, mainly in Africa (6.1). Indeed, internationally, the magnitude and intensity of refugee phenomena by the late 1970s was becoming well documented, notably by the UNHCR (D'Souza, 1980), and was evidently already affecting attitudes in Britain. In November 1977, the UNHCR's Executive Committee had unanimously urged governments to establish formal procedures for the determination of refugee status and recommended certain basic procedural requirements.[43] It is significant that the UK position was in favour of the new recommendations, a fact which may intimate that the international advantages outweighed any possible negatively perceived immigration implications.[44] In March 1978, the UK representative of the UNHCR sent a memorandum to the Home Secretary, the Foreign Office and the Solicitor General to urge the enactment of the main provisions of the Convention into domestic law, and to establish an independent body, who would not be the Secretary of State, to determine refugee status.[45]

When the issue of asylum procedures was discussed in Parliament, the battle lines for future legal debates were laid out. Of crucial importance was the perceived need for the involvement of legal mechanisms to control issues of refugee status. The debates also brought out the need to 'harmonise' controls as between Commonwealth citizens and 'aliens'. Lord Avebury, who introduced the matter in the House of Lords, summarised the implications for UK law of the Executive Committee's suggestions and the ongoing communications. He highlighted the UNHCR's point that, since refugees were treated as just another kind of immigrant, that was how they were seen by officials and by the public at large. While there had been a marked tightening up of controls over immigration in general, there was no change in the legal status of refugees. That meant an increasing number of persons coming to the attention of the UNHCR and the voluntary agencies as having been denied

---

43 Recommendation No 8 (XXVIII), UN doc A/AC96/549. A text can be found in the *Third Report from the Home Affairs Committee, Refugees and Asylum, with Special Reference to the Vietnamese*, HC 72-II (1984–85), p 85. For further explanation, see Goodwin-Gill (1983, pp 145–47, 204–05).

44 This question deserves further research as there appears to have been little investigation into the motivation to introduce requirements for procedures to determine refugee status beyond Goodwin-Gill's (1983, pp 145–47, 204–05) short explanation of the provisions of the recommendation. According to Qureshi (1988, pp 87–90), the presence of thousands of refugees in Africa and Asia by the late 1970s prompted the US to adopt the Refugee Act of 1980 which, by approximating the definition of refugees to the 1951 Convention and 1967 Protocol, apparently widened the categories of persons eligible to be recognised as refugees in US law.

45 Noted by Ivor Stanbrook, House of Commons Debates, vol 967, col 1367, 25 May 1979 and by the Minister of State, Timothy Raison, col 1375. The UK representative of the UNHCR referred to was Mr Heidler.

the rights supposed to be conferred on them by the Convention and Protocol. Exaggerating, he stated that they would have no recourse to the immigration appellate authorities or to the courts. He complained, possibly relying on the UNHCR survey, that, of 146 appeals determined since 1974, only one had been successful. Yet, the Government had dismissed as too expensive the prospect of keeping separate figures on refugees, and it had defended the last resort character of the Rules by refusing to consider creating a category of 'Convention refugees'. Lord Avebury argued that it would be simple to place in the Rules a paragraph stating that, where a person establishes that he comes within Art 1 of the Refugee Convention of 1951, he shall be permitted to enter indefinitely without conditions:[46]

> ... while the Rules do not prevent us from complying with our obligations, they certainly do not place any requirement on us that we should properly satisfy them as is suggested. It is now clear to me that we have been urging others to do the things that we have failed to carry out ourselves.[47]

Immigrants and refugees, argued Lord Sandys, had to be distinguished, in that immigrants had the possibility of returning to their country but refugees did not – hence the importance of protection from expulsion and travel documents under the Convention.[48]

The advocates of more transparent procedures sought to play down the prospect of an increase in numbers of applicants that any changes would bring. The UNHCR legal adviser's further memorandum had stated that the new suggestions would not be likely to lead to an increase in the number of refugees, but would rather speed up the process of recognition.[49] Lord Sandys noted that, out of 69,313 persons granted admission during 1977, only some 1,300 were said to have involved refugees or 1.9% of persons entering the country.[50] Baroness Elliot favoured the institution of some independent body that could co-ordinate all functions related to refugees. She argued that it would not necessarily lead to an increase in refugees, and would make for a faster and cheaper system of decision making.[51] Lords Avebury and Sandys mooted the possibility of the UNHCR being involved in the decision making process, as was already the case in Belgium and Italy, although not in Germany.[52] In the longer term it was thought that the UK should think about

46 Lord Avebury, House of Lords Debates, vol 393, col 802, 22 May 1978.

47 *Ibid*, col 803.

48 *Ibid*, Lord Sandys, col 808.

49 *Ibid*, Lord Wells-Pestel, col 817.

50 *Ibid*, Lord Sandys, col 808, who also said that the figure had been arrived at 'with very great difficulty'.

51 *Ibid*, Baroness Elliot, cols 811–12.

52 *Ibid*, Lord Avebury, col 803 and Lord Sandys, col 807.

possible harmonisation of the law on refugees throughout the EEC.[53] Lord Wells-Pestel argued for the Government that the latter were taking the discussions quite seriously: '... it is a matter between the Government and a representative of the UN, and therefore sets the whole thing on a much more important and, if I may say so, higher plane.'[54] However, he was quite dismissive of suggestions that the issues being discussed were a matter of EEC harmonisation. He pointed out that negotiations were going on within the Council of Europe and the UN, but it had to be admitted that harmonisation of procedures between the (then) nine members would be very difficult, partly because practice varied considerably.[55] He did not respond to the other issues as they were still apparently being discussed between the Home Office and the UNHCR.

By May 1979, when the emerging issues seemed to have been digested more thoroughly, the matter was debated in the House of Commons. Ivor Stanbrook, an expert in extradition and nationality law,[56] reiterated the complaints already discussed in the Lords by concentrating on the necessity for new legal procedures. For Stanbrook, the meaning of 'refugee' was nowhere defined and, since it had never been enacted into domestic UK law, the courts had never had a chance to recognise refugee status. All that British law provided was a passing reference to political asylum in the Immigration Rules which, strictly, were not legislation.[57] The effect of treating refugee status as a matter of last resort, he argued, meant that, even at the appellate stage, when time had run out, the question of refugee status was not brought to the attention of adjudicators and appeal tribunals, who seemed, in 'well documented cases' to give the most cursory examination of the UK's international obligations.[58] Desperate deportees may seek the help of MPs or voluntary organisations to prevail upon the Home Office at the last minute to prevent deportation. Instead, he argued that the correct result could be obtained on entry with a proper system of identifying refugees and their claiming refugee status.[59] The Refugee Convention of 1951 'should be enacted in some form into our law so that everyone may know his rights and

53 Lord Avebury, House of Lords Debates, vol 393, col 803, 22 May 1978 and Lord Sandys, col 809.

54 *Ibid*, Lord Wells-Pestel, col 813.

55 *Ibid*, col 818.

56 See Stanbrook and Stanbrook (1980) on extradition and Stanbrook (1982) on British nationality.

57 Ivor Stanbrook, House of Commons Debates, vol 967, col 1365, 25 May 1979. Lord Denning had taken a similar view of the rules in *R v Secretary of State for the Home Department ex p Hosenball* [1977] 3 All ER 452, although the matter of Rules, and their relation to more or less secret policies, have been seen as more complex since then (see, eg, Sachdeva, 1993, pp 29–31 and Jackson 1996, pp 16–19).

58 Macdonald (1983, p 242; 1987, p 277) makes the same point.

59 Ivor Stanbrook, House of Commons Debates, vol 967, col 1368, 25 May 1979.

obligations and be able to enforce them in the courts'.[60] Extradition, which, after all, involved political questions, was already handled by the courts: '... such problems have, with safety and complete confidence, been entrusted over the years to a judicial apparatus in this country.'[61] Stanbrook presented the contest as between the 'law' and raw executive power:

> The idea seems to be that this is a matter of executive power and that there should be no interference by a body of law controlling the determination of the status or by any authorities independent of the Home Office able to determine that status.[62]

Yet, advocacy for greater legal rights for refugees was also meant to achieve the extension of immigration control against non-European refugees. This is indicated in other passages in Stanbrook's speech:

> From time to time in the recent past we have been flooded with masses of foreign immigrants who have caused us acute social problems. We have admitted the majority of them because for far too long we have clung to the sentimental idea appropriate to our Imperial past ... we must not put obstacles in the way of genuine individual refugees. Large scale immigration is one matter, but individual cases of requests for political asylum are another. It is just because of the emotive nature of the immigration problems – the Vietnamese boat people being the current example – that the question of the definition of the word 'refugee' and the means of determining by law who is or who is not a refugee becomes urgent.[63]

The problems felt as a result of migration from the non-white Commonwealth obviously still rankled, an attitude that was symptomatic of the wider aspects of immigration control at this time. The case of the Vietnamese appears to be perceived as an 'immigration problem' and not as an issue of refugee protection. Importantly, Stanbrook advocated a stronger role for the State legal apparatus so that the separation of 'immigrants' from 'refugees' could be given legitimacy; a parallel task was already being performed by the legal system to police other categories of entrants. He further stated:

> All this time, several schemes have existed under which thousands of so called refugees, whose status has not been properly determined as refugees under the Convention, have been admitted in groups and in their thousands. That is plainly an unsatisfactory situation to all who cherish Britain's reputation for tolerance and the preference of the British for handling emotive questions in the proper way.[64]

---

60 Ivor Stanbrook, House of Commons Debates, vol 967, col 1371, 25 May 1979.

61 *Ibid*, col 1372.

62 *Ibid*, col 1368. At a later point, he stated (col 1372): 'Decisions under ministerial power are taken in a hidebound way.'

63 *Ibid*, cols 1364–65.

64 *Ibid*, cols 1370.

Therefore, a greater role for legal mechanisms was meant to neutralise the implications of refusing status to unwanted non-European refugees.

The Government's line at this stage was to brush off the need for further cumbersome procedures. Timothy Raison, Minister of State, argued that the 1977 Executive Committee recommendation suggested the setting up, wherever possible, of a single central authority, but it did not stipulate that such a body need be independent. The single central authority was the Secretary of State in the UK who considered cases very carefully. On appeals, it was argued that there was no requirement of a statutory right of appeal in the recommendation of the Executive Committee; the existing system was adequate since an applicant could always have his application reconsidered as long as it was not abusive. Nothing in the Convention required incorporation into the domestic law – the Government had decided in 1951 that the existing legislation was adequate and that remained the position. The UNHCR itself had after all stated that no refugee had been expelled from the UK in recent years.[65] However, Raison stated that, while in practice that was not the case, the impression given by the Immigration Rules was that eligibility under the Convention was a matter of last resort when other grounds had failed.[66] He also announced that the Home Secretary would consider an amendment of the Rules when an opportunity arose.

The topic of differential statuses for Commonwealth citizens was also raised in the same debates, marking a significant change in the long established legal distinctions between 'British subjects' and 'aliens'. The debates indicated that the 'problem' of Commonwealth migration was now sought to be assimilated to the means of controlling refugee migration although, again, the language of the debates only betrays an intention to enhance rights for Commonwealth citizens. Stanbrook identified the contradiction in the system of British nationality which led to their non-recognition: 'We have in the past treated all Commonwealth citizens as, legally, British nationals and, therefore, not eligible for the benefits of the convention on the status of refugees.'[67] Lord Avebury pointed out that Commonwealth citizens, such as the Ugandan Asians, were certainly Convention refugees but were not recognised as such. The UNHCR memorandum indicated that this amounted to a breach of Art 3 of the 1951 Convention, in that the Convention was being applied by discrimination on the basis of a refugee's country of origin. Persons who entered as students or

65 Minister of State, Timothy Raison, House of Commons Debates, vol 967, cols 1376–80, 25 May 1979. The Government's view of the need to incorporate the Convention and to have a right of appeal was consistent with that expressed by earlier governments (see 4.2.3).

66 In so stating, Raison contradicted evidence given by a Home Office official under the previous Government, that Convention status was, indeed, given as a matter of last resort (see 6.2.2).

67 Ivor Stanbrook, House of Commons Debates, vol 967, col 1365, 25 May 1979.

dependants could not get their status changed and, for students, the difference could lie in having to pay only the home rate for tuition at universities. Other advantages mentioned were protection from expulsion and the provision of travel documents.[68] Lord Wells-Pestel had already pointed out that the Government was already considering Commonwealth citizens as not 'own nationals' so as to bring them within the Convention, although there were still worries about international as well as domestic implications.[69] Raison further stated that Commonwealth citizens were treated as eligible under the Convention by the previous Home Secretary as a result of the UNHCR's representations and, while the UK already provided travel documents in line with the Convention, an identity paper would also be introduced.[70] Of course, the several legal rights mentioned would be contingent on recognition of individuals as refugees which, as further developments showed, tended not to be the case.

As promised by government ministers, there was a change in the Immigration Rules in 1980 which gave a much higher profile to refugee status. The new Rules, HC 394, were later carried into the 1983 Rules, HC 169. Grant and Martin (1982, p 324) summarised the new position as follows:

(a) where a person is a refugee full account is to be taken of the Convention and Protocol. Nothing in any section of the Rules is to be construed as requiring action contrary to the UK's obligations under these instruments;[71]

(b) leave to enter will not be refused if removal would be contrary to the provisions of the Convention and Protocol;[72]

(c) a person may apply for asylum in the UK on the ground that, if required to leave, he would have to go to a country to which he is unwilling to go owing to a well founded fear of being persecuted for reasons of race, religion, nationality, membership of a particular social group or political opinion;[73]

(d) a deportation order will not be made against a person if the only country to which he can be removed is one to which he is unwilling to go for

68 Lord Avebury, House of Lords Debates, vol 393, cols 803–04, 22 May 1978.

69 *Ibid*, Lord Wells-Pestel, col 817.

70 Minister of State, Timothy Raison, House of Commons Debates, vol 967, cols 1379–80, 25 May 1979. However, some four years later, Macdonald (1983, p 239) was still concerned about the 'enormous difficulties' raised due to an unusually wide definition of British nationality. He notes that, in the case of Cyprus, Uganda and Zimbabwe/Rhodesia, a compromise solution had been found by not expelling individuals, but at the same time, not extending to them the other benefits of the Convention. He hoped (pp 245–46) that the 1980 change in the Immigration Rules would change the situation.

71 HC 394, paras 16, 87, 138.

72 *Ibid*, para 64.

73 *Ibid*, para 120.

> reasons set out in the previous paragraph. This provision is said to be 'in accordance with the provisions of the Convention and Protocol'.[74]

The effect of the new Rules was given different interpretations, although it was clear that asylum featured prominently as a topic in immigration law textbooks (Grant and Martin, 1982, pp 322–46; Supperstone, 1982, pp 84–85, 111–12; Macdonald, 1983, pp 237–47). Gilbert (1983, pp 640–41) was of the view that this was a clear sign of incorporation into domestic UK law of the Convention and Protocol. Hartley (1980, pp 440–41) even went as far as to claim that the continual reference to the overriding nature of the Convention and Protocol made the position of those international instruments similar in UK law to EC law, which overrode the Immigration Rules. Other commentators were less sanguine due mainly to the ambiguous legal position of the Immigration Rules themselves. Goodwin-Gill (1983, p 182), then legal adviser at the Office of the UNHCR, was guarded about 'incorporation' as such, but stated that the Rules under the 1971 Act now acknowledged who should be admitted, allowed to remain, or not deported on account of a well founded fear, and that the Rules stressed that the immigration officer should refer a case to the Home Office for decision regardless of any grounds which could justify exclusion. This point was also emphasised by Paul Weis in 1980, as the UK representative on the UNHCR Executive Committee (Goodwin-Gill, 1983, p 182). Macdonald (1983, p 244) further argued that, since the Rules were binding on the appellate authorities, the Convention and Protocol must be treated in appeal proceedings and judicial review as part of domestic law. The Government's position came very close to this view, Mr Waddington, the Home Office Minister, arguing that the Convention was incorporated 'in effect, if not in law' through references in the Immigration Rules.[75] It was stated that the Home Office, in considering asylum claims, proceeded as if the Rules incorporated the relevant parts of the Convention and it was believed that appellate authorities would review cases on that basis, although judges had not yet pronounced definitively on the issue.[76]

The Rules were silent on other aspects of control to be applied to those seeking recognition as refugees. The circumstances in which extensions were granted and in which settlement could be obtained were also not given (Macdonald, 1987, p 281). There was no statement in the Rules or elsewhere as to the procedure to be adopted in the consideration of refugee cases, other than that the case of a potential refugee at port should now be referred to the Home Office for decision. This meant that, in practice, asylum requests were

74 HC 394, para 150.

75 *Third Report from the Home Affairs Committee, Refugees and Asylum, with Special Reference to the Vietnamese*, HC 72-I (1984–85), para 126.

76 Memorandum submitted by the Home Office, *Third Report from the Home Affairs Committee, Refugees and Asylum, with Special Reference to the Vietnamese*, HC 72-II (1984–85), pp 69–70. Guild (1986, p 27) also noted that it had not yet (judicially) been decided whether incorporation had taken place by reference in the Rules.

now dealt with by the Refugee Section of the Home Office's Immigration and Nationality Department. Although these rather formal changes had been introduced, their implications were becoming apparent only gradually as the monitoring of asylum claims revealed.

6.3.2 Impact of the changes

The issuing of statistics by the Home Office of the numbers of initial decisions made and appeals heard had become a norm, and was already a crucial factor in the so called 'numbers game' which showed a preoccupation especially with immigration from the Indian subcontinent. However, there were no separate statistics kept for asylum applications in the UK until 1979.[77] From that year, the number of persons, by nationality, who were granted (Convention) 'refugee status', 'asylum without refugee status', and those refused outright were issued. The initial years showed a marked decline in absolute and proportional terms of decisions in which Convention refugee status was granted. Increases could also be seen in the absolute and proportionate numbers of asylum applications which were refused outright (See Figure 6.1):

Figure 6.1

Year	Granted refugee status	Granted asylum without refugee status	Refused	Refusal rate (does not take into account exceptional leave)
1979	580	119	167 (85)	19%
1980	1217	196	486 (190)	26%
1981	1359	278	782 (300)	32%
1982	1755	613	1217 (700)	34%
1983	1018	389	1939	58%

The figures show the decisions made in each year and do not necessarily correspond to the applications made in the same year. The figures in brackets

77 Lord Sandys in the 1978 Lords' Debates mentioned with respect to the figures that 'the Home Office say that from their statistics they are unable to identify separately the refugees', House of Lords Debates, vol 393, col 808, 22 May 1978. See, also, Connelly (1984, p 14).

in the 'Refused' column show those who were granted exceptional leave to remain, and are based on estimates made by the UKIAS Refugee Unit. (Source: (1984) 171 *Race and Immigration*, September, p 9 and Connelly, 1984, p 14.)

The category of 'asylum without refugee status' was said by the Home Office to have been applied in the case of Commonwealth citizens (until 1979) or where granting Convention refugee status had not been thought to be appropriate for some other reason. This status was given one year at a time, but as with Convention status, indefinite leave could follow after four years. The use of this status was abandoned by the Home Office in July 1984.[78]

Not all applicants refused asylum 'outright' were necessarily denied the possibility to remain in the UK, although the Immigration Rules never reflected that. Policy decisions by the Home Office affected the position of several groups including Cypriots, Ugandans, Afghans, Lebanese, Salvadoreans, Poles and Iranians. They were not blanket policies but covered those expressing a fear of return to a country where it was impossible to decide who is or is not safe if they return and who had not committed a serious criminal offence. Such persons were normally given exceptional leave to remain without restriction on employment. Although exceptional leave to remain was renewable, so long as the policy motivating it remained in place, it was not considered as likely to lead to indefinite leave to remain being granted (Connelly, 1984, p 13).[79] The problem of the insecurity which this led to was considered by the Home Affairs Committee which recommended an upper limit of seven years by which time indefinite leave should be granted. However, the Committee did not envisage that more definite guidelines could be laid down, which would be general enough to preserve flexibility. It also feared that generosity by ministers in particular cases would be threatened by their becoming precedents to be used by a review body.[80] Official figures on exceptional leave to remain grants were only released from 1 July 1983 but unofficial estimates already showed that a greater number of applications were being given this status (see Figure 6.1). Thus, after the Rule changes in 1980, the policy of granting exceptional leave to remain continued to be used

78 House of Commons Debates, vol 64, col 85, 17 July 1984. Memorandum submitted by the Home Office, *Third Report from the Home Affairs Committee, Refugees and Asylum, with Special Reference to the Vietnamese*, HC 72-II (1984–85), pp 68–69.

79 There were differences in the way that exceptional leave was granted. For Cypriots, the Home Office began to issue six month extensions in January 1976, instead of the previously applicable three months (JCWI, 1976, pp 6–7). Connelly (1984, p 13) writes: 'Perhaps the main question to be asked about those granted permission to remain exceptionally is how long their stay should be considered temporary, and at what stage does it become permanent.'

80 *Third Report from the Home Affairs Committee, Refugees and Asylum, with Special Reference to the Vietnamese*, HC 72-I (1984–85), paras 121–22.

as a substitute category to place applicants on a slow track to settlement without granting Convention type protection. As the use of exceptional leave to remain fell outside the Rules, the avenues of legal challenge were also not clear. The Home Office thus continued to retain considerable discretion about the treatment of refugees, despite the apparent 'incorporation' of the 1951 Convention and 1967 Protocol in the 1980 Rules.

Significantly, the requirement to lodge applications with the Home Office involved greater monitoring and, therefore, the further problematisation of the origin of applicants. Before the Home Affairs Committee, which reported in April 1985, more detailed figures were revealed by the Home Office.[81] They showed that between 1979 and 1982 asylum applications had risen from 1,550 to 4,167. Regional and racial shifts in the composition of applicants were noticed. The recent increase was stated, in large measure, to reflect applications by Iranians, which constituted nearly half of all applications in 1983. The Home Office pointed out that:

> On a longer time scale it has been striking how, since the early days of the Convention, the main focus of asylum work in the UK has shifted from nationals of Eastern European countries (who accounted for only 215 applications in 1983) to those from other parts of the world, notably Africa and the Middle East.[82]

The wholesale advance of the legal system to frustrate the right of asylum for non-European refugees is examined in the next chapters.

Meanwhile, in March 1983, the case of Stancu Papusiou was debated in Parliament. Discussion of the case also revealed once more that European refugees' rights to settle in Britain were vigorously defended against government interference. Papusiou had been removed from the UK to Romania, whence he had fled. He had arrived in the UK 'illegally' in April 1982 and claimed asylum in a police station three days later, was subsequently detained in a police cell, and sent to Ashford Remand Centre until December 1982. He was later released to a hostel, but was arrested again and finally removed from the UK on 14 March 1983.[83] In Parliament, many questions were directed to the individual facts of the case: how Papusiou had been detained; on what grounds he had been refused asylum; that there had been problems of interpretation during interview; whether an opportunity was given to contact the British Romanian Association; his apparent

81 Memorandum submitted by the Home Office, *Third Report from the Home Affairs Committee, Refugees and Asylum, with Special Reference to the Vietnamese*, HC 72-II (1984–85), pp 80–84.

82 *Ibid*, p 71.

83 Papusiou had arrived in the UK with another Romanian citizen who subsequently managed to locate to France.

handcuffing.[84] Lord Avebury complained about the unavailability of instructions to immigration officers which apparently stated that they required the immigration officer to submit a case to a 'higher authority' as per the UNHCR Executive Committee's 1977 recommendation. Confirmation about whether that was really the case was asked for; and also about whether there were instructions about communicating with foreign embassies.[85] Further, the whole question of the security of various East European nationalities living in the UK – citizens of the Soviet Union, Poland, Hungary and Czechoslovakia – was raised. In particular, fears of Poles who could be returned to Poland's Martial Law regime came up. It was even noted that Iranians, Iraqis and Afghans were treated more favourably than the nationals of Soviet Bloc countries, judging by the official statistics on asylum decisions,[86] although, at the time, they did not show the frequency of exceptional leave to remain grants.

The Government also suffered criticism from the press reflecting the political spectrum because of the deportation.[87] The matter was so seriously regarded that there were even calls for the Home Office Minister, David Waddington, to resign.[88] The biased nature of the coverage which an East European case could bring was noted by Bevan (1986, pp 221–22):

> The controversy which surrounded the removal indicates both the power and the vagaries of publicity. Press and parliamentary coverage (notably from the Government's own backbenches) kept the Home Office on its toes. On the other hand, on its merits, Papusiou's case was not a strong one, necessitating a broad interpretation of 'persecution' and, compared to the many Iranians who were removed after the Islamic Revolution in spite of fierce criticism of its inhumanity, perhaps received undue attention.

Lord Elton, in his defence of the Government in the Papusiou case, stated that, in cases which carried no appeal, the possibility of review by the Home Office was available and 'may be considered of greater scope than a formal appeal'. He pointed out that there was also the possibility of judicial review.[89] Lord Elton admitted that there was no formal arrangement whereby an individual seeking asylum was referred to an agency such as the UKIAS or the UNHCR. He pointed out, however, that there were few cases which were unrepresented. He did promise to formalise the system of notifying an asylum

84 House of Lords Debates, vol 440, cols 1523–49, 29 March 1983.

85 *Ibid*, col 1531, 29 March 1983.

86 *Ibid*, Lord Bethell, cols 1523–27 and Lord Saint Oswald, cols 1533–34.

87 *Ibid*, Baroness Birk, col 1527.

88 *Ibid*, Lord Bethell, col 1527. Baroness Birk was moved to state (col 1529) about the *Papusiou* case that: 'The only encouraging aspect of this depressing drama is that so much outrage has been expressed.'

89 *Ibid*, col 1547.

applicant of the availability of advice in pursuing cases.[90] Thereafter, in cases where an asylum claimant was liable to be removed from the UK, or where he or she was in detention, a referral procedure with the Refugee Unit of the UKIAS was established, and it was stated that summary refusal of entry would not occur, and that a case would be reviewed at a higher level (Blake, 1983; Bevan, 1986, p 217).

The lacunae in the appeals structure remained, and lobbyists for reform began to focus on them. According to Home Office figures, applications for asylum made at ports of entry constituted some 7% of asylum applications in the UK in the 12 months ending 30 June 1984 while, in the same period, nearly 90% were made after entry to the UK. Another 3% were made at British posts abroad.[91] There is little way of knowing how many asylum seekers were rejected summarily by immigration officers or by entry clearance officers in posts abroad, although evidence of individuals and groups of refugees denied access to the asylum procedures has subsequently emerged. For those who claimed asylum 'in-country', an increasing number were being declared to be illegal entrants because they had obtained entry in some other capacity,[92] with the consequence that they also lost a potential right of appeal upon refusal of variation of leave, and were subject to detention and summary removal from the UK.

The question of extending a right of appeal to 'illegal entrants' generally had been mooted by the Government itself in its *Review of Appeals under the Immigration Act 1971* issued in 1981, but it was eventually dismissed by Lord Elton in January 1985.[93] The Home Affairs Select Committee also recommended that the right of appeal should be extended to all asylum applicants. It felt that the Home Office had been too dismissive of a comprehensive appeals framework, simply because it had observed what had happened in Germany and the US where the availability of appeals had resulted in a large numbers of spurious applications.[94] On the other hand, the Committee anticipated the use of fast track appeals procedures, which were eventually introduced by legislation in 1993. It recommended that the Home Office should look into setting up a procedure whereby leave to remain could

90 House of Lords Debates, vol 440, col 1548, 29 March 1983.

91 Memorandum submitted by the Home Office, *Third Report from the Home Affairs Committee, Refugees and Asylum, with Special Reference to the Vietnamese*, HC 72-II (1984–85), p 71.

92 Noted in *ibid*, p 213.

93 (1985) 178 *Race and Immigration*, April, p 4.

94 For the Home Office view, see the Memorandum submitted by the Home Office, *Third Report from the Home Affairs Committee, Refugees and Asylum, with Special Reference to the Vietnamese*, HC 72-II (1984–85), pp 76–77. For the Committee's recommendation, see HC 72-I (1984–85), paras 103–05. See, also, (1985) 180 *Race and Immigration*, June, p 7–8, for a summary of the Committee's main recommendations.

be refused in obviously bogus cases, and by which such refusals could be rapidly reviewed as in the Netherlands. At this stage, the Home Office maintained that a right of appeal before removal was unnecessary because of the possibility of judicial review and the fact that the Home Office had agreed the referral procedure with UKIAS for representations to be made in cases which were to be refused (Macdonald, 1987, p 281).[95] When a greater proportion of individuals claimed asylum at ports of entry, and a higher number of claimants were refused and/or declared illegal entrants, pressure began to shift to the High Court by way of judicial review applications, as that remained the only legal avenue to forestall removal. Already there was evidence of long waits for decisions from the Home Office. The Home Affairs Committee also found it unacceptable that decision making could take up to two years and recommended that in most cases six months should be the normal time.[96] However, no evidence was forthcoming that cases were being cleared any faster at the Home Office. Indeed, allowing a caseload to be built up further served to politicise the issue of asylum and, as later events have shown, the size of the caseloads became the main point of departure for further legislation against asylum seekers.

Although the Immigration Rules on asylum introduced from 1980 appeared to be minimal in their effects, several changes were introduced in the procedures applied to the consideration of asylum claims from the late 1970s. Maureen Connelly (1984, p 14), senior counsellor at the UKIAS Refugee Unit, stated: '... in the last six years the procedures for determination of applications for asylum have improved beyond recognition.' The main outcome of these changes was to allocate to the Home Office the task of monitoring the numbers of asylum claims, as well as the origin of applicants. Thus, asylum seeking was integrated as a specific category of immigration control on which figures were kept. A process of channelling asylum claims from the publicly funded UKIAS to the Home Office was also introduced after the Papusiou case. Meanwhile, the discretionary aspects of control were still present. The Home Office retained the possibility of granting exceptional leave to remain as a secondary status which raised the question of legal security. The extension of the right of appeal to port applicants and 'illegal entrants' was dismissed at this stage, probably because judicial review was not being used as significantly as it eventually came to be.

In the creation of new structures, there was an underlying consciousness that immigration of non-European people to Britain (as in other Western European countries) was too problematic to be addressed openly. There was still anxiety that Britain's non-white immigration commitments from the past

95 A possibility of obtaining the assistance of an MP to raise a case with a minister was also left open, although restrictions were soon placed on that avenue (Spiro, 1983; Owers and Shutter, 1984).

96 (1985) 180 *Race and Immigration*, June, pp 7–8.

had cost too much in social terms. That led to blanket declarations that the phase of primary immigration had ended. In practice, that meant that controls against non-white Commonwealth citizens were to be retained. At the same time, there was also a developing awareness that refugee flows had changed in their origin and direction, and that Britain could not escape these. Advocates for reform sought to bring the existing legal mechanisms of immigration control to bear on refugee migrations. Thus, although from a legalistic standpoint it appeared as if further rights were being made available to refugees, in fact, further structures of control were being erected for non-European refugees, the law being used to give legitimacy to an already reactionary system. Yet, in parallel to these events, from 1979, the UK accepted the admission of well over 10,000 refugees from Vietnam as part of an international arrangement. How is a commitment of such magnitude to be explained in the light of a growing antipathy toward non-European immigration to the UK?

6.4 VIETNAMESE REFUGEES

From 1975, refugees from Vietnam began to appear in Hong Kong, arriving in boats which had either transported them from their country of origin or which had rescued them at sea. A steady contingent of people – rescued by UK registered ships, some of those arriving in Hong Kong on boats, those who had to flee after the fall of Saigon, and some refugees in Malaysia and Thailand – were accepted in Britain. Most refugees were at first welcomed in Hong Kong (which was itself a popular destination) and provided asylum, but by 1979, when the exodus began to take on a greater intensity, the pressure on Hong Kong's resources induced the British Government to call for a UNHCR led resettlement programme. A quota of 10,000 people was agreed to by the UK at the international conference in Geneva in July 1979. In addition, a policy for boat rescues and a policy of family reunification was also committed to. In Hong Kong, a selection procedure was instituted to decide which refugees should be admitted, but each country set its own criteria and quota, while the UNHCR only vetted applicants in the first instance. The UK's criteria only demanded that the refugees wished to come to Britain, that, in the opinion of the voluntary agencies, it was possible for them to settle, and that the refugees were personally not unacceptable. In practice, these criteria were liberally applied and very few were rejected by the UK. Between April 1975 and September 1982, a total of 16,536 refugees from Vietnam were admitted to Britain (see Dalglish, 1989, in detail).[97]

97 The *Third Report from the Home Affairs Select Committee, Refugees and Asylum, with Special Reference to the Vietnamese*, HC 72-I (1984–85), p xx, puts the figure of people from Vietnam at some 19,000.

It is, at first sight, ironic to note that Britain, at the time it was accepting an immigration commitment of such magnitude, also had an official policy to restrict non-European migration. Indeed, the leading study on the Vietnamese refugees' reception in Britain is only too aware of this fact, pointing to the pre-election statements in 1979 by Margaret Thatcher that her Government would sympathise with those British people who felt 'swamped' by immigrants and had seen the character of their communities change as a result (Dalglish, 1989, p 63). But here was a sizeable group of refugees who were allowed to bypass the immigration controls that reflected an otherwise restrictive stance.

The role of the media has been emphasised in motivating Britain's reaction as the tragedy of the 'boat people' in the South China Sea unfolded. In fact, many refugees, especially those from North Vietnam, did not conform to this stereotype, although governments never investigated the validity of media images (Dalglish, 1989, pp 126–27). Many of the refugees applying for resettlement in Britain had been rejected by other countries and applied to Britain because choices were limited, underlining the fact that Britain was not the country they would have chosen. The quota programme effectively prevented them from achieving economic independence, which many of them had managed to set up in Hong Kong already by gaining employment and building new lives for their families (Dalglish, 1989, pp 36–38, 115). Upon closer examination, the treatment of the refugees once in Britain revealed a consistency with exclusionist political rhetoric cited above.

A dispersal policy, already proven as unworkable in the case of the Ugandan Asians, was adopted in the case of the Vietnamese refugees as well. Refugees were spread across the country by the voluntary agencies (Ockenden Venture, Save the Children and the British Council for Aid to Refugees) after offers of council accommodation were obtained from local authorities. 'The attitudes apparent in the 1960s and 1970s relating to Commonwealth immigrants and the perception of them as "problems" and the view of integration as similar to assimilation' were seen as lying behind the dispersal policy and the policy of asking for voluntary offers of council accommodation country wide to prevent secondary migration (Dalglish, 1989, p 77). Eventually, however, most refugees moved toward the established settlements of Vietnamese or Chinese in London, Birmingham and Manchester. Meanwhile, those who remained in what were for them culturally distant parts of the country showed heavy levels of unemployment and social isolation (Dalglish, 1989, pp 97–112).

Dalglish's detailed study also points to the motivation for the Government to sponsor the immigration of Vietnamese refugees besides the obvious pressure on Hong Kong:

> I see a group of individuals forced to flee to serve the political needs of their own country, and their flight used by many receiving Western countries to

> demonstrate the inhumanity of a government of which they did not approve. Using people as pawns in this way is unacceptable ... [Dalglish, 1989, p 137].

Thus, the factor that made the refugees acceptable was the international political situation fuelled by the media. Once on the doorstep, however, the material and psychological consequences had to be borne by the refugees themselves.

Wide criteria for family reunification had initially been applied to the Vietnamese, visas being granted to brothers, sisters, nephews, nieces and, sometimes, cousins of those already in the UK. That was altered in 1981 when only spouses, minor children and single dependent parents were admitted. Thereafter, British policy took a restrictive turn while pressure built up in Hong Kong's refugee camps which were coming to resemble penal institutions.[98] In April 1985, the Home Affairs Select Committee reported that: '... 6,000 refugees, not convicted of any crime, are being held in prison like conditions on British territory for a period which has no limit set.'[99] It was also argued by the Select Committee that only the promise of a new intake by Britain would motivate countries such as the US and Australia to accept more refugees as they regarded the refugees as primarily the UK's responsibility.[100] Meanwhile, the Government's observation with hindsight to the social problems experienced by Vietnamese settlers in Britain was that it had underestimated the difficulties 'which would result in bringing people from such a different culture and in such numbers in the UK'.[101] Thus, the blame for failure to settle without social difficulties was placed upon the refugees' culture, subtly resonating the theme rehearsed by Margaret Thatcher in 1979. JCWI's observation before the Home Affairs Committee put the problem in another way: 'We fear the British Government's reluctance to admit more refugees here from Hong Kong camps has nothing to do with refugee policy, as such, but everything to do with attitudes towards Asian immigration.'[102]

The case of the Vietnamese refugees is the last instance of non-European refugees being accepted as part of an international scheme involving substantial numbers. Even in this case, the numbers were not as large as in the Ugandan Asians' case, and a definite policy of restriction was adopted around

98 The restrictive turn and the consequent break up of families among refugee camps in Hong Kong is noted in (1985) 176 *Race and Immigration*, February, pp 4–5 and in the *Third Report from the Home Affairs Committee, Refugees and Asylum, with Special Reference to the Vietnamese*, HC 72-I (1984–85), p x.

99 *Third Report from the Home Affairs Committee, Refugees and Asylum, with Special Reference to the Vietnamese*, HC 72-I (1984–85), p ix.

100 *Ibid*, pp xv–xvii.

101 Home Office response to the Home Affairs Select Committee Report, *Refugees and Asylum, with Special Reference to the Vietnamese*, April 1985, quoted in (1985) 180 *Race and Immigration*, June, p 7.

102 Memorandum submitted by the Joint Council for the Welfare of Immigrants, *Third Report from the Home Affairs Committee, Refugees and Asylum, with Special Reference to the Vietnamese*, HC 72-II (1984–85), p 210.

the time that new Immigration Rules on asylum were published, although conditions in Hong Kong's camps worsened. The new Rules marked the increasing encroachment of legal activity, as the regulation of asylum began to be firmly established as part of immigration law in the UK. Indeed, Ivor Stanbrook had seen the elaboration of a refugee category clearly in law as part of a strategy to ensure that only some individuals, and certainly not culturally and racially distinct groups like the Vietnamese, were accepted in Britain in the future. While this strategy was not so obvious in the period examined, it came to be much more pronounced from the mid-1980s onwards, placing the law and lawyers in the centre of debates for protecting refugees.

CHAPTER 7

TAMIL MIGRATION AND THE LAW OF ASYLUM

7.1 BACKGROUND TO TAMIL EMIGRATION

Sri Lanka had been a British colony, attaining independence in 1948. That gave the floor to an increasing orientation towards policies of an aggressive State nationalism based on a fundamentalist Buddhist-Sinhala identity. Sri Lanka was, and continues to be, a plural society, which could roughly be described as consisting of the mainly Hindu Tamils who could trace their roots in India within a few generations, and those who claimed a much longer Sri Lankan ancestry, Sinhala speakers who are mainly Buddhist, Muslim inhabitants, and Burghers who were of mixed European and Asian ancestry. Areas of primarily Tamil settlement are to the east and north of the island and in the central regions. At first, State policies were confined to ensuring that the Sinhalese were able to enter educational and governmental institutions with greater ease, and organising the resettlement of Sinhalese in primarily Tamil areas, but these reforms began to take on a more aggressive tone. In response to increasing discrimination by the State and harassment by armed forces, Tamil resentment grew and by the early 1970s led to the constitution of, at first, pockets of armed militancy. In July 1983, there were island wide anti-Tamil pogroms backed by the armed forces of the State in which thousands of Tamils were killed and tens of thousands displaced. Many more Tamil youth joined in the armed struggle movements, which also recruited forcibly, with heavy punishments for perceived disloyalty. While the ethnic cleansing of Sri Lanka continued, a hostile anti-Tamil Muslim stance was engineered by the State, and fissures within Tamil militant movements were also exploited. These intensified when the Indian Peace Keeping Force (IPKF) occupied the Tamil areas in the north and east under an Indo-Sri Lankan Accord of July 1987, and attempted to influence Tamil militancy according to its own objectives, primarily against the strongest of the militant movements, the Liberation Tigers of Tamil Eelam (LTTE). Thus, by the late 1980s, a large part of the Tamil population had experienced forcible displacement, either as a result of State resettlement policies, or as a result of direct attacks on their houses, shops and villages. Refugee camps within Sri Lanka were liable to be searched and suspects were conducted away. Younger Tamils especially were subjected to brutal measures through arrest, detention and torture for indefinite periods, during which many simply disappeared. Many of the Tamil youth had joined militant movements, but became disillusioned with them, while others escaped possible ensnarement in fighting through forced recruitment or extortion. More recently, as reserves of adult men and women have become scarcer, an increasing number of children are forced to perform service in the LTTE. Although peace initiatives have been made, the conflict recommenced in a similar vein in 1994 and continues today (Hensman, 1993, pp 8–14; Daniel and Thangaraj, 1995, pp 231–40; Hoole, 1993; McDowell, 1996, pp 70–113; Steen, 1993, pp 25–96).

The migration from Sri Lanka can be linked to the vicissitudes of the conflict. After the July 1983 attacks against Tamils, Colombo became dangerous and many moved from there into the north and east of Sri Lanka, where economic opportunities had already diminished. Those working in the Middle East on short term contracts could not return to Sri Lanka. Working men decided to organise temporary sojourns in Western countries such as France, Germany, Switzerland or Canada to sustain families back home – Britain appears not to have been a significant destination, despite the English language link, and despite an established Tamil community.[1] As the LTTE consolidated its hold over rival Tamil militant movements in the north by 1986, the risk of coerced participation in the conflict became more pronounced, and the age of recruitment for boys (at first) and girls dropped to 15. These factors precipitated a further flight. Families who remained could be held to ransom to ensure a flow of money to the rebel groups. The Sri Lankan forces bombed villages and boats on the coast leaving with refugees for India. Later, émigrés were also caught up in the effects of the intervention of the IPKF in Sri Lanka, which turned its might on the LTTE, and the possibility of going to India as a safe haven began to appear more remote. By 1988, the costs of travel had doubled as compared to the period 1983–85. Since the recommencement of the war between the LTTE and the Sri Lankan armed forces in 1990, thousands of Tamil civilians continued to be killed in reprisals for LTTE killings of Muslim and Sinhalese policemen (Hoole, 1993; McDowell, 1996, pp 117–224).[2]

Although the Home Office's asylum statistics indicated a Tamil presence from the early 1980s, the new phase of Tamil migration to Britain was built on connections with Tamils already established (or staying temporarily) in Britain. Daniel and Thangaraj (1995, pp 240–48) divide Tamil migration in three phases. The first constituted, up to the 1960s, a mixed population of Sri Lankans who were engaged in professions such as law, medicine or engineering. The second phase constituted Tamils who came to Britain in the 1960s and 1970s primarily as students aiming for professional status, and who migrated partly as a consequence of anti-Tamil policies in Sri Lanka. The enactment of the Prevention of Terrorism Act in 1979 in Sri Lanka, which provided for summary powers of arrest and detention, marked the beginning of the third phase, as any Tamil male between 16 and 40 could be suspected of

1 Hoole (1993) notes that the cost of flying to Germany was far cheaper than going to Britain.

2 While McDowell's (1996) study concentrates on Tamils' settlement in Switzerland, it contains useful corroborative explanations for emigration patterns.

being anti-Sinhalese or anti-nationalist. In the immediate period after 1979, Tamils still attempted to come to Britain or another Western country as students, and would prefer not to apply for asylum; they only did so when circumstances forced them to. Thus, it was only since 1983 that a significant number of Sri Lankans appeared as asylum seekers in the Home Office's statistics. Some explanations as to why Tamils felt it necessary to apply for asylum are discussed in 7.5.[3]

7.2 INCREASING VISIBILITY, VISAS AND DETENTION

As already noted (6.3.2), the Home Office had begun to issue statistics of asylum applications from 1979. The presentation of those statistics before the Home Affairs Committee belied the underlying concerns. In particular, the Home Office pointed out that a definite increase was evident in claims from African and Middle Eastern countries. Further, Tamil asylum seekers from Sri Lanka, it was pointed out, were making applications in larger numbers, constituting 6.3% of all asylum applicants, and the third largest national group in 1983.[4] Since July 1983, the situation of Tamils in Sri Lanka also became a matter of concern for both Amnesty International, the Joint Council for the Welfare of Immigrants (JCWI) and other voluntary agencies in Britain. No announcement from the Government regarding a policy decision had been made about the status of the Tamils, although a request had been made by agencies which were handling Tamil cases in April and May 1984.[5] Before the

3 An alternative chronology is given by Taylor (1994, pp 99–110), which is generally consistent with that offered by Daniel and Thangaraj (1995). It divides up Tamil migration to Britain into four stages: 1948–58 – mainly students, some of whom decide to settle; 1959–72 – qualified professionals continue to migrate from mainly Jaffna, but some come to avoid anti-Tamil violence; 1973–84 – professionals continue to arrive, but also unqualified men sent by their families to escape escalating violence; post-1985 – asylum seekers flee arrest and torture by Sri Lankan forces and pressure to join militant organisations such as LTTE. The choice of the last stage may have been influenced by the political outcry and the legal changes which occurred when a group of Tamils arrived in 1985 claiming asylum. Grenier (1997, pp 6–7) provides a useful picture of the trends in asylum applications by Sri Lankans in the UK. He also links the highest number of applications with the phases of the conflict, beginning in 1983, when the 'civil war' is said to have started. However, a direct correlation with the phases of fighting and the rate of asylum applications in the UK must remain tentative due to a number of intervening factors such as the containment of people in refugee camps, the increasing prominence of Colombo as a staging post for emigration, the dangers and costs of making a long journey via other countries, dependence on connections who had already reached Britain, and the increasing legal restrictions against Tamils. The relevance of such other factors is shown most clearly by McDowell (1996).

4 Memorandum submitted by the Home Office, *Third Report from the Home Affairs Committee, Refugees and Asylum, with Special Reference to the Vietnamese*, HC 72-II (1984–85), p 71.

5 *Ibid*, Memorandum submitted by the JCWI, p 216.

Home Affairs Committee, the Home Office emphasised that the situation in Sri Lanka was serious and would continue to be monitored by ministers, but that it did not warrant an exceptional treatment policy.[6] The Committee, which reported on 16 April 1985, did not see the disparity in the operation of Home Office policies as between refugees from Poland and Sri Lanka. The JCWI had pointed out that, in 1981, Mr Whitelaw had announced, within 24 hours of the declaration of Martial Law, that all Polish citizens in Britain would be granted exceptional leave.[7] But the Home Affairs Committee did not believe that sufficient evidence had been advanced to show that exceptional leave was being been used in a discriminatory way – the situations in Poland in 1981 and Sri Lanka in 1984–85 were considered to be very different. The Committee also expressed doubts as to whether any review procedure could be established without damaging flexibility, which it saw as one of the chief merits of exceptional leave.[8] Already it was evident that non-European refugees would be treated quite differently to Europeans.

As a result of representations by the various agencies, a moratorium had been placed upon removals, but it led to problems of insecurity of status for some 900 Tamils. The vast majority were on temporary admission, but were liable to be detained and removed at any time, and with no right of appeal. Some individuals had been in the UK on such an insecure basis for over 20 months when the Home Office finally announced a policy on 20 May 1985, with the background of around 1,300 more entries in that month. Leon Brittain, the then Home Secretary, told the House of Commons that he saw 'no reason to believe that Tamils returning to Sri Lanka face persecution, and few Sri Lankan Tamils are likely to qualify for refugee status in this country'. All cases would be considered individually and there was no question of granting exceptional leave to enter or remain as a blanket rule.[9] The application of the policy was divided as between those Tamils who had arrived before 20 April 1985 and those who had arrived since that date. The former group (approximately 900) would be given exceptional leave to remain for six months and, if refused an extension of stay, they would have full rights of appeal. In the latter group, those who did not qualify for refugee status would be granted 12 months exceptional leave to remain only if they could show that they would suffer 'severe hardship' if they returned to Sri Lanka (Connelly, 1985, p 14).

6 Memorandum submitted by the JCWI, *Third Report from the Home Affairs Committee, Refugees and Asylum, with Special Reference to the Vietnamese*, HC 72-II (1984–85), p 79.

7 *Ibid*, p 216.

8 *Third Report from the Home Affairs Committee, Refugees and Asylum, with Special Reference to the Vietnamese*, HC 72-I (1984–85), para 122.

9 (1985) 181 *Race and Immigration*, July, p 3.

On 29 May 1985, while Parliament was still in recess, Leon Brittain changed the Immigration Rules to require Sri Lankan citizens to obtain visas in advance of travel to the UK, with effect the following day. Any concessionary issue of visas outside the Rules would be conditional on showing 'severe hardship'. Further restrictions were announced limiting MPs' right to make representations in Tamil asylum cases. While previously such representations had usually been accepted within 30 days of an applicant's arrival, they now had to be made within 24 hours of stating an interest in cases concerning Tamils. The UKIAS's Senior Refugee Counsellor commented that: 'This move, in effect, gave little time to interview Tamils under threat of being returned and no time whatsoever to collect background information needed to document individual cases' (Connelly, 1985, p 15).[10]

When the matter was debated by the House of Lords on 3 June 1985, Lords Avebury, Ennals and Mishcon questioned the Government's position and read out accounts of the atrocities against Tamils in Sri Lanka. It was pointed out that this was the first time a Commonwealth country had been under such a regime. For the Home Office, Lord Glenarthur, underplaying the implications of the change for asylum seekers, students or visitors, stated that entry clearance requirements for intending settlers (for example, for family reunion purposes) had already been in place.[11] Lord Avebury pointed out that the 24 hour time limit for interventions was not adequate, in response to which Lord Glenarthur stated that: 'I cannot say that 24 hours is a thoroughly dogmatic figure, and there will be some give and take' having in mind '30 hours or something like that.'[12] Questioned about the precipitate manner in which the visa requirement had been imposed and how some individuals had been caught out by it en route to the UK, Lord Glenarthur replied that 'there are always some people who fall between two stools'.[13] He argued that, had more notice been given, it would have encouraged a rush in the intervening period.[14] He was even able to portray the aim of the visa requirement in a humanitarian light, while signalling that further arrivals would be placed in detention:

> We were faced with a huge influx over the month of May, so sensible precautions for the welfare of not so much ourselves but of them in particular had to be taken so that they would be adequately looked after. The fact is that if they were to come here and were to clog up the centres where they are looked after and accommodation was not available for them, they would not be in the sort of position in which I am sure both noble Lords would like to see them.[15]

10 (1985) 181 *Race and Immigration*, July, p 3.

11 House of Lords Debates, vol 464, col 532, 3 June 1985.

12 *Ibid*, col 533.

13 *Ibid*, col 534.

14 *Ibid*, cols 532–33.

15 *Ibid*, col 535.

Lord Glenarthur justified the Government's position that the Tamils did not qualify within the terms of the 1951 Convention, although Lord Avebury pointed out that such a conclusion was unwarranted as they had not been given an opportunity to present their case. Lord Glenarthur responded by stating that the UNHCR shared the Government's view.[16]

On 23 July, a motion against the visa requirement was defeated in the House of Commons. David Waddington for the Home Office maintained that violence against Tamils was no longer widespread, although the flow continued.[17] But evidence of summary removals by immigration officers began to emerge. The Home Secretary admitted in the House of Commons that, in July, a Tamil who had been denied asylum was returned to Colombo before receipt of representations from the UKIAS due to an 'error in communications' with the Immigration Department.[18] By March 1986, the British Tamil Refugee Organisation had collected a dossier of cases in which refugees had travelled repeatedly between Britain, France, Jamaica, the Bahamas and India. A spokesman for the organisation, Pat Mylvaganam, cited the main cause of the problem as the introduction of compulsory visas. The Home Office had refused to consider requests for asylum on the grounds that Britain was not the first 'safe' destination reached by the refugees, in the early stages of what was to become the 'safe third country rule'. On the other hand, the visa requirement made it impossible to travel directly to the UK. The refusal rate in Colombo was extremely high, while seeking a visa would itself place applicants in danger (Rose, 1986).[19]

For those who did find their way to the UK and were refused, a quick removal was only legally preventable once a leave application for judicial review was actually heard in court. Thus, a promise by Home Office officials that removal would be deferred while leave was sought was not considered to be binding on the Home Office (Rose, 1987). Claiming asylum also became risky through the extension of the law on illegal entrants to asylum seekers. Judges had already approved its extension to include persons who entered by the use of false passports, under false names or by 'deception' and even those who, through the mistake of immigration officers, were initially given leave. Deception could include failure to disclose any facts later deemed to have been material to the decision to grant or refuse leave. Thus, if a person claimed asylum after having obtained leave to enter on a different basis, it became open to the Home Office to declare the person as an 'illegal entrant', thereby

16 House of Lords Debates, vol 464, cols 534–35, 3 June 1985.

17 (1985) 183 *Race and Immigration*, September, p 8.

18 *Ibid*, p 9.

19 Lord Mishcon had noted that (1985) *The Times*, 1 June reported that Sri Lankan security personnel stood by as 10 people were let at one time into the High Commission in Colombo, House of Lords Debates, vol 464, col 529, 3 June 1985.

making him or her liable to detention and summary removal (Macdonald and Blake, 1991, pp 408–11).

This practice of declaring applicants for asylum as illegal entrants was then challenged in the *Bugdaycay* case, which became the first of a series of refugee test cases to be dismissed by the House of Lords in recent years. It concerned three applicants – Turkish, Chilean and Ghanaian citizens respectively. They had initially been given leave to enter on visitor and student statuses, and were declared illegal entrants after they had applied for asylum and been rejected. In the Court of Appeal, Neill LJ argued that they could not contest their treatment as illegal entrants on the basis that, had they told the full story, their applications would have been accepted.[20] This view was ratified also by the House of Lords. An attempt was also made to argue that the liability to summary expulsion was against the UNHCR Executive Committee's recommendation in 1977 that a suspensive appeal to a judicial or administrative body should be available. Lord Bridge, who delivered the main speech, refused to consider the nature of the Executive Committee's statements as they had 'no binding force in either municipal or international law'. He held that the Immigration Act 1971 clearly did not provide a right of appeal in the manner contended, arguing that a person who had 'secured entry illegally' could not be in a position better than someone refused leave to enter. It was also held by the Lords that a court on judicial review could not make a substantive consideration of whether the applicants qualified as refugees; that was a matter solely for the Secretary of State.[21] The advocacy of such a detached function for the courts concerned with judicial review applications subsequently allowed greater executive freedom to challenge the validity of asylum claims with relative impunity.

Applying for asylum at a port of entry, or after having already entered, could lead to detention under the Immigration Act 1971 and, indeed, detention became increasingly used as a measure of deterrence. By 1986, there were reported to be a high number of Tamils in detention, often for long periods (JCWI, 1986, p 10).[22] The Immigration Act 1971 provided no right to bail, as available for detainees involved in criminal proceedings. A possibility of applying to an adjudicator for bail existed only where a person exercised his or her right of appeal, which was of no use where a person arrived at a

20 *R v Secretary of State for the Home Department ex p Bugdaycay* [1986] Imm AR 8, CA. Neill LJ quoted from Lord Denning's definition of 'material facts' in *R v Secretary of State for the Home Department ex p Jayakody* [1982] 1 WLR 405, p 408: 'They must be such that, if he had disclosed them, the Home Secretary would have been bound to refuse him entry or on which the Home Secretary would in all probability have refused him entry.'

21 *Bugdaycay v Secretary of State for the Home Department* [1987] 1 All ER 940, HL. The judgment was delivered on 19 February 1987.

22 JCWI (1986, p 11) reported that there were frequently more than 20 Tamils in Latchmere House remand centre and three had been detained there for 79, 86 and 93 days by April 1986.

port without a valid entry clearance or was declared to be an illegal entrant. The Act mentioned no sum of money which may be demanded of (two) sureties by adjudicators, and some of the Tamils who formed part of the group of 64 (see 7.3) were being released in the summer of 1987 on sureties of £2,000 each (Ashford, 1993, p 67). Bail could be granted by a judge upon a judicial review or habeas corpus application, but its use was severely limited in immigration and asylum cases since judges would look for 'exceptional circumstances', while applying for asylum was not in itself considered to be an exceptional circumstance. There was a flurry of Tamil cases which approached the issue in different ways: one admitting that delay in coming to a decision was a relevant factor, another concluding that a six month delay was not (Blake, 1988, p 14). In one reported case, bail was requested by two Tamil applicants 'in custody' since 30 July 1986 who were granted an adjournment, pending the decision by the House of Lords in *Bugdaycay*, but Macpherson J refused it on the basis that he had no jurisdiction to grant bail. On appeal, the Court of Appeal held that the judge could have granted bail, but that exceptional circumstances did not exist, and the fact that the applicants were claiming asylum was not a special case. Parker LJ stated that they 'were clearly rightly held in custody until that time, and for my part I can see no sort of circumstances which would justify their release'.[23]

By 1987, therefore, the Home Office had begun to build up a series of measures against refugees, including the imposition of visas, the use of detention and summary removal, powers asserted by the judiciary as already available under the Immigration Act 1971. These measures were particularly targeted against the arrival of Tamils from Sri Lanka, and were also to lead to a greater level of co-ordination among Western States who were generally looking for ways to deter further migrants from Southern countries. The early reaction of the courts in Britain was not only to enable the Home Office to continue to carry out these policies, but to assist it by extending the law on illegal entry to asylum seekers. Such measures did not have their desired effect, that is, to deter further arrivals from Sri Lanka. Tamils, on the other hand, continued to test UK policy further in the English courts and before the human rights bodies in Strasbourg, where reactions had evidently hardened.

23 *Victoria and Satkunam Thamathirupillai v Secretary of State for the Home Department* [1987] Imm AR 47, CA, p 50. The test of 'exceptional circumstances' came from the Court of Appeal's decision in *R v Secretary of State for the Home Department ex p Swati* [1986] Imm AR 88, which limited recourse to judicial review in visitor cases where there was no in-country right of appeal to an adjudicator.

7.3 COURT BATTLES, CARRIERS' LIABILITY AND REPATRIATION

In 1987, a lengthy and dramatic saga of court battles and legislative change occurred again as Tamils continued to arrive in Britain undeterred by the visa changes or detention policies. This time the Government was bent on repatriation. On 13 February 1987, 64 Sri Lankan Tamils, including 25 women, sought asylum at Heathrow airport. Six of them were given temporary admission while 58 were detained and scheduled for return to Bangladesh. In a break with normal practice, their claims were dealt with within four days. The refusals were made after superficial interviews and the referral procedure agreed with the UKIAS for representations to be made in cases which were to be refused was not adhered to. Faced with removal at Heathrow, some of the Tamils resorted to tearing off their clothes and laying on the tarmac. Forced inside the aircraft by three dozen police officers, they continued their demonstration by standing on the seats and refusing to wear seat belts. That enabled lawyers to obtain a stay of removal from the High Court. In the House of Commons, David Waddington, Minister of State at the Home Office, claimed that the Tamils were 'manifestly bogus' refugees although, within days, medical evidence was forthcoming that among the group were persons who had been subjected to torture (Burgess, 1991, p 50; Steen 1993, p 205).

On 24 February, the High Court granted leave to move for judicial review. Leave was granted on the basis that the Home Secretary erred in law in taking into account the fact that the applicants had used forged visas to arrive in the UK in determining the merits of their asylum claim (Macdonald, 1987a, p 277). Meanwhile, the Tamils, including women and young children, were being held in buses at the airport in order to defeat further court action should the Home Office succeed. After the decision to grant leave, they were dispersed to detention centres as far apart as Derby and Slough. By March 1987, there were reported to be 101 Tamils and 33 Iranians among the 160 asylum seekers in detention.[24] On 2 March, two days before the hearing of the substantive issues, the Home Office conceded that new decisions would be taken in the cases (Murtagh, 1987; Phillips, 1987; Blake, 1988, p 13; Burgess, 1991, p 50; Ashford, 1993, pp 64–65). The Home Office also gave an assurance that the fact that they had not been carrying valid visas would not influence the fresh decisions.[25]

Frustrated at the setback in the courts, Prime Minister Margaret Thatcher and Douglas Hurd, then Home Secretary, announced the intention of the

24 Ashford (1993, p 65) quotes a Tamil community worker: 'They've been taken from place to place. Their situation is terrible. In Derbyshire the men have to clean the toilets. In Harmondsworth, three women had to sleep in the telephone room, one just with a mattress on the floor.'

25 (1987) *Amnesty*, April/May, p 26.

Government to introduce legislation to fine airlines which flew in individuals without valid documentation.[26] As Steen observed, clearly, the determined asylum migrants were not deterred by the visa restrictions:

> As in the case of most Tamil asylum seekers from Sri Lanka, they had paid large sums of money to middlemen (or 'racketeers' in the British press), who on this particular occasion had organised their journey via Malaysia and Bangladesh to Britain [Steen, 1993, p 205].

On 3 March 1987, MPs were informed that they could no longer assume that 'stops' would be accepted in all cases.[27] David Waddington, Minister of State at the Home Office, defended this restriction on the basis that a delay in removing unsuccessful applicants led to the loss of the opportunity to remove them once and for all. He gave an example of 17 Tamils returned to southern India, who had been sent back by the Indian authorities on the ground that they had spent longer awaiting the outcome of the UK procedures than they had in India (Ruff, 1989, pp 487–88). The Immigration (Carriers' Liability) Act 1987 received royal assent on 25 May 1987, but with retrospective effect to 5 March 1987. The Government branded the recent arrivals as 'bogus' and, in justification of that view, it was stated that there had been a relative increase in applications being made at ports of entry, as compared to applications in-country, after admission under another category. The invalidity of their documents, and the fact that the Tamils had travelled three-quarters of the way around the globe, were also cited as justifications (Ruff, 1989, p 484). Douglas Hurd complained: 'If we turn a blind eye to abuse of asylum procedures and to unregulated and disorganised arrival in this country, we provide a ready market for the racketeer.'[28] The 1987 Act provided that, where a person requiring leave to enter the UK and arriving by ship or aircraft fails to produce a passport or identity card establishing citizenship or nationality, and a visa where one is required, the carrier is liable to a fine of £1,000. No exception was made on the face of the Act to exclude its application to asylum seekers. A set of guidelines establishing the circumstances in which a waiver could be made were issued by the Home Office in November 1987. These guidelines appeared to make airline staff responsible for sifting out 'genuine' refugees according to restrictive criteria, and a waiver of fines was made conditional on the passenger obtaining refugee status, and the carrier establishing that the UK was 'the only or clearly the most appropriate destination'. The guidelines also stated that fines would

26 Blake (1998, p 13) observes that it was due to the setbacks in the High Court that the Carriers' Liability Bill was 'swiftly laid before Parliament and hustled through'.

27 These changes were outlined in the judgment of the Court of Human Rights in *Vilvarajah and Others v UK* (1992) 14 EHRR 248, pp 274–75.

28 House of Commons Debates, vol 113, col 710, 16 March 1987, also quoted in Ruff (1989, p 484). The tendency to bemoan the irregularity of migration routes and methods began to assume greater importance in official discussions. See, further, 8.2.

not be waived for Sri Lankan, Libyan, Syrian and Iranian transit passengers (Cruz, 1995, pp 36–38).

In May 1987, a group of Tamils, mainly consisting of those who had resisted their removal at Heathrow, were taken on board the *Earl William*, a ferry moored in Harwich harbour about 100 km north-east of London and used as a floating detention centre for asylum seekers of all nationalities due to a shortage in other places of detention. In August 1987, the Tamils went on a hunger strike protesting against the internment itself, the miserable state of the amenities on board, the verbal racial abuse and physical attacks they suffered from the Securicor staff, and the length of time they were awaiting reviews of their cases by the High Court. The four Tamil women on board complained of being forced into the company of men and being denied sanitary towels for two months. Bail had to be secured for a group of 21 Tamils, including some of those on the *Earl William*, with fresh judicial review applications while all the asylum applications were being reconsidered. Timothy Renton, Minister of State, argued that 'the great majority of those on hunger strike had been refused asylum by the immigration service many months ago, and had prolonged detention in the hope of remaining in Britain by seeking judicial review'. Protests on the *Earl William* continued, but the detainees were only granted temporary admission when the ship broke from its moorings during a storm on 16 October 1987 (Ashford, 1993, pp 65–69; Steen, 1993, pp 205–06).

When some of the Tamils were refused asylum in late August and in the first week of September, the solicitors concerned were not even informed, and they learnt of the removals from the Press Association who had been briefed by the Government (Burgess, 1991, p 50). On 20 August, applications were made for leave to move for judicial review against the Home Office's rejection of some of the claims. That was refused by Rougier J who, however, granted another leave motion at his London flat to forestall removal over the weekend until a full Court of Appeal could be constituted (Scannell, 1987; Burgess, 1991, p 50). The substance of the applications was then dismissed by McCowan J in six joined cases on 25 September. The challenges were renewed in the Court of Appeal, but they were made on different bases by the various counsel, which underlined the fact that legal decisions were being made in a rarefied atmosphere and could not address the more fundamental issues at stake for the refugees. In a judgment dated 12 October 1987, the point which was taken up by Lord Donaldson MR in the Court of Appeal was whether the fear of persecution required in Art 1A(2) of the Refugee Convention of 1951 entailed an objective evaluation or a subjective one.[29] He decided that: 'Fear is an entirely subjective state experienced by the person who is afraid. The

29 This summary glosses over the subtle differences in the two approaches to 'subjectivity' which were made in argument.

adjectival phrase "well founded" qualifies, but cannot transform, the subjective nature of the emotion.'[30] He quashed the Secretary of State's decision on that basis and did not go on to examine whether, as McCowan J had thought, the Secretary of State had been entitled to take the view that the applicants' fears were not of persecution but of force inflicted in the course of measures taken against civil disorder in Sri Lanka. Donaldson did appear to have doubts about the Home Office approach to the cases. In a subtle passage he said:

> Nevertheless, the Secretary of State may wish to take note of some of the criticisms. For example, some of the applicants have expressed fears for their lives as a result of the indiscriminate shelling by the forces of law and order of villages believed to contain insurgents. Under the terms of the Convention this would not form a basis for claiming refugee status. But it might well be different if it appeared that these forces would not have resorted to indiscriminate shelling, but for the fact that all the villagers, whether insurgents or not, were of a particular race.[31]

In response to the Court of Appeal's ruling in favour of the applicants, Douglas Hurd said on BBC Radio Four that asylum applications could rise as a result from 4,000 to 100,000 a year, and this was repeated in a *Times* leader.[32] It was leaked to the press that, if the House of Lords did not overturn the Court of Appeal's judgment, the Government would introduce further legislation (Burgess, 1991, p 50).

Even Lord Donaldson's sympathy seemed to have turned into irritation when a further application was made to the Court of Appeal for bail. Remarks by the Master of the Rolls, in the Court of Appeal's initial judgment, that sureties for those in detention should not be set at unrealistically high levels, as that would be akin to a refusal of bail altogether (Scannell, 1987; Blake, 1988, p 14), were not printed in the reported versions of the decision.[33] When the successful appellants who were still in detention proceeded to apply for bail it was refused. The Master of the Rolls was obliged to question whether the Home Secretary and the media had understood the judgment or had chosen not to. He clarified that the Court of Appeal had not decided that the Tamils were refugees, nor that any were entitled to asylum. However, on the issue of bail, he did not find that the applicants before him had been treated unfairly, even though they had been in detention since 11 June, putting down

---

30 *R v Secretary of State for the Home Department ex p Sivakumaran and Others* [1987] 3 WLR 1047, CA, p 1052.

31 *Ibid*, p 1053B–D.

32 (1987) *The Times*, 15 October.

33 *R v Secretary of State for the Home Department ex p Vilvarajah and Others* (1987) *The Times*, *The Independent* and *The Guardian*, 13 October, as observed by Scannell (1987). The 'fully' reported version also does not refer to the remarks on detention, see *R v Secretary of State for the Home Department ex p Sivakumaran and Others* [1987] 3 WLR 1047, CA.

to good fortune the fact that detainees on the *Earl William* had been freed on temporary admission.[34] The Court of Appeal's decision was criticised for being 'a step backwards and an unwarranted reversion to the "review of the Minister's discretion" approach', implying a superficial review of the initial decision to refuse bail (Blake, 1988, p 14).

On 16 December, the House of Lords unanimously reversed the Court of Appeal's decision on the substantive issues. Lord Goff maintained that the arguments before the Lords had not shown much enthusiasm for defending the Court of Appeal's view: 'The manner in which the issue in the present case came before your Lordships' House was almost calculated to undermine confidence in the test adopted by the Court of Appeal'.[35] Counsel for only one of the applicants supported it wholeheartedly, although the UNHCR's representative made submissions in its favour based on the *travaux preparatoires* of the 1951 Convention. As in the Court of Appeal, the main emphasis was directed to the question of whether objective or subjective fear had to be shown; the five Law Lords thought that the well-foundedness of fear must be shown by a refugee demonstrating that there was a reasonable degree of likelihood that he or she would be persecuted. It was emphasised, as it had been in *Bugdaycay*,[36] that the court could not, on an application for judicial review, question the decision as to whether the applicants were entitled to refugee status; that was solely for the Secretary of State to decide.[37] One case headnote summed it up thus:

> Since the Secretary of State had had before him information which indicated that there had been no persecution of Tamils generally or any particular group of Tamils or the applicants in Sri Lanka he had been entitled to refuse the applications on the ground that there existed no real risk of persecution.[38]

A combination of the objective test and the detachment by which judges sitting on judicial review applications approached their task meant that there was no question of going to the substance of the Home Office decisions. According to Lord Keith, that became more so due to the manner in which arguments had been put before the court:

---

34 *Nadarajah Vilvarajah and Vaithalingham Skandarajah v Secretary of State for the Home Department* [1990] Imm AR 457, p 460.

35 *R v Secretary of State for the Home Department ex p Sivakumaran and conjoined appeals (UN High Commissioner for Refugees intervening)* [1988] 1 All ER 193, p 200a–b.

36 *R v Secretary of State for the Home Department ex p Bugdaycay* [1987] 1 All ER 940.

37 *R v Secretary of State for the Home Department ex p Sivakumaran and Others* [1988] 1 All ER 193, especially *per* Lord Templeman, p 199c–j.

38 *Ibid*, p 193h–j. Between 10–14 September 1987, Timothy Renton, Minister of State at the Home Office, had visited Sri Lanka, accompanied by the most senior asylum policy officer at the Immigration and Nationality Department and the head of the South Asia department at the Foreign and Commonwealth Office according to the judgment in the Court of Human Rights (1992) 14 EHRR 248, p 269. On the face of the reported decisions, no evidence appears to have been presented about the findings made during that visit at any stage in the English court proceedings.

> The Secretary of State has in his decision letters expressed the view that army activities aimed at discovering and dealing with Tamil extremists do not constitute evidence of persecution of Tamils as such. *This was not disputed by counsel for any of the applicants, nor was it seriously maintained that any sub-group of Tamils, such as young males in the north of the country, were being subjected to persecution for any Convention reason.* It appears that the Secretary of State, while taking the view that neither Tamils generally nor any group of Tamils were being subjected to such persecution, also considered whether any individual applicant had been so subjected and decided that none of them had been.[39]

Lord Goff also expressed sympathy with the Home Office view:

> Following the decision of the Court of Appeal, the Secretary of State is evidently concerned that this country, which is regarded as a suitable haven for many applicants for refugee status, may become flooded with persons seeking to acquire refugee status when, objectively considered, there is no real risk of their being persecuted for a Convention reason.[40]

The judgment of the Lords meant that the moratorium on decisions in refugee cases, in place since October 1987, was lifted and decisions were taken on outstanding applications (Blake, 1988, p 16). The Home Office at first agreed to defer any removals, while an indication that the Government desist from removal was being sought from the European Commission of Human Rights.[41] On 18 December 1987, the Commission refused to give any such indication and other representations from the BRC, the UKIAS and MPs were also rejected.[42] According to the Home Office, there were no strong compassionate grounds in the cases and removals were not deferred pending the outcome of a decision on admissibility by the European Commission of Human Rights (Blake, 1990, p 7).

The Tamils whose applications had been dismissed by the Lords in *Sivakumaran* were returned to Sri Lanka in February 1988, amidst 100 such expulsions recorded by the Tamil Refugee Action Group (1990) since that time. Lawyers for the six applicants kept track of their fate and launched an appeal to an adjudicator and, by the time they had won their appeals from Sri Lanka, four of them had been imprisoned and/or tortured.[43] At no point

39 *R v Secretary of State for the Home Department ex p Sivakumaran and Others* [1988] 1 All ER 193, pp 198j–99a (emphasis added). Burgess (1991, p 50n) states, however, that it was not denied in argument before the Lords that the Tamils might face persecution. Rather, the Home Office contention had been that the behaviour of the Sri Lankan authorities was attributable to their struggle to maintain the integrity of the State.

40 *Ibid*, pp 200j–01a.

41 Under the Commission's Rules of Procedure, r 36.

42 A chronology of the events leading to the removal of five applicants is given in the judgment of the European Court of Human Rights, *Vilvarajah and Others v UK* (1992) 14 EHRR 248, pp 263–66.

43 Five of the applicants had their applications heard in Strasbourg. The judgment of the Court of Human Rights documents their fate upon return to Sri Lanka (1992) 14 EHRR 248, pp 250–62.

during the appeal hearings did the Home Office produce any evidence to support its version or materially dispute any of the evidence given for the Tamils. The adjudicator, RG Care, decided that the Tamils faced persecution in Sri Lanka and should be re-admitted 'with a minimum of delay'.[44] Care's decision was challenged by the Home Office, but the notice of appeal had been wrongly addressed and, when it eventually found its destination, the Immigration Appeal Tribunal decided that the notice had been given out of time and it had no jurisdiction over the matter. The Home Secretary then decided upon judicial review of both Care's and the Immigration Appeal Tribunal's determinations. However, in the High Court both Lloyd and Auld LJJ thought that the Immigration Appeal Tribunal did not have jurisdiction, as the notice was out of time. The Home Office also argued that, since two applicants had initially been refused entry as visitors, the adjudicator had no jurisdiction to hear an appeal on the asylum issue. On this point, the court divided, Lloyd LJ finding for the view taken by the Home Secretary. However, since Auld LJ thought otherwise, Care's decision stood.[45] The Court of Appeal also upheld that decision,[46] and an attempt to suspend the ruling pending further appeal was turned down by the High Court on 31 July 1989 (Scannell, 1989, p 18; Burgess, 1991, p 51; Steen, 1993, p 207). Only then were five of the applicants granted entry clearance on an exceptional basis for 12 months and returned to the UK.[47]

In the wake of the heavy administrative reaction, levels of detention, and the failure of the English courts to provide meaningful safeguards, five of the cases were contested in the Commission and Court of Human Rights in Strasbourg. These applications occurred in a context which had seen many other European governments take hostile measures against the Tamils' attempt to establish themselves on their territories. The initial motivation towards increasing restrictionism in the asylum field, as a development parallel to the European Single Market was, at least in some measure, to control the movement of Tamil refugees. Similar motivations have led European and North American States, as the leading donors, to influence the UNHCR not to accord Convention status, and to adopt a co-operative attitude in repatriation programmes, for Tamils. This background may provide part of the explanation for the eventual decision of the European Court of Human Rights in the *Vilvarajah* case.

---

44 *Sivakumaran and Others v Immigration Officer, Heathrow*, 13 March 1989, adjudicator.

45 *R v Immigration Appeal Tribunal and an Immigration Appeals Adjudicator ex p Secretary of State for the Home Department* (1989) *The Times*, 10 August; *The Independent*, 25 August, DC.

46 *R v Immigration Appeals Adjudicator (RG Care) ex p Secretary of State for the Home Department* [1990] Imm AR 1990, CA.

47 Four applicants returned to the UK on 4 October 1989, while one returned on 28 August 1989, having fled to France from Sri Lanka in the interim.

7.4 TAMILS IN EUROPE

From the mid-1980s, governments of Western States tried to identify common interests and began to move international policies towards the containment of non-European refugees. For Western European States, there has been a trend, on the one hand, towards the curtailment or limitation of the settlement of communities of non-Europeans (see 6.3). On the other hand, regional arrangements such as the European Community, European Free Trade Area, the Benelux Union, and the British-Irish-Channel Islands Common Travel Area guaranteed the free movement of citizens between various countries. The project of creating a single market among States of the European Community, involving the elimination of individual States' control of borders by 1992, focused the policy of European Community Member States towards the greater regulation of the outer frontiers of the Community. The regulation of asylum seeking, already begun in the Council of Europe framework, was increasingly taking place on the fringes of the Community by means of the inter-governmental process (exemplified in the Schengen process), not directly susceptible to the Community's constitutional or jurisdictional framework, as well as in wider fora involving a greater number of Western States. After the fall of the Berlin Wall in 1989, some of the former Eastern Bloc countries were brought into the process of controlling the eastern flanks of the Community, pending their own membership of the Community.[48] At the global level, the UNHCR's policies, dictated by the mainly Western donor States, also changed to reflect their priorities of containment and repatriation. While the UK lies to the far west of the European continent and is an island State, and thus did not experience the level of asylum migration as a country like Germany, British governments nevertheless realised the usefulness of using inter-governmental mechanisms in achieving their own aims of limiting the settlement of 'culturally alien' peoples, and actively promoted their own policies through them. One avid lawyer and observer of developments in UK asylum law in the 1990s was obliged to point out at the start that: 'A consideration of an asylum policy for the UK raises the question of how long there will be distinctive national procedures at all, rather than a common European one'

48 On free movement in the European Community/Union/Economic Area, see Hartley (1978) and Guild and Martin (1996). On the Benelux Economic Union, see Kruijtbosch (1993). Macdonald and Blake (1991, pp 122–32, 1995, pp 151–62) provide details on the British-Irish Common Travel Area. For an unrelenting apology for harmonisation among the (then) 12 European Community States, see de Jong (1993), who was at the time Head of the Aliens Affairs Department, Ministry of Justice, The Hague. For the impact of the Schengen agreements of 1985 and 1990 and the Dublin Convention on asylum seekers, see Jessurun d'Oliveira (1993) and Bolten (1991). On the various inter-governmental fora dealing with aliens issues among the European Community Member States, see De Zwaan (1993). On the role of the Council of Europe, see Hondius (1993). On the shifting focus to the eastern flanks of the European Community, see King (1993).

(Randall, 1994, p 202). Indeed, under the Amsterdam Treaty agreed in 1997 among the European Union States, such possibilities are already beginning to take concrete legal form.

In the early 1980s, the UNHCR, which had grown since its establishment, became critical of Western governments' discouragement of refugees. In particular, the United States of America was criticised over its policies towards Salvadoreans and Germany was criticised for its detention of asylum seekers in inhumane conditions (Lawyers Committee for Human Rights, 1991, pp 45–48). In August 1984, the High Commissioner, Poul Hartling, had sensed that many developed States had adopted 'a clearly perceptible policy of discouraging the arrival of further asylum seekers' (quoted in ICIHI, 1986, p 39). The High Commissioner convened the first of the Inter-Governmental Consultations on Asylum Seekers and Refugees in Europe and North America in Geneva on 28–31 May 1985, to argue against the growing intolerance towards asylum seekers in Western Europe. Various European States showed irritation at the High Commissioner's position. Representatives of Germany, France, and Britain emphasised that the new asylum seekers were not European. The number of applications and the 'misuse' of procedures in Germany was also emphasised; the Netherlands complained about the misuse of procedures and the use of false documents. Britain and France argued for a greater responsibility on 'countries of first asylum' and favoured regional measures to keep inter-continental refugees at bay. For the United States it was stated that the UNHCR must lend the weight of its moral authority in helping to implement hard decisions, even if that meant returning people to situations – 'safe situations' – in countries of first asylum or elsewhere.[49]

The UK Government had imposed the requirement for visas for Sri Lankans during the Geneva meeting and UK officials defended the Government's actions. Roy McDowall, head of the Home Office's Refugees and Special Cases section, voiced the view that the vast majority of Tamils had arrived for economic reasons, and did not appear to be genuine refugees. A team from his office had reached that conclusion after having interviewed about 80 persons and deciding that only one came within the Convention definition of a refugee. They were to be returned to Sri Lanka within a few days. This view provoked surprise from a German diplomat who stated that Germany, with some 10,000 Tamil asylum seekers, had accorded refugee status to 95% of applicants. On the other hand, there was a feeling that restrictive policies by one State affected other States. It was asserted that most of the 2,000 recent arrivals in the UK would have made for Holland had the

49 Extracts from the speeches by various participants at the meeting appear in 'Asylum in Europe' (1985) *Refugees*, July, pp 19–28.

Dutch not started handing out food tokens instead of money, and put the Tamils into grim housing (Guest and Keel, 1985).[50]

Individual European countries continued to apply measures against further Tamil settlement amidst a series of restrictions against refugees.[51] The Danish Government suspended family reunion for Tamils in autumn 1987. In Germany, an offer was made by the interior ministry of £100 per family and a one way ticket to Sri Lanka for a voluntary repatriation scheme. Tamils also emerged as a test case for the refugee policy of European Community States.[52] Since 1985, asylum policy was also dealt with increasingly among the then 12 European Community Member States, although outside the Community legal framework, as the Community institutions did not have specific legal competence as this stage. That question became more urgent as the Single European Act of 1986 looked to 1992 as the deadline for the abolition of the Community's internal borders controls, and the focus shifted to controlling movement into the Community.[53] The UK Presidency of the European Community Council took steps in October 1986 to organise a regular programme of meetings of ministers responsible for immigration, matters to be prepared by an 'Immigration Group' of civil servants (sometimes referred to as the 'Ad Hoc Group on Immigration'). Since that meeting, the Immigration Group began to tackle 'abuses' of the asylum process. On 27 April 1987, European Community immigration ministers agreed on a series of measures to assign greater responsibility on air carriers bringing in asylum seekers, to curb activities of operators organising traffic in refugees and to co-ordinate the processing of asylum requests. In the same year, four European Community Member States – Germany, Belgium, the UK and Denmark – introduced laws to increase responsibility on carriers to control the entry of asylum seekers, making them liable to fines (Cruz, 1995, p 5).[54]

50 A background to the problems faced by Tamils in the Netherlands from the spring of 1985 is given by Ephimenco (1985), who recounts the forcible evictions of Tamils, forced relocation to areas outside of Amsterdam, the replacement of social security payments by bed and breakfast allowances, and the speech of Ruud Lubbers, the Prime Minister, who announced in mid-June that most Tamils would be 'sent back'. These events are said to have sparked off a flight from the Netherlands into Germany, France and Belgium. The question of the numbers of Tamil asylum seekers in various European countries is highly problematic and wide variations of estimates exist within each country (Steen, 1993, pp 150–54).

51 For a comparative study of restrictions against asylum seekers in Belgium, Denmark, Germany and the Netherlands, and associated human rights concerns, see Fullerton (1988).

52 Steen (1993, p 10) quotes a French newspaper, *Le Monde Diplomatique* which wrote in November 1987 that: '... *le probleme Tamoul est revelateur et lourd de consequence dans la question des refugiés pour les années à venir.*'

53 The need to co-ordinate rules on the grant of asylum and refugee status had already been identified in the Single Market White Paper of June 1985 on the removal of internal frontiers, cited in Communication of the Commission to the Council on the abolition of controls of persons at intra-Community borders COM (88) 640 final, Brussels, 7 December 1988, p 41.

54 In Denmark, the law did not come into effect until 1989.

Since the controls on the Community's external borders would have to serve the whole Community, it was thought necessary to have clear rules for determining which State was responsible for dealing with asylum applications. Thus, European Community immigration ministers arrived at political agreement to place responsibility on a State which issued a residence permit or a visa to an applicant, subject to the presence of family members in another State by May 1989.[55] Adrian Fortescue of the European Community Commission gave an idea of the aims of co-ordinating asylum policy in a frontier free Europe in this way before the House of Lords Select Committee on the European Communities:

> If a Sri Lankan wants to seek asylum in Denmark, he has to go to Denmark and ask and the Danish authorities will have to decide the matter. That in itself produces quite enough traffic for them to be able to deal with. They would not welcome the prospect – I used Denmark as an example, it would be true of any country – of indirect traffic, and that would increase if border controls were removed, because the same Sri Lankan refugee could fly to France enter without seeking asylum, and then start heading for his real target.[56]

Co-ordination efforts among Member States have gathered pace since the signing in 1990 of the Schengen and Dublin Conventions. These and further developments at the European level and their implications for UK laws are examined further in 8.2.

From 1986, UNHCR policy took a decisive turn by the appointment of a new High Commissioner, Jean-Pierre Hocke, at the insistence of the United States. Hocke appointed Jonas Widgren, Swedish Deputy Minister for Immigration, as the Co-ordinator for the Inter-Governmental Consultations. This signalled a change in UNHCR policy towards closer co-operation with North American and European States, amidst fears among human rights groups that it would accelerate Europe's regional policy of deterrence. Especially since the UNHCR's engagement in repatriating Tamils from Tamil Nadu, following the India-Sri Lanka Accord of 1987, strong criticisms came from NGOs and refugees' organisations in Europe and there was widespread concern about the position of UNHCR on the Tamil repatriation question, as well as its ability to actually provide protection for returnees. A major fear was that the programme might be used as a precedent for involuntary repatriation of larger numbers of Tamils from Europe. Indeed, Widgren has since stated that the UNHCR hoped to follow the repatriation from India with

55 Communication of the Commission to the Council on the abolition of controls of persons at intra-Community borders COM (88) 640 final, Brussels, 7 December 1988, pp 45, 49–50. The Dublin Convention had received approval by the immigration ministers by May 1989 according to Mr Langdon of the Home Office, House of Lords Select Committee on the European Communities, 22nd Report, *1992: Border Control of People*, with evidence, HL 90 (1988–89), minutes of evidence, 7 November 1989, p 147.

56 House of Lords Select Committee on the European Communities, 22nd Report, *1992: Border Control of People*, with evidence, HL 90 (1988–89), minutes of evidence, 7 November 1989, p 10.

a similar 'pilot' project for the voluntary return of 500 young Tamils from Europe (Lawyers Committee for Human Rights 1991, pp 68–73; Steen, 1993, p 9).[57] The attitudes of the UNHCR and individual European governments were crucial elements in the first case on refugees dealt with by the ECHR.

Before five of the six Tamils in the Sivakumaran case had returned to the UK (see 7.3), the European Commission of Human Rights made an admissibility decision in their cases on 7 July 1989.[58] The main bases of the applications against the UK Government were that there had been a violation of Art 3 of the European Convention on Human Rights (prohibition on torture, inhuman and degrading treatment or punishment) and of Art 13 (obligation to provide for an effective remedy with respect to breaches of the rights in the Convention). On 8 May 1990, the Commission's report on the cases was adopted.[59] Despite the evidence of suffering, including the deaths of family members, bombardment and burning of houses and shops, repeated arrests, beatings and torture prior to initial departure from Sri Lanka and subsequent to the removals from the UK, the Commission rejected, by the casting vote of the President, the contention that the UK Government had violated Art 3 of the Convention on Human Rights. A significant factor in the Commission's decision appears to have been the 'success' of the UNHCR backed repatriation programme organised in response to the Accord between the Sri Lankan and Indian Governments in July 1987: 2,746 Sri Lankans had been repatriated between late December 1987 and 11 February 1988. By August 1988, a total of 23,000 had been repatriated and an estimate of a further 12,000 had made their own arrangements by the same month. Some Western European countries (France and the Netherlands) had also started to remove Tamils since August 1987, while others still maintained a policy of no return (Germany and Italy).[60] By December 1987, however, Amnesty International, the BRC and the UNHCR had urged the UK Government not to return Tamils due to uncertainty, in particular, about the effectiveness of the July 1987 India-Sri Lanka Accord.[61] But this factor was taken into account only by the minority opinion in the Commission.

The crucial point taken by the Commission was with respect to the availability of an adequate remedy under Art 13 of the Convention on Human Rights. The Government had contended that the combination of judicial

57 The UNHCR itself was sharply divided on the issue of Tamils who, more than any other group, had fuelled internal disagreement (see Steen, 1989, p 9, who attributes this information to Jonas Widgren, October 1989).

58 An extract of the admissibility decision is given in Stevens (1992, pp 54–55). The Government argued that the incidents occurring after their return to Sri Lanka as related by the applicants were 'random' and were, in any case, not verifiable and not to be taken into account in assessing its liability.

59 *Vilvarajah and Others v UK* (1992) 14 EHRR 248, pp 276–85.

60 *Ibid*, pp 267–69.

61 *Ibid*, p 269.

review, the UKIAS referral system, the possibility of representations by MPs and an appeal to an adjudicator (albeit available from outside the country), satisfied the requirements of Art 13. But the majority (13:1) of the Commission maintained that referral to UKIAS and representations by MPs were not mandatory, while the appeal to an adjudicator was not effective because it had to be exercised after leaving the country. Crucially, it found that the High Court had not sought disclosure of the material upon which the Secretary of State's decision was based. This view of the Commission put into question the UK system of judicial review as the only legal remedy available for many rejected asylum seekers.

More than a year later, on 30 October 1991, the ECHR issued its judgment. By a majority of 8:1, it found that the repatriation programme was a strong indication that, by February 1988, things had improved sufficiently for repatriation to take place despite the continued existence of 'civil disturbance'. Further, it found that the background of the applicants and the general situation in Sri Lanka did not show that their personal situation was worse than the generality of other Tamils and other young male Tamils returning, and that the Secretary of State had carefully considered the personal circumstances and the prevailing situation in Sri Lanka. The Court felt that the mere possibility of ill treatment was not in itself enough to give rise to a breach of Art 3 – 'substantial grounds' had to be present for that to occur. But 'there existed no special distinguishing features in the applicants' cases that could or ought to have enabled the Secretary of State to foresee that they would be treated' in the way that they were.[62]

On the question of judicial review, the European Court was referred to the *Bugdaycay* judgment of the House of Lords where Lord Bridge had made remarks to the effect that administrative decisions which could imperil life or liberty would be subjected to 'the most anxious scrutiny',[63] although in the same judgment the Lords had emphasised that, on judicial review, the courts could not examine the substance of the decisions (and the same detached attitude had been reiterated by the Lords in *Sivakumaran*). Macdonald and Blake (1995, p 454) described as 'bold' the submission to the Court by the UK Government, which could have been read by the Court as indicating that English courts, on judicial review, could substitute their own fact finding for that of the executive and that they could evaluate whether the European Convention was breached, which was not the case.[64] The deceptive

62 *Vilvarajah and Others v UK* (1992) 14 EHRR 248, pp 289–90.

63 *R v Secretary of State for the Home Department ex p Bugdaycay* [1987] 1 All ER 940, p 952. The European Court was also referred to the speech by Lord Templeman where similar remarks were made, p 956, and to the decision of May LJ in *Gaima* [1989] Imm AR 205, p 207 where he advocated a 'rigorous examination' test.

64 The Government's submission was since 'spotted' by Sedley J in *R v Secretary of State for the Home Department ex p McQuillan* [1995] 4 All ER 400, p 409f–g, and used to base an argument that a more robust examination may be available on judicial review.

formulation of words used by the UK Government may have influenced the European Court's decision on the effective remedies point since, by a majority of 7:2, the European Court found against the applicants. Only the Irish judge of the European Court, Walsh, who was joined in his dissent by Judge Russo, pierced the veil: 'The English courts will not review a decision by reason only of the fact that the deciding authority failed to consider whether or not there was a breach of the Convention.'[65]

The Court thus managed to overlook the significance of the experiences of the Tamils by privileging the UK Government's perspective. It also overlooked the fact that domestic courts had clearly failed to provide adequate remedies. As in the *East African Asians* cases, the European Human Rights machinery again did not seem very interested in protecting non-European refugee groups, and signalled to European governments that their hostile policies against Tamil settlement could continue. Since June 1992, the UNHCR assumed the role of further repatriations from India, amidst fears from Tamils about the ability of the UNHCR to guarantee protection for refugees who were returned there through its adoption of 'passive monitoring' of returnees.[66] Dramatic developments took place more recently in Switzerland, where the Federal Office for Refugees had, with the UNHCR, taken the view since 1990 that Tamils and Sinhalese whose asylum applications had been rejected could be safely returned to the south of Sri Lanka. This gave way to a full blown repatriation programme under the Swiss-UNHCR-Sri Lanka tripartite agreement of 1994, which was reported to have sparked the flight of some 600 Tamils to other European countries (McDowell, 1996, pp 59–65, 206–08).[67] McDowell writes that the repatriation agreement:

> ... sent a signal to other refugee receiving countries that the return of Tamils and Sinhalese to Sri Lanka was acceptable. The repercussions of the UNHCR's involvement were quickly felt throughout Europe and North America, and directly influenced determination procedures in Western countries faced with applications for asylum from Sri Lankan Tamils. Once an internal safe flight alternative had been formally and widely recognised by Western governments and the UNHCR, the more difficult it would be for a Sri Lankan national to prove, beyond reasonable doubt, that persecution had rendered his or her continued stay in Sri Lanka impossible [McDowell, 1996, pp 60–61].

Indeed, the recent pattern of refusals given by the British Home Office indicates the insistence that applicants should go to Colombo which is regarded as a place where they will be safe from persecution (see 7.5).

65 (1992) 14 EHRR 248, p 294.

66 See, eg, 'Tamils fear UNHCR involvement in Sri Lanka will lead to refoulement' (1993) *Tamil Information – Special Issue*, January.

67 It is apparent now that many Sinhalese have also left Sri Lanka and settled in various European countries, amidst press reports relating the increasing pressure to join the State military forces.

The *Vilvarajah* proceedings meanwhile demonstrated that, in a hostile Europe, there was little chance of the Strasbourg machinery leaping into action to protect asylum seekers, despite the obvious facts of the cases involved, and widespread doubts within and outside the Strasbourg organs about repatriation. Despite the negative findings on both points by the Court of Human Rights, the wheels of legislation had already begun to move. The government, fearing that it would lose before the Court, issued proposals to include a right of appeal for asylum applicants, which were finally incorporated in the Asylum and Immigration Appeals Act 1993. The eventual decision by the Court, reversing the Commission, has allowed the Government to withdraw from these commitments more recently in the Asylum and Immigration Act 1996. These developments are considered in Chapter 8. The next section examines in more detail the problems that were created for successful Tamil settlement in Britain as a result of the UK's restrictive policies.

7.5 THE EFFECTS OF THE CONTROLS UPON TAMIL REFUGEES

Any attempt to ascertain in general terms the process of finding asylum for Tamils in Britain is bound to be tentative, given the absence of a privileged historical perspective (Tamils continue to migrate for asylum purposes today), the constantly shifting international scene, including the implementation of restrictive policies by other European States, as well as the decisions made by 'agents', airline staff, immigration officials or police, detention staff, lawyers, adjudicators and the Immigration Appeal Tribunal, judges at all levels, and other agencies, all of which have contributed to the conditions of asylum in Britain in one way or another. On the other hand, the psycho-social costs of migration on the Tamil community have certainly been heavy as the few studies on Tamil asylum settlement in Britain – Hensman (1993); Steen (1993); Daniel and Thangaraj (1995) – have shown, and from which most of the synthesis in this section is drawn.

The difficulty of pinpointing the reasons for the transformation of the British Tamil population into 'asylum seekers' were alluded to in 7.1. Some applications for recognition of refugee status were being made from 1980, and further cases began to appear in 1983 at the JCWI 'and other agencies' of individuals who were seeking leave to enter as visitors or students, and who applied for asylum when refused on the basis that they did not intend to remain for a limited period (JCWI, 1984, p 11). Earlier migrants also kept up to date with the changing legal situation and were able to advise on the course of action to be taken. Some had come as visitors or students and could remain within a legal category which prevented them obtaining employment. Some were forced to apply for asylum because of the impossibility of surviving otherwise. From 1983, Tamils therefore began to appear more visibly as 'asylum seekers' as the Home Office figures showed. Similar processes continued to force Tamils into the asylum procedures as further restrictions bit. Lord Avebury pointed out in the House of Lords that, due to the visa requirement imposed in 1985, persons already in the country under another form of leave, for example, as students, would, upon their return to the UK after a brief absence abroad, be forced to apply for asylum unless they satisfied the immigration officer that they would return to Sri Lanka after their studies. Others may not want to apply for asylum but may be content to remain as visitors.[68]

Difficulties were invariably experienced in obtaining the correct documentation and visas once they were being demanded and asylum could not be applied for from Sri Lanka. No 'refugee' visa category existed and there were, in any case, delays in the issuing of visas by the British High Commission in Colombo. Even before the enactment of the Immigration (Carriers' Liability) Act 1987, Sri Lankans were normally stopped from boarding aircraft bound for Britain in Colombo if they did not have visas. Removal from Britain would result in a mark on a passport which, in at least one case, was used to prevent a man who had already been removed from Britain from boarding an aircraft from Colombo, this time heading for Ireland. He was shot dead by an army patrol in Jaffna in November 1985 (Rose, 1986). A Tamil woman with two small children, among a group of 23 Tamils, was stranded in the transit lounge at Dubai airport. They had been prevented from continuing their flight to safety in Britain by British Caledonian airline staff who 'spotted' their false documents.[69] As already noted (7.3), no exception was allowed for asylum seekers in the 1987 Act and, instead, the Government stressed the liability of carriers when they transported asylum seekers (Burgess, 1991, p 51n). The restrictions associated with documentation provoked reliance on 'agents' and, in the post-1985 phase of flight, the prices to get to Heathrow rocketed and agents often left the passengers stranded *en route*.

If arrival and disembarkation in Britain was successful, Daniel and Thangaraj (1995, p 243) found that:

> Phase III Tamils who arrived at Heathrow Airport knew that they were supposed to walk up to the immigration counter and request political asylum. After being processed, and if they were lucky enough to be spared deportation, they would be asked if there was anybody in London who could care for them. The asylum seeker would have the name and address of a friend or a friend's friend ready.

68 House of Lords Debates, vol 464, col 531, 3 June 1985.

69 (1987) *Refugee Community News*, April/May.

From that stage a person was dealt with under an official legal regime for 'asylum seekers'. Through contact with fellow Tamils, temporary admission (TA) could be granted, and such a pattern has been characteristic of the Tamil community response to detentions.[70] Any number of other courses could also follow: the person could be detained; there could even be a refusal to take an asylum claim or a refusal of asylum within a short time, followed possibly by removal. In detention, the conditions and the level of abuse and beatings also contributed to a desolate existence. The psychological stress of awaiting release from detention (legally indefinite, and often for months) or awaiting a decision on a claim led to many cases of mental breakdown, depression or suicide, a pattern repeated amongst other groups.

Waiting for a decision could also take many months. Daniel and Thangaraj (1995, p 243) state that even acknowledgment from the Home Office that an asylum claim had been made could take one and a half to two years, and they thus distinguish between a 'potential asylum seeker' who still awaits such an acknowledgment and an 'asylum seeker' whose claim has been acknowledged. For those under temporary admission, conditions could be applied for reporting once a week, and failure to do so could result in action to enforce removal being taken. Unlike those in previous streams of Tamil settlement in Britain, many of the asylum seekers were married men, although entire families arrived too in the wake of the July 1983 events in Sri Lanka; unaccompanied individuals were soon followed by dependants; marriages were made quickly and in-laws followed spouses. Preoccupied with employment, so that families in Britain and in Sri Lanka could be supported and sisters married, many rushed straight into low paid work, often with the assistance of earlier arrivals. Where a person was granted exceptional leave to remain, as most Tamils were, leave to enter or remain was given for one year first and then for two successive periods of three years. After seven years, the leave could be made indefinite. At each stage, an application had to be made to the Home Office. Family reunion could only be allowed after seven years. Refugee status under the Convention, which carried an 'outside the rules' possibility of family reunion, was rarely granted.[71] The Home Office refused to consider issuing a policy on family reunification, and only made the concession that, where an individual had been in the UK for longer than four

70 The Tamil Refugee Action Group (1990, p 4) reports that, in most cases, the community responds to find suitable accommodation for refugees. Steen (1993, p 112) refers to the activity of three Hindu Saiva temples in London which had been actively involved in accommodating the newcomers.

71 The Tamil Refugee Action Group (1990) reported that more than 7,000 Tamils had applied for asylum in the UK up to 31 March 1990 and only 49 had been granted Convention refugee status. Restrictive attitudes are also evident in the granting of visit visas to relatives already settled in the UK. *R v Secretary of State for the Home Department ex p Selliah Kurumoorthy* [1998] Imm AR 401 concerns a judicial review of a refusal of entry clearance for a husband and wife to visit the wife's 75 year old sister in London.

years, family reunion could be considered if 'exceptional and compassionate circumstances' were present:

> Many of the men who came to Great Britain after 1985, having left their wives and children, now hold little hope of seeing them. And they live in a state of heightened anxiety as they await the seven year limit, at which time they will know, by law, whether their application for asylum has been accepted or not. Many are those who, unable to bear the strain, have returned home regardless of the consequences awaiting them. And some have met their death there. Others have gone back after learning that the reason for which they came to Britain in the first place no longer exists; their family has been wiped out by one armed guard or another, soldiers or militants [Daniel and Thangaraj, 1995, p 248].

The increasing legalisation of the process meant that applicants had to rely at each stage on advisers, often fellow Tamils, who have legal qualifications or who merely have some knowledge of the process involved.[72] Individuals could be cheated of their claims by the unsuspecting use of advisers who could determine the fate of their claims. The Home Office is known to use some advisers to deliberately destroy an applicant's chances.[73] Otherwise, an applicant may be asked to renew a passport from the Sri Lankan High Commission so that exceptional leave to remain could be granted. A person who followed this advice could then find it being used to undermine the asylum claim. A constant fear of Home Office interviews remained for those awaiting decisions, since they served as occasions to serve refusal and enforcement notices.

In the Home Office version of events, Sri Lanka is portrayed as a democracy, increasingly observant of human rights norms.[74] In one recent judicial review application, it was argued that the Immigration Appeal Tribunal should have taken into account the fact that rape was being used as an instrument of repression by the Sri Lankan army and therefore should have concluded that the woman applicant was in fear of persecution. Collins J refused to quash the decision on the basis that rape did not necessarily amount to persecution. Probably anticipating further claims on the same evidence, he argued that not all female Tamils had a well founded fear of persecution.[75] Partly due to such stances, there is mistrust of British officials

72 It appears that most Tamils do not resort to the publicly funded advice agencies, but consult solicitors in private practice or other advisers within the Tamil community.

73 Daniel and Thangaraj (1995, p 249) note that: 'The Home Office is known to use such ill trained and prejudicial agents as a means of denying applicants asylum.'

74 A recent example can be found in a letter from Graham Watt, Country Information and Policy Unit, Asylum and Appeals Policy Directorate of the Immigration and Nationality Directorate to Mike Kaye, Parliamentary Officer, the Refugee Council, 15 July 1998, which reads, in part: 'The Foreign Office's assessment is that there has been a general improvement in the human rights situation in Sri Lanka, particularly with regard to disappearances in Jaffna and that the Sri Lankan Government is showing greater willingness to bring members of the security forces to trial ...'

75 *R v Immigration Appeal Tribunal ex p Subramaniam* [1999] Imm AR 359, QBD.

whom many Tamils suspect of collaborating with the Sri Lankan Government.[76] The tendency to resent the settlement of Tamils in Britain is also evident in attempts by the Home Office to claim that applicants ought to have sought asylum in India or some other country through which they passed. Alternatively, the credibility of claimants was attacked on the basis that they chose to come to Europe rather than to India. From 1993, the number of Sri Lankans recognised under either exceptional leave to remain or refugee status declined dramatically, as with applicants of most other nationalities. A preponderance of refusals of Tamil applications by the Home Office now concentrates on the possibility of returning to Colombo (Storey, 1997), in line with the trend in other Western countries already discussed. Such measures have forced applicants into the appellate system which has repeatedly been redesigned to frustrate a meaningful challenge of the position taken by the executive.

The kind of hostility directed at Tamils was soon routinely being applied to other groups of refugees from Asia and Africa. At first, the measures which were applied in the case of Tamils, including the imposition of visa controls, summary removals and detention, were applied to these other groups as well. Progressively, however, the Government sought to tighten the possibilities of entering Britain, by criminalising some of those who did attempt to enter, and generally allowing the greater intrusion of legal mechanisms into the lives of refugees. The result has been the consolidation of the new repatriation focused law on 'asylum seeking' that is premised on the intervention of lawyers at various points so that some mediation between the State and refugees can take place, but which further degrades and oppresses refugees.

76 A Tamil newspaper ((1998) *Eelamurasu*, 2–8 July) reported that the Sri Lankan Government had introduced legislation imposing a fine of Rs200,000 or five years of imprisonment to those who leave the island illegally (without emigration clearance) or try to enter a foreign country and are deported back to Sri Lanka. The law was said to have been introduced consequent to repeated complaints made by Britain, Canada, Australia and the US.

CHAPTER 8

RULING THE REFUGEES

8.1 DETENTION, EXPULSION AND THE ROLE OF JUDICIAL REVIEW

By the late 1980s, Tamils were being joined by several other groups of refugees from Africa and Asia. A flight of larger numbers of Alevi Kurds from south-eastern Anatolia in Turkey to European countries began in 1988, in response to repression by the Turkish State and the dominant Sunni majority. The UKIAS claimed that, by September 1988, Kurds had replaced Tamils as the foremost group claiming asylum in the UK (Ashford, 1993, p 69). The Home Office figures showed that applications by Turkish citizens had risen from 50 in 1985 to 700 in 1988, and to 4,600 in 1989.[1] Applications by Somalis had also been rising from 50 in 1983, to 400 in 1988 and 2,660 in 1989.[2] These reflected the conflict situation in Somalia in the lead up to the collapse of the Siad Barre regime which, from May 1988, turned to all out civil war in the northern part of the country (El-Solh, 1991, p 541). While only 450 Sri Lankans had applied for asylum in 1988, a drop from the peak of 2,300 in 1985, there had been a rise again in 1989 to 2,060. Asylum applications by Ugandans had risen by 900 to 1,580 in 1989. Other significant nationality groups which were mentioned as applying in 1989 were Indians (680), Ethiopians (520) and Zaireans (450).[3] The statistics also mentioned the relative proportions in overall applications between 1979 and 1989 by nationality group – Iranians (25%, and they also constituted 25% of all refusals in that period), Sri Lankans (14%), Turkish citizens (11%), Somalis (7%) and Ugandans (6%).[4]

The imposition of visa regimes to deter refugees arriving from particular countries became commonplace. In 1980, visas were required from nationals of Iran. The imposition of a visa requirement for nationals of Sri Lanka in 1985 has already been noted (7.2). Nationals of several other Commonwealth countries – Ghana, Nigeria, India, Pakistan and Bangladesh – were required to

1 Home Office Statistical Bulletin, issue 22/90, 24 July 1990. The statistics are in an extremely crude form and do not give indications of whether any dependants were included, nor do they provide a breakdown in terms of gender or age. The same document also confirms that the Turkish applicants were Kurds. The suggestion that most of the Turkish applicants were, indeed, Alevi Kurds from Anatolia is made by Ashford (1993, p 69).

2 *Ibid*, Home Office Statistical Bulletin.

3 *Ibid*, Home Office Statistical Bulletin. Tatla (1999, pp 59–60) cites a ministerial statement to the effect that a majority of the 5,900 Indian citizen applicants between January 1984 and September 1992 were Sikhs.

4 *Ibid*, Home Office Statistical Bulletin.

have a visa in 1986, amid increasing refusals by immigration officers at the airports and agitation by the Immigration Service Union (White, 1987; JCWI, 1987; Drabu and Bowen, 1989). These were followed by similar restrictions on nationals of Turkey in 1989, directly in response to the arrival of the Kurdish refugees from May onwards. In 1990, immigration officers were stationed at check in desks at Turkish airports apparently to advise airline staff on the validity of passenger documents, indicating a shift to official control at the embarkation stage. A requirement for visas was imposed on Ugandans in 1990; nationals of the former Yugoslav Republics in 1992, when applications from those countries had reached 5,000 that year; and Sierra Leoneans and Togolese in 1994, also in response to a number of asylum applicants arriving from those countries (Grenier, 1996, p 13). While visa restrictions, combined with carriers' sanctions already in place, have not necessarily prevented refugee groups from attempting to secure asylum in the UK, it has considerably increased the risks and costs of travel, pushing them into reliance on trafficking networks, upon which government policy has been focused more recently.

If an asylum claim was made at the port of entry, a *pro forma* interview was held and, where there was evidence that a person passed through a third country deemed 'safe', there was a possibility of quick removal. Removal would theoretically follow after the case was referred to the Home Office which would fax an authorisation. Then other grounds of entry could be taken into consideration. The UKIAS or (since 1992) the Refugee Legal Centre could make representations before removal within 48 hours. In any other case, temporary admission could be granted or detention could follow. A decision to detain had to be ratified by a Chief Immigration Officer. The detainee would have to go through a medical examination and would be strip searched by customs officers, often under the pretext that the person may be carrying drugs. These procedures were not necessarily followed in all cases and evidence began to emerge of persons not being allowed to disembark from aeroplanes. Once asylum applications made at port were increasing in the later 1980s, the Immigration Service response was not to issue temporary admission where an applicant had no address, indicating a routine use of detention (Ashford, 1993, pp 3–5).[5] The increase in detentions in immigration cases had already been highlighted by d'Orey in 1984, but Cohen (1989) and Ashford (1993, p xi) noted that it had became much more serious since then. Some refugee communities, as with the Tamils, attempted to arrange accommodation for fellow arrivals, but it was not possible to provide a

5 The increase in applications at ports from 1,600 in 1988 (30% of the total) to 9,480 in 1989 (60% of the total) was noted in the Home Office Statistical Bulletin, issue 22/90, 24 July 1990.

comprehensive service and that option could be frustrated by the refusal of the Immigration Service to grant temporary admission.[6]

Monitoring of detention practices was carried out by the Latchmere/Haslar Project which was set up in 1987 (first at Latchmere Prison, Richmond and then at Haslar Prison near Gosport), but it was wound up when the Home Office withdrew funding in April 1992, and other agencies followed suit in protest (Ashford, 1993, p xii). The Immigration Service insisted that it was under no obligation to give reasons for detention, but several reasons were uncovered by the Latchmere/Haslar Project and were not restricted to the lack of an address. They included the use of deception (the use of forged documents, or attempt to entry initially as a visitor); 'gross deception' (trying to enter on a forged British travel document); having a weak asylum case; lack of community ties; having no money; the expectation of a quick decision on an asylum claim; doubt about identity or nationality; attempt to abscond from the airport; suspicion that a person would not abide by the conditions of temporary admission; or the person was 'clearly an economic migrant' (Ashford, 1993, p 6).

The arrival of Kurdish asylum seekers from May 1989 led to another policy of mass internment in prisons and Immigration Service detention centres around the country, amounting to more than 180 Kurdish detainees by June 1989, some of whom began hunger strikes. One such detainee, who had been released and had been diagnosed as suffering from deep mental depression about being returned to Turkey, was detained again in October 1989 after his asylum claim was refused. He and another Kurdish detainee also awaiting removal set fire to themselves. The former perished from the burns and his fellow detainee suffered 30% burns. It was only then that the Home Office appeared to change its policy to detain Kurdish asylum seekers (Ashford, 1993, pp 48, 70–71). The level of detention suffered by Zairean applicants between 1989 and 1991 was also high and releases began to hurriedly occur in March 1991, mainly as a result of the threat of media exposure. Ashford (1993, pp 47–50) also records the deaths of a Ugandan man and two Zairean men which occurred while they were in detention.

Where temporary admission was refused by the Immigration Service, a representative would have to go before an adjudicator or the Immigration Appeal Tribunal to secure bail, or to attach a request for bail with a judicial review or habeas corpus application in the High Court. In early 1991, it appears to have been normal practice to demand £500 from each surety, but after a meeting of adjudicators in Thanet House, on The Strand in London, a decision was made to increase that amount to £2,000 from each surety, making bail a remote possibility (Ashford, 1993, pp 8–9). On the other hand,

6 *Ad hoc* measures to secure accommodation for refugees continued. The Refugee Arrivals Project (RAP) was set up in 1988 at Heathrow, and later at Gatwick. It could arrange for accommodation in association with refugee community groups and could provide initial orientation regarding welfare and further sources of advice.

the response of the courts continued to be discouraging. In *Re Maybasan and Others*,[7] the reported facts reveal that seven Kurds from Turkey had arrived in the back of a lorry from Belgium in July 1990 and had claimed asylum. A decision was made to remove the applicants to Belgium under the so called 'safe third country' rule. After a judicial review action had been threatened, the Home Office decided to consider the substance of the asylum claim, leaving the applicants detained. They applied for bail to an adjudicator who refused it. An application for a writ of habeas corpus was made before Otton J who refused it on the basis that the only remedy lay in making another application to the court asking for a judicial review of the adjudicator's decision.[8]

Nevertheless, the courts came to be seen as remedies of last resort where the raising of fine legal points could, at least, lead to a deferral of removal frustrating the Home Office's aim of quickly turning cases around. The possibility of judicial review was already perceived to be an obstacle since the early 1980s when immigration cases began to feature significantly in the High Court's caseload (Bridges *et al*, 1995 p 11).[9] The then Lord Justice Woolf warned in 1986 that, if judicial review was used too much, the Government would get so frustrated that it would try to prevent the courts from having any powers to curb the excesses of its actions. Reporting on this, Phillips (1986) noted that: 'The conclusion has been formed that judicial review has got to be curbed, and all new legislation is being framed with that consideration in mind.' On the other hand, a senior specialist immigration barrister, as well as the author of the most significant immigration law textbook, maintained that judicial review remained important for immigration cases (Macdonald, 1987b).

The attitude of officials was, however, adamant against allowing easy recourse to the courts. In some of the Tamil cases immigration officers took to suggesting that a bare grant of leave would not result in a stay of removal in the absence of an injunction and, at the time, it was thought that no injunctions could lay against the Crown (Blake, 1988, p 13).[10] By 1990, it

7 [1991] Imm AR 87.

8 Ironically, Otton J, [1991] Imm AR 87, also held that the adjudicator had no power to grant bail in the situation, as the applicants were detained as persons against whom removal directions could be given. The possibility of applying to the High Court for habeas corpus was circumscribed by the Court of Appeal in *R v Secretary of State for the Home Department ex p Muboyayi* [1991] 3 WLR 442 (see, further, Macdonald and Blake 1995, p 546).

9 Blake (1983, p 304) already commented on the usefulness of judicial review: 'It is well known amongst immigration practitioners that the reasons for granting or refusing leave to appeal [to the Immigration Appeal Tribunal] in discretionary cases are almost impossible to divine. Yet judicial review is the only remedy where it can be shown that exercise of discretion is plainly wrong or erroneous in law.'

10 Blake (1988 p 13) states that this was the prevailing view notwithstanding the decision in *Ex p Herbage* [1986] 3 WLR 504, a non-immigration case. After the case of *M v Home Office* [1993] 3 All ER 537, HL, in which a Zairean asylum seeker was removed after an undertaking had apparently been given to the High Court, it was established that the Home Secretary could be restrained by interim or final injunctions and would be guilty of contempt of court if an injunction or undertaking given to the court is breached (Macdonald and Blake 1995, pp 23, 546).

became clear that airline staff were engaged in conducting unlawful removals of asylum seekers, even involving minors and torture victims (Burgess, 1991, p 51). Amnesty International gave a figure of a hundred people wrongly expelled as a result of not being allowed to get off aircraft.[11] Burgess (1991, p 51) and Stanley (1992) record that Kurdish asylum seekers were being removed unlawfully, with the number of removals running into three figures. Twenty three judicial reviews of unlawful removals were settled by the Home Office with reparation to include compensation and return where individuals were still out of the country. As with the failure to remove Tamils in 1987, the Government put further pressure on airlines. From 1 August 1991, the fine levied on carriers for each undocumented passenger admitted was increased to £2,000.[12]

As a source of law, judicial review decisions provided fertile ground for legal speculation. The balance of cases in the *Immigration Appeal Reports* (the 'Green Books') had shifted, still with considerable delay, far towards the reporting of judicial review cases and away from tribunal decisions which gave information on the working of particular Immigration Rules. The latter could only be found in the Supreme Court Library (Macdonald and Blake, 1991, p viii), a problem which has fostered a whole range of other reporting efforts.[13] Most High Court decisions reported in the Green Books were applications for leave that had been refused. This creates the impression that judicial review was generally unsuccessful in outcome although, where leave was granted and the case settled, no reasoned decision was issued.[14] However, empirical research (Sunkin *et al*, 1993a, pp 433-435, Sunkin *et al*, 1993b, pp 8–13; Bridges *et al*, 1995, pp 21–22) shows that judges generally did react negatively to the increased number of judicial reviews. Between 1987 and 1989 and in the first quarter of 1991, two-thirds of immigration applications, a substantial proportion of which were made on behalf of Tamils and Kurds, were refused leave and, ultimately, only 11% reached past that stage. Immigration cases, of all categories, were the least likely to succeed at the leave stage during the same period, which is important, considering that

11 Cited by Jeremy Corbyn, House of Commons Debates, vol 181, col 717, 26 November 1990.

12 Immigration (Carriers' Liability Prescribed Sum) Order 1991, SI 1991/1497.

13 The *Bulletin of the Joint Council for the Welfare of Immigrants* and the journal *Immigration and Nationality Law and Practice* already carried notes of unreported cases. The Immigration Law Practitioners' Association commissioned the writing of case reports between 1993 and 1996. Various other efforts have followed. The Immigration Advisory Service produces an *Immigration Law Digest* noting many cases not reported elsewhere. A new set of law reports, the *Immigration and Nationality Law Reports*, began in 1997. An initiative was also set up by the Electronic Immigration Network to provide an internet site for case reports and exchange of information.

14 This was pointed out to the writer by Raza Hussein, Barrister.

the grant of leave was itself a significant factor in influencing settlement.[15] These data suggest that the hostile reaction of judges evident from the Green Books is more than just impressionistic.

Rather than providing leave to enter for people who claimed asylum, the Home Office appeared to be pursuing a policy of keeping their claims in cold storage, leaving people in detention or with the insecurity of temporary admission. The problem of waiting times for decisions on asylum claims was raised in an adjournment debate introduced in the House of Commons by Jeremy Corbyn. Figures published by the Home Office showed a total of 27,170 applications awaiting a decision on a claim for asylum by 30 September 1990. Out of 'European' countries, the largest, by nationality, were said to be from Turkey at 1,690. From African countries the largest group waiting for a decision were Somalis at 2,990, while out of the Asian countries the largest group of outstanding applications were from Sri Lankans at 4,950.[16] Indeed, the figures further broken down did show quite a high number of Asian and African applicants waiting for decisions (see Figure 8.1).

Clearly, cases involving thousands of people were being held up by Home Office decision makers and, by 1991, the Government introduced a Bill in order to reject them *en masse*, while attempting to frustrate possibilities of resorting to the courts. The focus also shifted to the control of legal advice, a key determinant of litigation in the courts. In July 1991, the Government decided to force an expansion of the UKIAS to establish it as the monopoly supplier of legal assistance for immigrants and asylum seekers, while it threatened to withdraw the 'Green Form' legal aid system of public funding from all independent solicitors. Juss (1993, p 140) suggested that: 'The decision by the Home Secretary, Kenneth Baker, may have been influenced by the way in which independent solicitors succeeded on more than one occasion in embarrassing the Home Secretary in judicial review proceedings.' As a result of criticism from the legal professions and other advice groups, the Government withdrew by making an announcement in February 1992 during the second reading of the abortive asylum Bill. Meanwhile, the UKIAS refused to comply with the Government's demands and, in January 1992, the Home Office stripped it of its asylum work (Juss, 1993, pp 140–41), transferring it to the newly established Refugee Legal Centre. Since this time, the question of funding and control of legal assistance has gained in prominence amidst further government controls.

15 Bridges *et al* (1995, pp 21–22) give the figures of asylum related applications in the High Court which, since 1987, rose to over 300. Their sample showed 258 Tamil applications in 1987, 23 in 1988, four in 1989 and one in the first quarter of 1990. Kurdish applications in the sample were 11 in 1987, six in 1988 and 55 in 1989.

16 The statistics in question were published in the House of Commons Debates, vol 178, cols 451–52, written answers, 30 October 1990, and not at cols 452–53, as Jeremy Corbyn stated in the adjournment debate, House of Commons Debates, vol 181, cols 716–24, 26 November 1990.

Figure 8.1

Region	Number waiting for decision	Country	Number waiting for decision
Africa	13,500		
		Somalia	2,990
		Uganda	2,910
		Zaire	2,460
		Ethiopia	1,910
		Ghana	1,290
Asia	8,190		
		Sri Lanka	4,950
		India	1,890
Middle East	2,780		
Europe	2,080		
		Turkey	1,690

Source: House of Commons Debates, vol 178, cols 451–52, 30 October 1990

The figures are not stated as including dependants but, in line with normal Home Office record keeping practices, it can be assumed that they do not.

These developments in the domestic scene were also tied to discussions at the European and international levels about the problems experienced by Western countries in trying to avoid the settlement of non-European refugees. One experienced solicitor suggested that European influences would grow all the time on both substantive and procedural levels, and, even if the UK did not participate in European developments, it would affect (and be affected by) their course (Randall, 1994, p 202). While the UK appears to have adopted a 'Euro-sceptical' attitude with respect to certain questions on European integration, it has also taken advantage of certain parts of that process in order to consolidate controls against non-European refugees.

8.2 THE HEART OF EUROPE

The realignment of the UNHCR's focus in the 1980s and 1990s, from emphasising the international legal norms of 'protection', towards repatriation and the containment of refugee flows in the regions of origin and, if necessary, in refugee camps is noted by several commentators (Chimni, 1993; Aleinikoff,

1995; Goodwin-Gill, 1999). This shift, pushed for by Western States, was already illustrated in the case of Sri Lankan Tamils. It can also be seen in the approach of the British Home Office and in the case of other Western countries participating in the European Community/Union and other international fora. Roy McDowall, the Home Office civil servant who defended the UK's imposition of the visa requirement on Sri Lankans in 1985, wrote a few years later:

> The solution to the present refugee problems seems to lie in a direction which is presently being actively pursued by the UNHCR, namely, the linking of development aid with regional settlement. It is to the long term advantage of the major donor States – which are also the prime receivers of today's irregular movements – to share UNHCR's view since funds which are now used to support extra-regional arrivals in a developed State can be put to far wider use within a developing or Third World region. As has frequently been stated in recent years, funds can only be used once, and it is beyond question that local resettlement, as well as being less expensive, has the added advantage of making voluntary repatriation much more simple than from distant countries of resettlement ... It is unlikely that States would agree to increasing their overseas development aid and, at the same time, tolerate within their boundaries those whose case for asylum is perceived to be marginal, at least within the terms of the 1951 Convention [McDowall, 1989, pp 185–86].

This was an indication of several aspects of newer developments in thinking. First, 'developed' countries were reconceptualised as primary receivers of refugee movements, although they were not. In global terms, the proportion of refugees from outside Europe who actually arrived in Europe was minuscule, hence the qualification of their movements into 'developed' countries as 'irregular', which could more appropriately have been described as 'not susceptible to regulation in the manner which had been hoped'. The statement also indicates the distancing of the new refugees from the criteria of the Refugee Convention of 1951, a tendency that has increasingly become fashionable. As Chimni (1993, p 443) points out in a similar context: 'The relevant language game here is that of contemporary international refugee policy which is principally articulated by the developed countries to contain and manage the global refugee problem in the light of their interests.' A document prepared more recently by the Austrian Presidency of the European Union States:

> ... it can be perceived that, for instance, the UNHCR is now clearly committed to the repatriation of displaced persons, in contrast to earlier positions, and increasingly emphasises local solutions to problems, rather than resolving problems by accepting flows of refugees into third States.[17]

17 Presidency to K4 Committee, Strategy paper on immigration and asylum, Brussels, 1 July 1998, para 35.

The policy implied by the change of emphasis internationally was also promoted domestically in the UK. Peter Lloyd, Parliamentary Under Secretary of State for the Home Department, responded to a House of Commons adjournment debate on asylum in 1990 by citing the budget of £60 million that had been allocated to the Overseas Development Agency in the same year, of which £20 million went to the UNHCR and £40 million in 'direct aid', including that which was channelled through the British voluntary organisations and the 'UN refugee relief agency' as well as £5 million which went to the Red Cross. Reflecting the shift of terminology already taking place at the international level, that allocation of funds was claimed to have been to address the 'long term root causes that create migratory pressures'.[18]

More detailed policies have developed on the margins of the European Community (and, from 1993, the European Union). The reunified Germany, in particular, was concerned about its exposure towards the east as the previous controls on movement by the Eastern Bloc States did not apply to the same degree, and favoured a Community approach to asylum questions. Meanwhile, the British attitude was to maintain border controls in the run up to 1992 and the UK did not participate in the Schengen system initiated in 1985 and supplemented by a Convention in 1990. Marshall (1996, p 30), in a comparison of British and German refugee policies, explains Britain's ambivalent attitude towards co-operation in the European Community by pointing to its image as an island State with worldwide connections, and the possible need to introduce identity cards to recompense any loss of control at the ports. The British response was also lukewarm to accepting a distribution formula for refugees from the Yugoslav war, which Germany advocated strongly (Marshall, 1996, pp 32–33). However, in a parliamentary debate on the asylum Bill in 1992 the Home Secretary, Kenneth Clarke, assured that:

> We quite rightly receive large numbers of people from Yugoslavia. No one has been forced to return to a war zone and no one will be. My recollection is that, of the 30,000 or so who have come here already this year, we have returned about 40 who came from third countries. They had not come from Yugoslavia. We returned them to countries in which they had been living ... Nothing in the Bill affects our ability to make an effective response to the Bosnian and Yugoslavian problem. Even leaving Yugoslavia aside, however, the trend in applications has been steeply upward over recent years.[19]

This may indicate that, while there was a British unwillingness to enter into open-ended commitments in Europe, refugees from Yugoslavia were

18 House of Commons Debates, vol 181, cols 720–21, 26 November 1990. For an academic view which seriously considers the prospect of reducing migration flows by linking the subject to development issues, see Gilbert (1994).

19 House of Commons Debates, vol 213, cols 24 and 26, 2 November 1992. A quarter of Yugoslavs were said to be from Bosnia, while large numbers were also said to be from Croatia and Serbia, as well as some from Slovenia and Macedonia and some Albanians from Kosovo, col 25.

considered acceptable amidst the legislative fury which was unleashed for other, non-European refugees. Layton-Henry (1992, p 277) makes the point that, while the substantial increase in refugee numbers in the 1990s was due to the wars in Bosnia and Croatia, the perception conveyed by the media and politicians is not of large numbers of European refugees but of rising numbers of 'Third World people' trying to circumvent the immigration laws.[20] Busch (1999, p 20) argues, however, that, during the NATO invasion of Kosovo in 1999, a policy of containment was adopted, as refugees were kept in mass reception camps in Macedonia and Albania, put up by NATO, UNHCR and NGOs. 'For those not handpicked by UNHCR for evacuation, it was all but impossible to leave these camps, with their internment like conditions. They were virtually trapped in areas close to the border, which could easily have become combat zones.' There is also growing evidence of the difficulties of legal recognition in the UK for Albanians from Kosovo in the months preceding, and which outlives, the temporary sympathy widely expressed for the refugees during the NATO invasion.[21]

There were, in any case, meeting points between the British position and that of other European Union States which overrode the apparent differences. There was 'considerably greater agreement on a more restrictive approach to the issues of asylum and migration than on the question of borders' (Marshall, 1996, p 32). Another commentator has suggested that the British approach to harmonisation of certain issues related to asylum seekers was very positive (Boccardi, 1993, pp 41–43). As noted in Chapter 7, political agreement had been reached by 1989 on determining the State that was to be responsible for examining a particular application for asylum. In June of the following year,

20 Gurung's (1992, p 11) suggestion, that the imposition of a visa requirement against nationals of former Yugoslavia may have been motivated by hostility against Bosnian Muslims, requires further research. Also uncertain is whether Roma from former Yugoslavia reached Britain.

21 In *R v Secretary of State ex p Besnik Gashi* [1999] Imm AR 231, DC, the facts reveal that a Kosovar Albanian was to be returned to Germany on the basis that it was considered a safe third country by the UK Home Office, although the applicant's claim for asylum had already been rejected in Germany. The Court of Appeal reversed the dismissal of the application for judicial review: *Besnik Gashi v Secretary of State for the Home Department* [1999] Imm AR 415. In *Mentor Berisha and Another v Secretary of State* [1999] Imm AR 4000, the Court of Appeal refused to quash the Home Office decision to remove the Kosovar Albanian applicants to Greece. *R v Secretary of State for the Home Department ex p Gecaj and Others* [1998] Imm AR 11 is an unsuccessful judicial review application in which lawyers claimed that six Kosovar Albanian clients should benefit from a rapid decision by the Home Office in reliance on an extremely favourable Immigration Appeal Tribunal decision, *Gashi* (13695). The argument was based in part on the fact that the money wasted by the State in legal fees charged for processing the claims of all Kosovars through the Home Office and the appeals system would exceed £4 million. Even the group of some 4,000 Kosovars airlifted to the UK in 1999, and granted exceptional leave to remain, were expected to return to Kosovo (Bamber, 2000).

the Dublin[22] and Schengen[23] Conventions were signed. While the UK remained outside the Schengen system, the Dublin Convention, to which it did accede, featured almost identical provisions on the issue of State responsibility. An order of priority to allocate responsibility was devised: the presence of (nuclear) family members who already possessed Convention refugee status in a particular State; residence permits, visas or transit visas issued by a State; lawful entry into a State without a visa; irregular entry from a particular State; and finally the country where the application was lodged. The obligation on any particular State was not to grant asylum but simply to accept the person when removed from the expelling State in order to examine an asylum application. The measure was intended to prevent what States saw as 'asylum shopping' between various European Community Member States, and the decision to refuse by one State would effectively become the decision of all States (Bolten, 1991; Macdonald and Blake, 1991, pp 308–11; Macdonald and Blake 1995, pp 411–13). David Waddington, Minister of State, announced the following month in a written answer in *Hansard*, that all Western European countries which were signatories to the 1951 Convention applied 'safe third country' procedures consistently with the Dublin Convention:

> It is an internationally accepted concept that a person fleeing persecution, who cannot avail himself of the protection of the authorities of a country of which he is a national should normally seek refuge in the first safe country reached. I entirely agree with this concept. [The 1951 Convention] is an instrument of last resort – not a licence to travel the world in search of an ideal place of residence.[24]

While the practice not to consider asylum claims substantively was already in operation before this announcement, many judicial review applications to contest safe third country refusals reached the courts soon after. The courts tended to disregard the fact that the Dublin Convention was not even in force (it did not come into force until September 1997), and continued to approve Home Office refusals even where lawyers provided evidence that a particular European country would not accept them, and would simply return them to the UK or expel them to another destination (Shah, 1995c).

Meanwhile, three documents prepared by the Ad Hoc Group on Immigration received the approval of the 30 November–1 December 1992 Edinburgh meeting of Community immigration ministers, under the UK Presidency. On the 'Resolution on a harmonised approach to questions

22 Dublin Convention Determining the State Responsible for Examining Applications for Asylum Lodged in one of the Member States of the European Communities, 15 June 1990, 30 ILM 425 (1991).

23 Agreement for the Execution of the Agreement Concerning the Gradual Abolition of Controls at the Common Borders Concluded Between the Governments of States of the Benelux Union, the Federal Republic of Germany and the French Republic at Schengen 14 June 1985, 19 June 1990, 30 ILM 84 (1991).

24 House of Commons Debates, vol 177, cols 262–63, written answers, 25 July 1990.

concerning host third countries', Guild (1993, p 91) explained that: 'The principle is that, if there is any country outside the Community (other than a country of origin) to which an asylum seeker or refugee can be returned, Community States should so return the person.' Another document, the 'Conclusions on countries in which there is generally no serious risk of persecution' provided an elliptical formula to identify 'safe' countries of origin, on the basis of previous refusal figures of applicants from those countries. Both these documents were complemented by a third 'Resolution on manifestly unfounded applications for asylum'. This document outlined factors which should enable a State to process claims for asylum through summary procedures. Not only did it include those claims which fell under the first two instruments, but it listed a number of other circumstances in which the same procedures could apply, for example: the applicant's story is inconsistent or not credible; effective protection could be sought in another part of the country of origin; destruction, damage or disposal of any passport or ticket; failure to comply with substantive obligations relating to asylum procedures (Guild, 1993; Fernhout and Meijers, 1993). To various degrees, the criteria in these documents were subsequently adopted in the 1993 legislation in the UK, with further fine tuning in the 1996 and 1999 legislation.

Co-ordination of asylum policy among the 12 Member States received formal recognition in the Treaty of European Union signed at Maastricht on 7 February 1992, while the actual deliberations on policy were formally transferred to the 'K4 Committee', so called after the Treaty Article on which it was based. Since then another document, a 'Joint position' on the harmonised application of the term 'refugee' in the 1951 Convention, was produced in 1996. This document, while stated to be non-binding on judiciaries, has already received some judicial approval in the UK.[25] In the Amsterdam Treaty, signed on 18 June 1997 and which came into force in May 1999, an arrangement was made to move decision making formally into the Community framework in a new Title on 'free movement, immigration and asylum', and to incorporate the Schengen '*acquis*' into the Union (and potentially Community) framework. The latter provisions would involve the possible application of the 200 plus decisions and measures of the Schengen Executive Committee and parts of the Schengen Agreement in the European Union as a whole. The British, Irish and Danish Governments worked out an 'opt in' provision to retain discretion as to whether and when to participate in

25 *Secretary of State for the Home Department v Adan* [1998] Imm AR 338, *per* Lord Lloyd, pp 345–46, a Somali case concerning the requirement of current fear of persecution even where there is inability to return; *R v Secretary of State for the Home Department and Immigration Appeal Tribunal ex p Robinson* [1997] Imm AR 568, CA, a Tamil case on internal flight alternative. The headnote in the reported version, p 569, reads: '3. The appellate authorities should follow the conclusion in the Joint Position paper of the European Union.'

these events, as it was accepted that there was no prospect that any future British Government would abandon national frontier controls.[26]

The co-ordination of policy among the Member States has also had significant implications for the international relations of the Union. The Austrian Presidency document of July 1998 stated:

> Europe's relationship with the traditional host States in the migration policy context has changed completely: although the USA (together with Canada and Australia) was a major host country for onward migrants up to the 1980s, it has lost this function and is now important more in the political context of the causes of emigration movements and as a co-operation partner in crisis management.[27]

Recent emphases by the Member States have been on encapsulating within the European Union framework some States in Central and Eastern Europe. These States, in a waiting lounge which is also being converted to a first line of defence against flows of asylum migrants from further east and south, have already been tied to readmission agreements which oblige them to receive expellees (Lavenex, 1999).[28] Busch (1999, p 22) refers to the probability that Balkan States will be transformed into heavily guarded NATO and European Union protectorates where the activity of international military and police forces, and local authorities acting under their orders, will focus on forcibly preventing refugees and other migrants from leaving the region. Turkey, now itself a candidate for membership of the European Union, is seen as a major transit point for people moving from further south in Iraq, Iran, Egypt, Sri Lanka, Pakistan and Bangladesh. Discussions between the EU's K4 Committee and the Turkish Government have proceeded on the basis of tackling these flows.[29]

---

26 (1997) 7(3) *Statewatch*, May–June, pp 13–17.

27 Presidency to K4 Committee, Strategy paper on immigration and asylum, Brussels, 1 July 1998, para 30.

28 'The States of Eastern and Central Europe have grown into a new role. For Western Europe they are no longer the States which produce refugees, but co-operating neighbours gradually adjusting to the standards of Western European States.' Presidency to K4 Committee, Strategy paper on immigration and asylum, Brussels, 1 July 1998, para 30. This evaluation of Eastern and Central European States certainly does not account for the treatment of gypsy Roma refugees from those countries in Britain.

29 The acceptance of Turkey into the European Union fold will forseeably not be without difficulties on the subject of free movement rights for Turkish citizens. Webber (1998, p 79) sees resistance from European Union Member States by citing a European People's Party declaration of 4 March 1997 which stated that Turkey 'is not a candidate for membership of the European Union in the short or the long term because of differences of civilisation'. Çiçekli (1998, pp 62–63) explains that concern about the increasing number of Turkish immigrants, notably in Germany, has been an important factor in the non-implementation of freedom of movement for them and was indeed a factor in the non-acceptance of Turkey's European Union membership. For discussions between the European Union and Turkey on controlling migration, see (1998) 8(1) *Statewatch*, January–February, pp 1–3; (1998) 8(3) and (4) *Statewatch*, May–August, pp 1–2.

Political interest is now focused on the more general questions of curbing migration at source, problems of combating facilitator networks and expulsion issues. The document produced by the Austrian Presidency of the European Union in July 1998 explicitly assumes that every other immigrant in the 'First World' is there illegally. It advocates the establishment of mass fingerprint files, and reflects the continuing concern to process asylum claims quickly so that claimants do not get a foothold in a particular country. It proposes an European Union migration policy belying an unprecedented control mania with global implications:

> Here, a model of concentric circles could replace that of 'fortress Europe'. For obvious reasons, the Schengen States currently lay down the most intensive control measures. Their neighbours (essentially the associated States and perhaps also the Mediterranean area) should gradually be linked into a similar system which should be brought increasingly into line with the first circle's standards, particularly with regard to visa, border control and readmission policies. A third circle of States (CIS area, Turkey and North Africa) will then concentrate primarily on transit checks and combating facilitator networks, and a fourth circle (Middle East, China, black Africa) on eliminating push factors.[30]

The perspective outlined in the Austrian Presidency document can be expected to inform the European Union's relations with third States as they are brought in to enforce the system of global apartheid already anticipated by Richmond (1994). In February 2000, European Union States managed to include in the terms of the new Lomé Convention that the 71 African, Caribbean and Pacific (ACP) member countries shall accept the return of and admit their nationals illegally present on the territory of Member States, while the admission into ACP countries of third country nationals was left to be regulated by the conclusion of bilateral agreements.[31] These terms, reported to have been accepted hesitantly by the ACP States, represent the export of a formula to guarantee expulsion, a formula that has already undergone significant testing in the European context.

Crucially, the days of the 1951 Refugee Convention and 1967 Protocol, which have been interpreted to the most restrictive degree possible, are now numbered. One European Union Commissioner, Anita Gradin, described the 1951 Convention as out of date,[32] and the Austrian Presidency document advocates that Member States should initiate discussions in international 'opinion-forming' bodies for supplementing, amending or replacing it altogether.[33] Thus, we have a picture of European States in the 1990s arming

30 Presidency to K4 Committee, Strategy paper on immigration and asylum, Brussels, 1 July 1998, para 60; paras 115–21 are also crucial in this respect.

31 (2000) *Migration News Sheet*, March, p 2.

32 (1998) 8(1) *Statewatch*, January–February, p 21.

33 Presidency to K4 Committee, Strategy paper on immigration and asylum, Brussels, 1 July 1998, para 103.

themselves against the intrusion of non-European migrants through the implementation of a new international migration order, in contrast to the years after the Second World War when Western European countries (and other 'white' countries outside Europe) united to provide protection for European refugees.[34] At least in the case of Britain, the 1951 Convention is *being made* out of date by the administrative and judicial re-characterisation of refugees. That is part and parcel of a policy which has created, in the 1990s, a *lex specialis* on 'asylum seeking' designed to facilitate expulsions and to control the lives of Asian, African and an increasing number of Latin American refugees, without granting security of legal status which, in turn, marks them out as an indefinitely marginalised group in law and in the wider society.

8.3 REFUGEES AND RULE BY LAW

It has been noted already (8.1) that, by the early 1990s, the Home Office had overseen the build up of a large caseload of asylum applications. It was the existence of this caseload that provided a further opportunity to politicise the question of asylum, by creating images of abuse which the refugees were allegedly perpetrating in a pattern that has become increasingly familiar since. At the same time, the courts were already reacting against the increase in applications from rejected or detained asylum seekers. From subsequent events, it is clear that the Home Office's plan was to refuse the applications waiting there in massive numbers, and yet to frustrate resort to the courts. New procedural and substantive laws were being developed in the context of the European negotiations and in the light of the decision in the *Vilvarajah* case. These factors combined to produce provisions in three subsequent statutes, the Asylum and Immigration Appeals Act 1993, the Asylum and Immigration Act 1996 and the Immigration and Asylum Act 1999.

The impact of these new laws is indicative of what one commentator has called the '"strong State" approach to asylum seeking' (Young, 1998, p 42). The three pieces of legislation were introduced in a political atmosphere extremely hostile to the presence of refugees. This hostility has not subsided with the fulfilment of political demands for further restrictions. Instead, the issue of asylum seekers has been catapulted to one of the top three concerns for voters in the UK (Ford, 2000). A main concern of the legislation has been the diversion of State investment to the creation of an appeals system based on the premise that access to the courts be limited. At the same time, judges

34 The Australian Immigration Minister, Philip Ruddock, expressed views in London on 21 March 2000 to the effect that the 1951 Convention was too open to interpretation and abuse, and urged its amendment, after a meeting with British Immigration Minister, Barbara Roche, AAP, 21 March 2000.

have also participated in the increasing restrictionism, generally leaving immigration officers, Home Office officials and the appellate authorities with a large measure of discretion to operate restrictive policies. Yet, for refugees, simply obtaining legal recognition has made them dependent on lawyers to an unprecedented degree, thus raising questions about the exploitation of refugees by the legal system itself.

While it is the case that several critiques of the recent legislation exist, they have to read with caution, as they generally represent the sectional interests of professionals, including a preponderance of lawyers, and only indirectly represent the refugees. They are what Randall (1994) terms the 'protection community' or what Kaye (1992) terms a refugee 'policy community', effectively constituting a separate layer of government over the refugees. The protection community includes organisations such as the Immigration Law Practitioners' Association, the Refugee Legal Centre, the Immigration Advisory Service, Amnesty International, the Joint Council for the Welfare of Immigrants, the Bar and the Law Society, the Refugee Council and the UNHCR. These organisations are limited by their corporate rules and funding conditions. Some of the extreme tend to view as legitimate the Government's problematisation of 'bogus' refugees and tend to blame the failure of the Government to deal with caseloads and to provide speedier expulsion measures as a betrayal of its promises (for example, Dunstan, 1998a). Others concentrate on the formal legal aspects and recommend changes in the procedures applicable to refugees (for example, Justice *et al*, 1997). The influence of these policy actors in this field has been instrumental in creating an image of refugees that is, first, deemed as determinable through the deployment of 'appropriate' legal mechanisms and, secondly, as objects of charity. Consequently, they do not reveal much about the experiences of refugees themselves. Few commentaries acknowledge the institutionalised racism that has been entrenched by the State to control refugees, even though it is clear that the State has sought to target, in particular, groups of Asian, African and Latin American refugees by creating a separate law on 'asylum seeking'. On the other hand, studies concerning the impact of the controls on particular groups of refugees, comparable to the few studies made on Tamil asylum migration to Britain, have yet to emerge. The following account of the recent controls therefore relies quite heavily on reports produced by the UK 'protection community'.[35]

35 For exceptions, see El-Solh (1991); Toal (1997a; 1997b; 1998); and Farah (2000) on Somalis; Katsapaou (1997) on Kurds from Turkey; Wahlbaeck (1999, pp 72–74) on Kurds from Iran, Iraq and Turkey; and the reports by Asylum Aid (1995a; 1995b; 1999). Clearly, this is an area that requires further research. Disappointingly, a recent fieldwork study by Travers (1999) carries a detailed discussion of the asylum appeals process from the point of view of civil servants, legal practitioners, adjudicators and 'campaigners', but excludes discussion of the experiences of refugees in negotiating the appeals process.

8.3.1 Legal power and the misrecognition of refugees

The Government introduced a Bill in 1991 which would have granted a right to apply for leave to appeal to an adjudicator on the papers, access to a full hearing premised upon leave being granted. The reasons for this change of stance by the Government require some elaboration as, on the face of it, rights, at least for port applicants and those declared illegal entrants, were being increased not decreased. Randall (1994, pp 221–22) cites three reasons, culled from the views of civil servants, for this change of attitude which appeared to accommodate pressures from the lobbying organisations, whom the Government had thus far managed to avoid.[36] They reveal the Government attempting to balance the possible outcome of litigation in Strasbourg with its own bureaucratic requirements. First, the Government had already taken the view, by the early part of 1991, that it was likely to be defeated in the European Court of Human Rights, in the *Vilvarajah* proceedings. This consideration is not apparent from the parliamentary debates on the Bill, however. The policy change may, nevertheless, have been a pre-emptive device to limit damage in Strasbourg, with details left sufficiently flexible to depend upon the result. Secondly, Randall suggests that the result of some judicial review actions had been to place certain procedural requirements to be observed by the Home Office and immigration officers, which effectively frustrated the key aim to reduce the amount of time spent on dealing with applications. The concession of a limited right of appeal may have been thought as capable of achieving a faster determination process. Thirdly, the existing determination system was breaking down under the increased numbers of applications with massive delays occurring. The second and third of Randall's suggestions were certainly cited by the Government in the parliamentary debates on the asylum Bill, and they were repeated in the second, successful attempt to legislate after the 1992 general election. It appears that some kind of decision had been made that thousands of cases would be rejected. Giving a possibility of appeal to an adjudicator so that he or she could deal quickly and more cheaply with an application could, it was thought, obviate resort to the High Court, which was already facing a higher caseload of asylum litigation.

When the Bill was re-introduced in October 1992, the familiar theme of branding asylum applicants as 'bogus' was repeated, the recent drop in the number of successful applications and the prevalence of the use of forged

36 Randall (1994, pp 218–19) cites the proposals of reform made by the European Council for Refugees and Exiles (ECRE) published in October 1990 and by Amnesty International which were published in May 1992. Both advocated the institution of a right of appeal to an independent adjudicator for asylum applicants rejected by the Home Office. The position of the UNHCR does not appear to have been so clearly determined.

documents being cited in support.[37] Government Ministers also stated, in the now familiar vein, that good race relations were dependent on strict administration of immigration controls for the benefit of those genuinely persecuted, but not for those who were fleeing merely because of civil wars and political strife.[38] According to Lord McKay, the Lord Chancellor, the economic crisis in African countries was a primary motivator of the wish to escape.[39] Such statements revealed the new concepts that began to be used to distance refugee groups from the criteria of the 1951 Convention and they became particularly evident in practice after the Bill was passed into law. Kenneth Clarke, Home Secretary, claimed that a faster decision making system and an effective way of filtering the caseload were needed so that people could not put roots down in Britain by abusing inefficiencies in the process.[40] He claimed that, although only a tenth of the proportion of applications had been accepted as coming under the Refugee Convention of 1951, as compared to a half 10 years earlier, two-thirds were eventually allowed to remain because 'it has usually taken so long to decide'.[41] Five hundred new staff were stated to be doing asylum work in the Home Office, managing to clear 20,000 applications in 1992. But administrative changes, it was felt, were not enough, and legislation was needed.[42]

The change that was promoted by Kenneth Clarke as the key one, however, related to the appeals system. The requirement in the earlier Bill, to obtain leave to appeal from an adjudicator on the papers, was dropped. For cases described as 'without foundation' a fast track system of appeals was to be administered by adjudicators, alongside a slow track one for cases in which there could be further appeals. It was explained that the Government was looking to resolve groundless cases, especially those in which another 'safe' European country could be identified, within a week or 10 days. In other cases it was intended that initial decisions and appeals would be exhausted within three months. The different treatment of cases was justified on the basis that, within the appeals system itself, there was a backlog of 23,000 cases.[43]

37 House of Lords Debates, vol 541, col 1165, 26 January 1993.

38 See Kenneth Clarke, Home Secretary, House of Commons Debates, vol 213, cols 21–23, 1 November 1992; Lord McKay, Lord Chancellor, House of Lords Debates, vol 541, col 1166, 26 January 1993.

39 *Ibid*, Lord McKay, col 1164.

40 *Ibid*, Kenneth Clarke, col 24.

41 *Ibid*, Kenneth Clarke, col 27. This view of exceptional leave to remain is disputed in the light of how that status was granted after the 1993 legislation (Grenier, 1996, pp 39–41; Justice *et al*, 1997, p 23).

42 *Ibid*, Kenneth Clarke, col 30.

43 *Ibid*, Kenneth Clarke, col 32.

Kenneth Clarke claimed: 'The new appeal rights will be the key to procedural simplicity and decision making finality. Strict time limits, together with a streamlined channel for clearly groundless cases, will prevent abuse.'[44]

The proposals were enacted as the Asylum and Immigration Appeals Act 1993, and supplemented by the introduction of new procedure rules and by changes in the Immigration Rules.[45] In fact, it is more appropriate to consult the changes in the Immigration Rules first since they demonstrate the change in the attitude to consideration of claims by the Home Office which had already been taking place in previous years. This attitude was then meant to carry over into the appellate system designed in the Act itself. A distinct repatriation focus was evident from the Rules. A claim for asylum would be granted if the Secretary of State was satisfied that the person applying was in the UK already, that he or she was a refugee under the 1951 Convention and 1967 Protocol, but only if a refusal of the application would result in the person *being required to go to a country* where their life or freedom was threatened. A similar emphasis was evident in another provision which enabled the service of removal directions, a notice of intention to deport or a deportation order, together with a notice of refusal. Such a possibility was envisaged in the 1993 Act itself which provided for the curtailment of existing leave after refusal of an asylum claim.[46] Claiming asylum therefore became extremely risky.

The Rules also now warned that failure to disclose factors material to the claim, failure to report for fingerprinting, failure to complete an asylum questionnaire or failure to attend an interview could lead to a refusal. They also listed circumstances in which the credibility of an applicant would be damaged: failure to apply forthwith; making false representations; destroying, damaging or disposing of a passport or other document or ticket relevant to the claim; undertaking activities in the UK considered to be inconsistent with previous activities and calculated to enhance a claim; the lodging of concurrent applications either in the UK or in another country. From evidence of decisions made after the 1993 Act came into force, it became apparent that such factors were overwhelmingly used in refusing a huge number of claims. Further, the Secretary of State was not obliged to consider the substance of a

44 Kenneth Clarke, Home Secretary, House of Commons Debates, vol 213, col 32, 2 November 1992.

45 The new procedure rules were issued as the Asylum Appeals (Procedure) Rules 1993, No 2227. The new Immigration Rules were issued as HC 725 (1993), which amended the previous restatement of the Rules in HC 251 (1990). They were then incorporated in another restatement, HC 395 (1994). The relevant paragraphs in HC 395 are paras 327–52.

46 Asylum and Immigration Appeals Act 1993, s 7. In the debates on the Bill, Charles Wardle confirmed that the curtailment of leave power, upon refusal of an asylum claim, was to enable notification of refusal, of curtailment of leave and a deportation order to be made against a person in one instance, House of Commons Debates, vol 216, col 697, 11 January 1993.

claim if removal to a third country was a possibility. The criteria for such a country would be met if the applicant had an opportunity to make contact with the authorities in a country through which he or she passed to seek their protection, or if there was other clear evidence of admissibility to a third country. Another provision allowed summary refusal on the basis that a person had had his or her claim already considered and rejected by another State party to the 1951 Convention and 1967 Protocol. Cases in the courts prior to these Rules already indicated that merely transiting through it would satisfy the relevant connection to another country. The Rules now specifically stated that the Secretary of State was under no obligation to consult the authorities of the third country before removing an applicant, again incorporating the results of earlier case law (Shah, 1995c, pp 272–80).

An appeal to a 'special adjudicator' for most asylum cases refused by the Home Office was now available on the basis that consequent expulsion may be in breach of the UK's obligations under the 1951 Convention and 1967 Protocol (no other international treaty or other instrument was mentioned as relevant).[47] This formula again indicated that the focus of the legislation was expulsion, rather than on making an assessment of the case for refugee status.[48] From that stage a further appeal could be made to the Immigration Appeal Tribunal, but only after leave to appeal was first obtained, by application to be made within five days of the adjudicator's decision.[49] After a substantive decision from the Tribunal, a possibility of appeal on a point of law now lay with the Court of Appeal, with leave to be obtained from either body, a measure which was also designed to take the pressure off the High Court.[50] Cases certified as 'without foundation', being either regarded as not raising 'any issue as to the UK's obligations under the Convention', or as 'frivolous and vexatious', were diverted to appeals before special adjudicators who would decide whether the Secretary of State's certificate should be upheld.[51] The main class of such 'without foundation' cases were those which carried a certificate that declared that the applicant should be removed to a third country considered safe.

The new asylum regime introduced under the Asylum and Immigration Appeals Act 1993 was thus designed around administrative priorities and preconditioned on access to lawyers which could not, in any case, be guaranteed. Some critics of the Bill (which became the 1993 Act) had argued that a right of appeal would not in itself help and it would be important to take into account the 'culture of decision making' at the Home Office (Juss,

47 Asylum and Immigration Appeals Act 1993, s 8(1)–(4).

48 Although each of the sub-sections caters for the various possibilities of expulsion the terminology nevertheless consistently implies a repatriation focus.

49 Asylum Appeals (Procedure) Rules 1993, para 13.

50 Asylum and Immigration Appeals Act 1993, s 9.

51 *Ibid*, Sched 2, para 5.

1993, p 143). The 'culture', however, immediately swung further against the refugees, as the Home Office started to refuse cases outright in large numbers, forcing thousands of cases into the appeals framework. Refusal by the Home Office to grant either refugee status or exceptional leave to remain increased from 46% in 1993 to 79% in 1994 (Justice *et al*, 1997, p 15). Figure 8.2 further indicates that, while a huge rise was evident in the numbers of decisions being made since 1992, there was also a noticeable increase in the number of outright refusals.

Figure 8.2

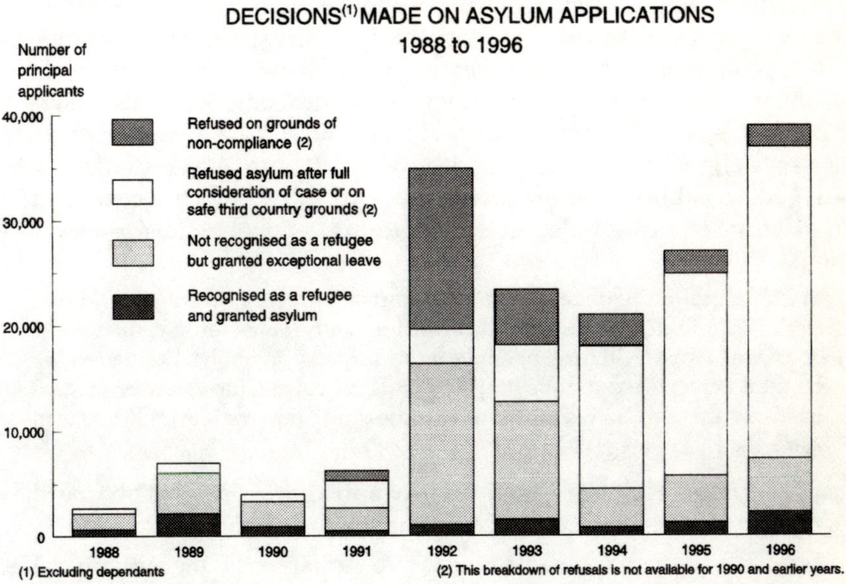

Source: Home Office (1997, p 8)

Despite the upward trend in refusals, the Home Office was building up a backlog of more cases. By March 1994, the number of cases pending decision was 42,170 and they rose to 55,255 in December 1994, and to 69,650 by the end of 1995. The Home Office continued to retain the power to determine which groups of cases would be decided and when. Similarly, many cases became simply 'stuck' somewhere in the appellate system. The number of cases awaiting appeals or the result of an appeal was 11,690 at the end of 1995, thus giving a potential 80,000 claimants a completely insecure legal status that year

(Grenier, 1996, p 5). This figure would not, of course, include people against whom refusals were made and who simply 'disappeared' from the figures.

As already indicated, the introduction of a right of appeal and a channel for appealing to the Court of Appeal in the 1993 Act was meant to reduce the pressure of judicial review applications on the High Court. Placing limits on legal aid funding (Jackson, 1996, p 28; Bridges *et al*, 1995, p 84) was also presumably intended to result in less litigation. However, an upsurge of leave applications were seen after the 1993 Act came into force, probably linked to the number of asylum applications which were also refused since the Act. On the other hand, leave applications came to be refused as a higher rate, an indication that the courts broadly supported the aims of the legislation by making it more difficult to obtain access to judicial review (Bridges *et al*, 1995, pp 25, 149). Even so, a major contribution to the Home Office's concerns was the lack of litigation success with safe third country cases, for which the fast track appeals process had primarily been established. McKee (1999) shows how the process of removing appellants could sometimes be slowed down to the point of frustration using the appeal and judicial review mechanisms. This was especially so in cases dealt with by the Refugee Legal Centre which managed to achieve a 40% success rate in third country cases before adjudicators. If a case failed at the adjudicator stage, judicial review was sought.

> The Immigration Service would set Removal Directions very soon after a special adjudicator had upheld a certificate, with the result that the Crown Office was awash with urgent applications for leave to apply! The deferral of Removal Directions consequent upon getting a Crown Office number made it less likely that the applicant could be successfully removed, even if he failed before the High Court [McKee, 1999, p 107].

Clearly, far from resulting in a reduction of applications in the High Court, the 1993 Act procedures were leading to further cases.

Another asylum Bill was introduced into Parliament in the autumn of 1995 as government ministers indulged in another bout of stigmatising refugees as 'bogus' (Young, 1998, pp 39–42). The ensuing Asylum and Immigration Act 1996 (in force from 1 September 1996) contained provisions to further restrict possibilities of appealing by subjection to even stricter time limits and by fast tracking a greater number of refused claims, thereby limiting access to the Immigration Appeal Tribunal. The Procedure Rules of 1996, which accompanied the Act, gave greater discretionary powers to, and even pressured, adjudicators to dismiss claims faster, and appeals have been increasingly dismissed summarily.[52] Several classes of claims were made

52 The Asylum Appeals (Procedure) Rules 1996, SI 1996/2070 came into force on 1 October 1996. For an explanation of the provisions of the 1996 Rules, see McKee (1996); Care (1998); and Travers (1999, pp 143–51).

subject to the faster appeals procedure. They included claims by persons from countries chosen by the Secretary of State 'in which it appears to him that there is in general no serious risk of persecution'. In practice, countries were selected on the basis of negative Home Office decisions, underlining the circularity of the claim of safety in a particular country of origin. The States of origin initially listed under this provision were Bulgaria, Cyprus, India, Ghana, Pakistan, Poland and Romania. Other situations in which claims could be certified for fast tracking included failure to produce a valid passport, the perceived merits of a case and its timing (for instance, making a claim after a refusal as a student has been issued). Claimants could have their cases placed on the slow track only if evidence of torture was forthcoming, or there was some factual circumstance which contradicted the basis of a certificate (Gillespie, 1996, pp 86–87; Winterbourne *et al*, 1996).[53]

In 'safe' third country cases, the right of appeal to a special adjudicator was removed in cases where return was proposed to an European Union State (which constituted the vast majority of third country cases) or any other State nominated by the Home Secretary in a statutory instrument. The States initially listed under this provision were the United States, Canada, Switzerland and Norway. Instead, a virtually useless possibility to appeal once removal had already taken place was instituted (Gillespie, 1996, pp 87–88; McKee 1999, pp 107–11).[54] This measure obviously reflected the Government's concern to remove applicants without further delaying matters through appeal. The initial reaction of the courts was to approve the practice of removing applicants to other European countries. A series of reported cases reveals the considerable lack of success on judicial review, even where there is information that applicants will be returned to the UK or removed to yet another State, and even where it is clear that applicants have already been rejected after going through asylum procedures in the third State.[55]

53 The main provision is the Asylum and Immigration Act 1996, s 1, amending the Asylum and Immigration Appeals Act 1993, Sched 2, para 5. For the countries designated under s 1, see the Asylum (Designated Countries of Destination and Designated Safe Third Countries) Order 1996, SI 1996/2671. See *R v Special Adjudicator ex p Mohammed Zaman* [2000] Imm AR 68, a Pakistani Ahmadiya case establishing that adjudicators have no power to overturn the listing of a particular State.

54 Asylum and Immigration Act 1996, ss 2 and 3. Countries other than European Union States are listed as safe third countries in the Asylum (Designated Countries of Destination and Designated Safe Third Countries) Order 1996, SI 1996/2671.

55 *R v Secretary of State for the Home Department and Immigration Officer, Waterloo International ex p Canbolat* [1997] Imm AR 281, concerned the removal of a Kurdish woman to France. In *Kerrouche* [1997] Imm AR 610, CA, the argument that France applies a different interpretation of the Refugee Convention and therefore would not admit the Algerian applicant to asylum procedures was rejected. In *R v Secretary of State for the Home Department ex p Sirghi* [1998] Imm AR 310, a Moldovan was certified for removal to Germany although there was evidence of a risk of onward removal to Poland. In *R v Secretary of State ex p Besnik Demaj* [1998] Imm AR 147, QBD, it was held that it was not unreasonable to remove the Albanian Kosovar applicants to Germany although there was evidence of expulsions of Kosovars from Germany. The facts of *W v Home Office* [1997] Imm AR 302, CA, a pre-1996 Act case, reveal that the Liberian applicant ...

This practice will foreseeably be even more difficult to challenge in the light of the decision by the European Court of Human Rights in the case of *TI v UK*. This case concerned the question of the 'safety' of Germany whence the Sri Lankan Tamil applicant had arrived in the UK, after an unsuccessful challenge before the German courts against the rejection of his asylum claim. His claim on arrival in the UK was certified and two judicial review applications were rejected in turn. Both the UK and German Governments made submissions before the European Court convincing it that their respective asylum systems were watertight, and that the applicant was not therefore at risk of inhuman and degrading treatment.[56] The Immigration and Asylum Act 1999 now directly incorporates the implications of readmission agreements like the Dublin Convention or more informal 'standing arrangements', allowing removal upon certification of a claim by the Home Office without a possibility of appeal with suspensive effect.[57]

The process of asylum seeking has become increasingly dependent on having access to legal advice. One report maintains that community advisers should win trust and bring clients to the 'experts' (Justice *et al*, 1997, pp 33–34). Jackson (1996, p 28), a Vice President of the Immigration Appeal Tribunal, states that legal advice should be sought as soon as possible, also warning that applicants should not normally attempt to present their cases to adjudicators or the tribunal; nor should they vest the responsibility in a friend. Indeed, success rates at any stage of the application or appeal process are affected by having legal representation. Unrepresented, an applicant will usually not have access to evidence to rebut the Home Office refusal letter, which is all he or she can discern as to reasons why the application is refused. The source and quality of legal representation varies and is constantly changing, especially in the light of changes to the public funding of legal advice and the competition for control among various professional groups. Together, the Refugee Legal Centre and the Immigration Advisory Service were estimated to provide assistance to 25% of all appellants. The other major source of legal advice is through solicitors, most being concentrated in London. No legal aid provision was made for representation beyond initial case preparation, for which 'Green Form' funding, though reduced through pressures from the Legal Aid Board,

55 [Contd] had embarked from Nigeria, transited though Gatwick airport before flying to Dusseldorf where he was refused entry. He was returned to Heathrow airport and claimed asylum. His claim was certified and he lost his appeal as well as an application for judicial review. He was returned to Germany from where he was again returned to the UK and detained on arrival. See, also, *Mentor Berisha and Another v Secretary of State* [1999] Imm AR 400, *R v Secretary of State ex p Abdu Cherife* [1999] Imm AR 317, QBD; *R v Secretary of State for the Home Department ex p Juan Carlos Arias* [1999] Imm AR 225, QBD; and *R v Secretary of State for the Home Department ex p Guhad* [1997] Imm AR 1 (a pre-1996 Act case).

56 *TI v UK*, Appl no 43844/98, decision of 7 March 2000. For the domestic proceedings, see *Iyadurai v Secretary of State for the Home Department* [1998] Imm AR 470, CA and *R v Secretary of State ex p Iyadurai (No 2)* [1999] Imm AR 202, QBD.

57 Immigration and Asylum Act 1999, ss 11 and 12.

was available. The gaps have led to the phenomenon of solicitors 'dropping' clients, or crucial stages of the appeal process not being attended to, such as requests for adjournments. Not surprisingly, because of the overall shortfall in legal assistance provision, a high proportion of appellants had remained unrepresented (Grenier, 1996, pp 25–26; Harvey, 1998; Justice *et al*, 1997, pp 32–33; Shah, 1995a; Smith, 1993).[58]

Recent years have also witnessed the emergence of a politics around 'bogus' advisers, with some lawyers' groups seeking to distance themselves from others regarded as exploiting asylum seekers, as falsely making asylum claims, or as needlessly pursuing appeals and judicial review remedies. Responses have included the potential criminalisation of some advisers and the institution of tighter surveillance on those allowed to practice. The Asylum and Immigration Act 1996 carried a provision to criminalise assisting the entry into the UK of a person believed to be an asylum claimant. Although an exception was included for *bona fide* advisers, the provision criminalises persons who give advice to a person who is in the UK 'illegally' or to someone abroad (McGuire, 1999, p 72). The Immigration and Asylum Act 1999 now institutes the office of an Immigration Services Commissioner who is supposed to maintain a register of persons qualified to provide immigration advice and services, and to administer disciplinary powers.[59] There is also increasing State control of legal assistance provision. This is reflected in provisions brought into force early in 2000 restricting access to legal aid budgets to contracted law firms and other providers, while extending their eligibility to access funds for representation in the appeals system.[60] The Refugee Legal Centre and the Immigration Advisory Service, which are more prone to government pressure, obtain increasing amounts of money.[61] Plans

58 Grenier (1996, p 26) points out that, for applicants who are detained, the problem of getting legal assistance is even greater due to some of the same reasons, but also because under the Procedure Rules of 1993, the obligation to comply with time limits was more onerous than hitherto. He also points out that representatives from the communities affected find it difficult to reach detention centres. See, also, Witherow (1995) and Trost and Billings (1998, p 88) to similar effect. Bridges *et al* (1995, p 40) found that 85% of immigration judicial review applications were made by solicitors based in London. Harvey (1998, p 181) found, in a sample survey of 622 determinations by special adjudicators promulgated in the second half of 1995 that 31% of applicants were unrepresented at the hearing, although only 4.5% had no representatives on record at all. She found that 49% of solicitors and 44% of immigration consultants did not attend the oral hearing, while the figure was 20% for unpaid voluntary organisations.

59 Immigration and Asylum Act 1999, ss 82–93.

60 A press release of 2 March 2000 from the Lord Chancellor's Department quotes the Lord Chancellor as follows: 'The Government has been concerned about the number of unscrupulous advisors operating in this area. All advice and representation is now provided by quality assured firms through contracts. I want to encourage existing firms to expand and more quality firms to move into this area of work to meet genuine need. This will help to meet the Government's targets for efficient handling of asylum claims.'

61 A letter from Lord Williams, Minister for State in the Home Office, to Lord Dholakia, 9 July 1999, states that the two organisations would receive £6.681 million in 1999–2000, an increase of 11% over the previous year.

are also in train for the Home Office to extend its team of Presenting Officers. These measures reflect the institutionalisation of a class of 'legitimate' professionals to service the expanding appeals apparatus. For refugees, they represent the ever narrowing channels for accessing legal advice and representation in a process at the end of which they are likely to be rejected.

From initial decision, appeals and further challenges in the courts, the asylum process is calculated to result in a high rate of refusals. From February 1995, the power to curtail existing leave, introduced in the 1993 Act, has been applied more frequently (Grenier, 1996, p 28). From the spring of 1995, a 'short procedure' scheme was initiated and extended to most points of application, whether in-country or at port, in which the interview and information gathering process was effectively shortened and tied to time limits for most nationality groups, without enabling access to lawyers (Jagmohan, 1996).[62] Apart from refusals based on third country grounds, the Home Office often issues refusals on the basis that the person was not credible. Such allegations are backed by pointing to the use of false documents, failure to claim immediately upon arrival or to claim asylum in a country of transit, or to inconsistencies between information given at an initial interview, which could be taken within hours of arrival if the claim was made at port, and a self-completed questionnaire later filled in.[63] Various studies of Home Office decision making reveal the extremely poorly argued refusal letters, which did not take applicants' histories seriously, but were focused on undermining the facts given (Asylum Aid, 1995a, 1995b and 1999; Grenier, 1995 and 1996, pp 31–38; Justice *et al*, 1997, p 41; Katsapaou, 1997 on Kurds from Turkey; Refugee Legal Centre, 1997b; Toal, 1997a on Somalis). These factors no doubt contributed to the 'culture of disbelief' which advisers continued to experience in their dealings with Home Office officials (Justice *et al*, 1997, p 12).[64]

62 The courts had already approved the practice of immigration officers refusing access to lawyers at interviews. See, for example, *Celik and Celik v Secretary of State for the Home Department* [1991] Imm AR 8, CA. For a non-asylum case, see *R v Secretary of State for the Home Department ex p Vera Lawson* [1993] Imm AR 58, QBD. Trost and Billings (1998, p 87) note that immigration officers can no longer be considered as mere gatekeepers following the introduction of the short procedure; 'their role is now crucial in shaping the flow of information passed on to caseworkers, which can materially affect the outcome of the application'.

63 Judges had generally tolerated these grounds of refusal even before the 1993 Act came into force. This can be seen, for example, in *Victoria and Satkunam Thamathirupillai v Secretary of State for the Home Department* [1987] Imm AR 47, CA, a Tamil case, where Parker LJ supported the reasons for refusal which were based on the use of forged documents.

64 Several reported cases on 'fresh claims' reveal the difficulties that applicants face in getting the Home Office to reopen their cases. See *Yolanda Ward v Secretary of State for the Home Department* [1997] Imm AR 236, CA; *R v Secretary of State for the Home Department ex p Hamid Habibi* [1997] Imm AR 391, QBD; *Mehmet Kabala v the Secretary of State for the Home Department* [1997] Imm AR 517, CA; *Secretary of State for the Home Department v Coskun Bobeyi* [1997] Imm AR 491, CA; *R v Secretary of State for the Home Department ex p Senathirajah Ravichandaran and Another (No 3)* [1997] Imm AR 74, QBD.

Immigration lawyers report that, with the knowledge that there is general access to the appeal system, the Home Office's Asylum Division prepares a 'case for the prosecution', more readily giving refusals which can then only be contested at the hearing (Grenier, 1996, p 25). Thus, the more arcane legal discussions about lower standards of proof to be applied in asylum cases become 'inextricably linked with issues of credibility' (Macdonald and Blake, 1995, p 383). Indeed, Jackson (1996, pp 377–78) points out that 'credibility will lie at the centre of most asylum pleas'. Adjudicators are thus free to make findings against credibility and this is done in the vast majority of appeals. Such decisions are extremely difficult to reverse on appeal or judicial review, even when there may be other legal points at issue.[65] In fact, the Home Office's refusal letters are often disregarded in the hearing, which therefore becomes a trial on any issue which the Home Office Presenting Officers wish to raise, and the applicant or representative has to anticipate this. Even positive findings can be turned around. Inconsistencies in an account given possibly years ago, about events which date even before that, can be used to brand applicants as liars. Even in cases taken by the Refugee Legal Centre, 300 pages of scrupulously prepared evidence can be dislodged by adverse credibility findings.[66] Discussions with lawyers reveal that adjudicators are increasingly becoming contemptuous of facts and law and are adopting a hostile attitude to appellants. A snapshot of appeals decided in 1996 (see Figure 8.3) unsurprisingly reveals that the vast majority of appeals are refused.

65 Debbie Winterbourne, Legal Officer, Refugee Legal Centre, interview, 12 September 1998. The Asylum Rights Campaign (1996, p 34) found from a sample of cases that, 'in a majority of cases, as soon as an adjudicator disbelieves one part of an appellant's account, s/he disbelieves the whole and dismisses the appeal on that basis'. Sarah Young, Barrister, confirmed to the writer her preliminary findings in ongoing research, that the High Court has shown great reluctance to interfere with an adjudicator's assessment of an asylum seeker's credibility. See, eg, *R v Secretary of State for the Home Department ex p Kingori (aka Mypanguli)* [1994] Imm AR 539, CA; *R v Immigration Appeal Tribunal ex p Zola Nolongala* [1996] Imm AR 626; *R v Secretary of State for the Home Department ex p Makanguru* [1998] Imm AR 141. See, further, Weston (1998) and Harvey (1998) on the role of credibility in asylum appeals.

66 *Ibid*, Debbie Winterbourne. Sarah Young, Barrister, confirms that only the evidence presented on behalf of the applicant tends to be subjected to rigorous examination and tested in cross-examination.

Figure 8.3

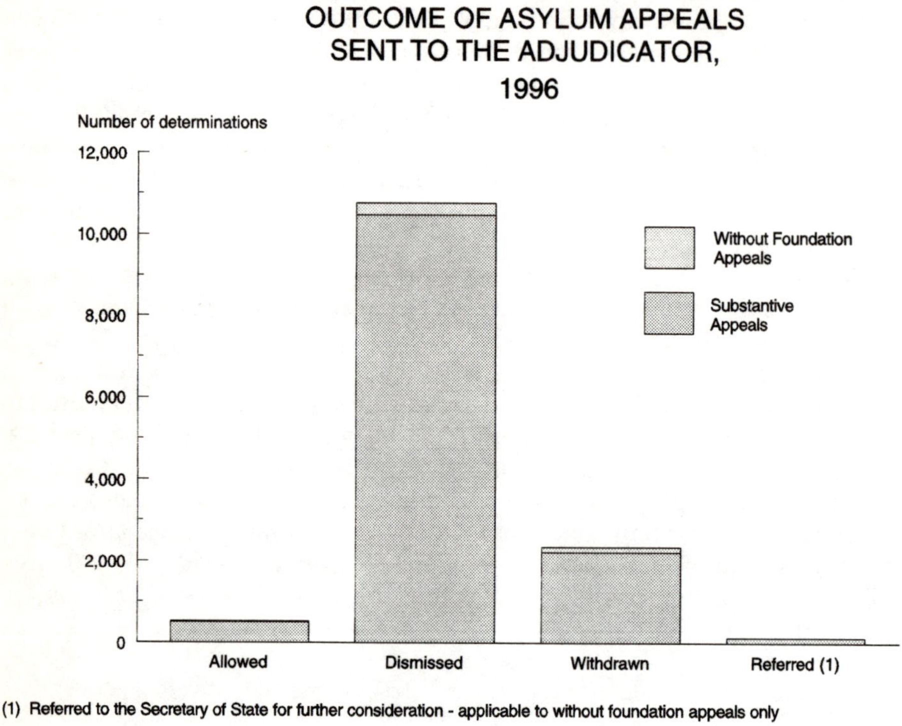

Source: Home Office (1997, p 12)

The 'mainstream' of asylum appeals remain without much apparent alteration on the face of the Immigration and Asylum Act 1999, as does the increasing number of 'certified' claims that attract a truncated appeal as introduced in the 1996 Act.[67] Broad powers are given in the 1999 Act to make Rules to regulate the determination of appeals.[68] The details are awaiting publication in revised Immigration Rules and Procedure Rules. The powers may reflect practices already in operation, such as the imposition of strict time limits, insistence on mandatory forms in which evidence must be presented and

67 Immigration and Asylum Act 1999, s 69 is the main provision. For the certified appeal, see Sched 4, para 9.

68 *Ibid*, Sched 4, para 5.

dismissal of appeals when applicants are not able to attend. Such rules create further obstacles for accessing an already highly legalised system. The main apparent change is the inclusion of a possibility to invoke the European Convention on Human Rights in an appeal, in parallel to provisions already applicable in the Human Rights Act 1998.[69] These powers are due to come into effect in October 2000 and, while much excitement is evident among lawyers about them, it may be premature to evaluate their impact. However, in the light of the interpretation of the rights of refugees by the UK judiciary and the European Convention organs to date, there are no serious grounds for thinking that the invocability of the European Convention in domestic fora can have a significant impact.[70]

The legal system thus keeps up the appearance that remedies are available for refugees to contest unfavourable decisions by the Home Office, retaining the idea of the rule of law. In practice, however, the hostility that has been politically generated against refugees has been incorporated into the appeals system, and tens of thousands of cases of unrecognised refugees have resulted. They will not obtain appropriate legal status until some indeterminate date when they may be considered eligible to remain legally in the UK. Meanwhile, they remain in an insecure legal status making them liable to arrest, detention, prosecution and expulsion at the discretion of government bodies. Recent changes in the already tenuous legal and social position of the refugees are examined in the next section.

8.3.2 Legalised marginalisation of refugees

As already evident in the foregoing discussion, the combination of visa restrictions and carriers sanctions were among the first steps taken in recent years to prevent the arrival of refugees seeking asylum. Several provisions now appear in statutes that have bolstered the policing system before refugees arrive in the UK. Police powers have also been given to immigration and police officers to maintain close control of asylum seekers once in the UK. Detention has been used as a measure specifically targeting asylum seekers,

69 In particular, Immigration and Asylum Act 1999, s 65.

70 Before the passing of the Human Rights Act 1998, the legislative omission of the relevance of other international human rights instruments led to criticisms (eg, Justice *et al*, 1997, pp 23–24). On the other hand, and with particular reference to the *Vilvarajah* case, Randall (1994, p 204) provided a less sanguine view: '... the [European Convention on Human Rights] has not proved to be the useful tool for migrants and particularly refugees for which many advisors had hoped.' The subsequent case of *Chahal v UK* (1997) 23 EHRR 413 may have led to some optimism, especially because of the finding by the European Court of Human Rights that Art 3 of the Convention provides greater protection than the terms of Arts 32 and 33 of the Refugee Convention of 1951, since the latter provide for exceptions to the principle of non-expulsion (Art 32) and non-refoulement (Art 33). Nevertheless, optimism is probably misplaced as very few cases actually tend to turn on this jurisprudential point.

and is being expanded rapidly. The expulsion of 'failed' asylum seekers is being conducted at a greater pace. Besides these extreme measures, recent legislation also focuses on welfare and housing provision, ending up in the institutionalisation of a dispersal scheme as attempted earlier with the Ugandan Asians and the Vietnamese.

The 1993 Act had already introduced some more provisions designed to extend the visa and carriers liability system to passengers travelling on transit, to avoid the possibility of further claims for asylum.[71] The Immigration and Asylum Act 1999 imposes further restrictions on carriers, and an intensification of the control of travel routes is evident. The Immigration (Carriers' Liability) Act 1987 is replaced by a provision allowing the charging of £2,000 per person carried without a valid passport or document establishing identity and nationality/citizenship, and a visa if required, and the new provision applies to ships, aircraft, vehicles or trains.[72] New penalties are imposed for carrying clandestine entrants who claim asylum or attempt to evade immigration control.[73] Obligations are placed upon carriers to pass on information on passengers on the demand of immigration officers.[74] For refugees, these provisions are likely to increase the cost of reaching the UK by pushing them further into reliance on trafficking networks.

From the latter part of 1994, prosecution, conviction and imprisonment of an increasing number of people began to take place when they were stopped at Heathrow airport while seeking to transit through the UK to the United States or Canada using a false or altered passport. There were 53 arrests in the financial year 1993–94, 126 in 1994–95 and 376 in 1995–96. The prosecutions which took place in Uxbridge magistrates' court resulted in sentences of between 14 days and three months being given (Dunstan, 1998b). In August 1998, the National Association of Probation Officers (NAPO) reported that more than 800 asylum seekers *en route* to the United States were arrested and charged 'for being in possession of false travel documents' in 1997. Those convicted were sentenced to an average of three months in prison. The Assistant General Secretary of NAPO claimed that, 'everyone that works in the system says that black foreigners get higher sentences than Europeans'.[75]

71 Asylum and Immigration Appeals Act 1993, s 12. The Order accompanying the Act listed Afghanistan, Iran, Iraq, Lebanon, Libya, Somalia, Sri Lanka, Turkey, Uganda and Zaire as countries the nationals of which were required to obtain transit visas: Immigration (Transit Visa) Order 1993, SI 1993/1678. The power to designate transit visas by order is retained in the Immigration and Asylum Act 1999, s 41.

72 Immigration and Asylum Act 1999, s 40. Although £2,000 is mentioned in the section, the amount is actually alterable. Under s 42, the carrier (ie, vehicle, etc), may be detained until payment of charges is made.

73 *Ibid*, ss 32–39.

74 *Ibid*, s 18.

75 (1998) *Migration News Sheet*, September, p 16. Bye (1999) estimates a total of 1,000 prosecutions in connection with passports annually since 1995. She cites research by Liz Hales who found that, among those taken to Wormwood Scrubs prison from Heathrow, 91% were fleeing for political reasons.

Challenges to three such prosecutions were upheld by the Court of Appeal in July 1999 under Art 31 of the 1951 Refugee Convention.[76] To limit the impact of the judgment, the Government inserted a provision into the 1999 Act to circumscribe the applicability of defences for illegal entry based on Art 31, while keeping open the possibility of prosecutions on a variety of charges.[77]

Further worrying signs of hostility can be seen in the extension of criminalisation of refugees under the immigration laws. The 1996 Act extended offences already existing under the Immigration Act 1971, and introduced new powers to arrest without warrant and obtain entry, search and seizure in cases of illegal entry, entry by deception and breach of conditions of entry, all of which have already been defined widely in the courts (McGuire, 1999, p 72). Under the 1999 Act, deception exercised in obtaining leave to enter or remain in the UK or in securing postponement or revocation of enforcement action can be punished by up to two years imprisonment.[78] The penalty for 'assisting illegal entry' has been increased from seven to 10 years imprisonment.[79] A series of powers has also been given to arrest and search persons and to enter and search premises without warrant.[80] The new powers are intended to assist immigration officers in detecting and detaining 'absconders'. Those not detained or subject to illegal entry or deportation action are required to report regularly to immigration officers or police stations, and the establishment of new reporting centres is aimed at increasing the number of people required to report.[81]

There is a greater focus on detaining asylum claimants with the number of detainees on the rise. In early 1998, there were more than 700 detainees at any time, most of whom tended to be asylum seekers.[82] In 1999, detention places were announced to be up to 1,000, three-quarters of which were used for asylum seekers.[83] There is a diversification from prisons and detention centres to camps with the opening of a former army barracks at Oakington, near

76 *R v Uxbridge Magistrates' Court ex p Adimi*, CO/2533/98; CO/3007/98; CO/2472/98; CO/1167/99, 29 July 1999, noted at (1999) 13(4) *Immigration and Nationality Law and Practice* 149, pp 149–51. See, also, Bye (1999).

77 Immigration and Asylum Act 1999, s 31.

78 *Ibid*, s 28.

79 *Ibid*, s 29.

80 *Ibid*, ss 128–46.

81 Home Office, Immigration Research and Statistics Directorate, July 1999.

82 It was revealed at a Refugee Legal Group meeting, 2 June 1998, that there were 750 detainees in February 1998, of whom 200 were not asylum seekers.

83 Home Office, Immigration Research and Statistics Directorate, July 1999. In Northern Ireland, more than 85 out of a total of between 200 and 300 asylum seekers were held in detention in 1998. They were held in high security prisons at Maghaberry for women and Magiligan for men. At the latter centre, the men could not receive telephone calls, and the prison being located some 112 km from Belfast made visits difficult. There were no facilities for those requiring interpreters, and detainees, placed alongside convicts including sex offenders, have been victims of racist insults and bullying: (2000) *Migration News Sheet*, January, p 13.

Cambridge, in March 2000 which is supposed to hold 400 asylum seekers and their dependants, and used for detaining persons who are likely to be removed within a few days of arrival.[84] Further plans include military or hospital sites in Kent, Yorkshire and the West Midlands expected to be converted and run by private security firms where claims of 40,000 people are supposed to be assessed each year (Rufford, 2000). Detaining persons on ships was also being considered at the time of writing.[85]

The regimes in detention centres unsurprisingly provoke protests by the detainees, but also harsh reactions. The trial of nine West Africans charged with riot and violent disorder, at Campsfield immigration detention centre near Oxford, collapsed in June 1998 after video evidence contradicted the testimony of the prosecution witnesses who were Group 4 detention staff. In August 1997, some detainees at Campsfield had become worried about the removal of two of the detainees by squads of guards who refused to say where they were being taken, but stonewalled and abused the detainees. The Group 4 staff then put on riot gear, and a baton was used on at least one of the detainees, when a protest ensued at one of the gates. A fire alarm was set off:

> Staff congregated inside, detainees outside. According to the defendants, despite the fact that people of all races had joined the protest, detainees were allowed back into the centre by ethnic group, until the only group left outside were the Africans. The rest were shipped out to other centres, but the Africans were held in the centre's gym for several days. Thirteen of them were arrested, interviewed and charged with violent disorder. Later, charges were dropped against four of the men, but the remaining nine had the more serious charge of riot added – a charge used to mark the most serious and life threatening situations. Group 4 injuries totalled a few minor bruises.[86]

This incident shows the vicious racism that is inherent in the pattern of detentions and prosecutions against asylum seekers.

Legal remedies against detention remain weak, and representatives are not likely to apply for bail because of the lack of legal aid funding to go before adjudicators or the Immigration Appeal Tribunal. Another reason is the high cost of sureties which may be demanded – a total of £5,000 was considered to be normal in 1998.[87] Bail for Immigration Detainees (BIDS), a voluntary

84 ILPA information for members, February 2000.

85 'Asylum seekers could stay in "floatels"' (2000) Press Association, 27 February. The report cites Securicor as having made a proposal to the Home Office, after a project run in Germany by one of Securicor's sub-contractors.

86 (1998) 8(3) and (4) *Statewatch*, May–August 1998, pp 21–22. Thackray (1998) reports that the month following the trial, five of the men were detained in Rochester prison facing deportation. Two men had had made suicide attempts, while a third of the group was on 'suicide watch'.

87 Debbie Winterbourne, Legal Officer, Refugee Legal Centre, interview, 12 September 1998. If bail is granted, a requirement to report to the police up to three days a week can be imposed.

organisation set up in June 1998 to help immigration detainees to make bail applications, gives a more recent scenario:

> In a majority of cases, adjudicators continue to ask for sureties and continue to seek large sums of money. For example, recently, an extremely experienced and respected adjudicator refused to grant bail without substantial sureties in a case in which the Immigration Service had simply left blank the section of the bail summary entitled 'reasons for detention' – indicating they had no reasons for detention. In other recent cases, one adjudicator indicated that he felt bound to require substantial sureties on the basis of what he perceived to be the tradition of the IAA, while in another case the adjudicator indicated that some kind of collegiate decision has been made by the judiciary of the IAA regarding levels of sureties.[88]

The practice of granting liberty in exchange for money is thus becoming an institutionalised feature of immigration control.

The 1999 Act makes provision, due to come into effect in April 2001, for routine bail hearings to take place within seven days and one month of detention. Written reasons for detention are also to be obligatory, although they can be anticipated to cover situations in which persons are already detained.[89] There will not be any upper limit on the time spent in detention as, according to a government minister, that is considered to frustrate chances of removal and to incite non-co-operation by detainees in order to force their release:

> Our commitment to increase the number of failed asylum seekers who are removed may mean that there is an increase in the number detained immediately prior to removal. We would much prefer that those whose applications for asylum have failed and whose appeals have been dismissed should go voluntarily. But, if people in this position refuse to leave, then we may have to use our powers of detention to achieve the objective of increasing the number of failed asylum seekers who are removed.[90]

Detention is therefore seen as a key to forcing people to leave the UK.

Between January 1992 and September 1996, a total of 90,350 'asylum seekers' were refused any sort of status by the Home Office and 81% of all subsequent appeals were dismissed; some 72,000 had therefore reached the

88 Letter from BIDS to Dunn J, Chief Adjudicator, dated 11 February 2000. Anecdotal evidence indicates that Chief Immigration Officers demand up to £10,000 from sureties.

89 Immigration and Asylum Act 1999, ss 44–50 and 147–59. A letter from Lord Williams, Minister for State in the Home Office, to Lord Avebury, 9 July 1999, lists the circumstances in which detention will be allowed. They include: likelihood of failure to comply with bail conditions or of any recognisance or bail bond; likelihood of commission of a criminal offence; likelihood of danger to public health or public order; involvement in entering the UK in breach of the immigration laws; suffering from mental disorder; being under the age of 18 without any satisfactory arrangements for care having been made; lack of sufficient information as to whether to grant temporary admission or leave to enter or remain; and being subject to removal.

90 Letter from Lord Williams, Minister for State in the Home Office, to Lord Avebury, 9 July 1999.

end of the asylum process and became liable to be expelled during the same period; 10,888 or one in every seven of those were actually removed or departed 'voluntarily' from the UK. Dunstan (1998a, p 69), Refugee Officer at Amnesty International between 1986 and 1997, uses these figures to argue that, with the chances of removal being so low, 'the incentive for those seeking only to circumvent the immigration controls to make an unfounded claim is strong ... the problems associated with such misuse of the asylum process will not be remedied until this failure is addressed'. The number of removals has also therefore come to be seen, significantly by a representative of a human rights organisation, as another way of reducing the number of asylum claimants. Recent ministerial statements also now boast of the Government's record of expulsions, particularly against asylum seekers:

> ... removals are increasing on all fronts and at a substantially increased rate for failed asylum seekers. Over 7,100 principal applicants were removed in 1997, and just over 7,000 in 1998. Those figures are more than double the total for 1995, and five times the 1992 figure.[91]

In a bid to reduce the number of asylum applications, much of the recent legislation has restricted access to State welfare and housing. The 1993 Act contained a provision to enable local authorities to refuse public housing to asylum seekers who were deemed to already have 'reasonable accommodation'. In regulations passed in February 1996, most forms of public support for asylum seekers were removed. In particular, provision was made to exclude in-country asylum applicants, who constituted the majority of applicants, and all failed asylum applicants, including those whose cases were in the appeals system, from means tested State benefits (Feria, 1996). The *vires* of these regulations were successfully challenged in the Court of Appeal, which stated that primary legislation would be needed for the changes to be immune from challenge by judges. Meanwhile, a state of total confusion about the position regarding benefits was created. In reaction to the quashing of the social security regulations, the Government legislated in the 1996 Act for benefit restrictions, and introduced further measures which allowed local authorities to prevent asylum seekers from accessing housing under the Housing Act 1985.[92] Legal battles then ensued to establish a minimal duty

91 Letter from Lord Williams, Minister of State in the Home Office, to Viscount Astor, 9 July 1999. The Immigration and Asylum Act 1999, s 13 ensures removal by giving powers to provide identification data to ensure acceptance in the country of destination.

92 In particular, see ss 9 (housing) and 11 (benefits) of the 1996 Act. Of that measure, Grenier (1996, p 19) writes: 'The housing options for asylum seekers without benefits are extremely limited. Most night shelters do not accept children. Mother and baby hostels require Housing Benefit payments. It has already been well documented that the children of asylum seekers suffer because of living in poor temporary accommodation on very low incomes. Experts in the field have warned that the introduction of this clause could lead to hypothermia (to which small children are particularly vulnerable), frostbite, tuberculosis, nutritional deficiencies, vulnerability to disease, asthma, low birth weights, difficulties of accessing the NHS (because of having no address), resulting in begging, prostitution, theft and dangerous illegal employment.'

upon local authorities under the National Assistance Act 1948 to provide for asylum seekers who became destitute, although obligations on authorities had to be newly established each time through further court battles, as they continued to resist (Webber, 1997a).

The linking of asylum seekers with public funds has taken on much more drastic shape in the Immigration and Asylum Act 1999, with its institution of a 'dispersal' policy. The dispersal campaign appears to have started when groups of Roma gypsies arrived from Slovakia and settled in Dover in late 1997. Since then, public hysteria about asylum seekers has reached a heightened state, as London and south-east England have been identified as 'full'. The 1999 Act gives power to the Home Office to allocate housing and to make welfare payments to asylum applicants.[93] Welfare payments, a substantial part of which are paid in the form of vouchers rather than cash, can be made conditional on a person accepting to be moved to wherever housing is allocated. The Home Secretary is specifically obliged not to have regard to a preference that the supported person or his dependants may have as to the locality in which the accommodation is provided.[94] These measures are aimed at moving asylum applicants away from London and Kent, and placing them in sub-standard accommodation.

Since before their implementation in December 1999, stories from the press show how racist campaigns are appearing at local levels as residents reportedly resent the presence of refugee groups who are frequently portrayed as being criminals. The fear of racial attacks against refugees and anyone who is not white has grown, while commentators have stated that decisions to move people are being made in response to racist campaigns against the settlement of refugees.[95] The implementation of the 'dispersal' scheme through the 1999 Act represents the institutionalisation of the methods that were deployed by the State in response to the arrival of the Asians from Uganda in 1972, and the arrival of the Vietnamese from the late 1970s. As with those earlier precedents, they can be seen as a kind of assimilation policy which does not respect the decisions of refugees themselves, as this probably means an unacceptable assertion of their ethnicity. Also, in line with the earlier precedents, it is not likely to work unless coercion is exercised upon the applicants, and significant 'secondary' migration can be expected.

---

93 Immigration and Asylum Act 1999, ss 94–127.

94 *Ibid*, s 97(2)(a).

95 (1999) 9(6) *Statewatch*, November–December and *Campaign Against Racism and Fascism*, March 2000, generally; Burrell (1998) on Roma in Kent; *Searchlight*, January 1998 and Dodd (2000) on Dover; Gillan (2000) on people 'dispersed' to Glasgow. Burrell (1998) cites Alasdair Mackenzie, co-ordinator of Asylum Aid, who rightly predicted that public antipathy towards asylum seekers would grow as the Government pursued its policy of dispersing them to towns and cities around the country.

With the institutionalisation of arbitrary power against refugees, especially by the dispersal programme, a legal image of 'asylum seekers' as potentially permanent wards of the State has been created. This has allowed the possibility of the freedom to work to lapse into a non-debate further undermining possibilities of self-determination for refugee communities. By controlling the issue of documentation to asylum seekers, the immigration authorities can effectively control the possibility of obtaining employment. Tens of thousands of people who are either in the process of seeking asylum or have been rejected remain without documentation allowing employment. The legal system has thus allowed the growth of a *sans papier* population who can be marginalised economically. Instead, new criminal offences were created by the 1996 Act to penalise employers of persons without work permission, unless document checks were performed on prospective employees (Berkowitz, 1999; McGuire, 1999). This pushes many refugees further into a legal twilight zone and potentially no recourse to the employment laws. When State benefits were removed for most categories of asylum applicants in 1996, a test case was brought to challenge the practice of withholding work permission until the lapse of six months after a claim was made. However, the challenge was rejected by the Court of Appeal,[96] and the grant of work permission therefore remains a discretionary power of the Home Office or immigration officers.

A highly restrictive law on 'asylum seeking' has therefore developed in recent decades. The State has sought to frustrate chances of obtaining access to British territory by imposing visa requirements, sanctions on carriers, and the criminalisation of refugees who do make it to Britain. It creates a large number of persons without any valid immigration status, who are therefore liable to arrest, detention, prosecution and expulsion. This has been accomplished by the large scale intervention of lawyers servicing the appeals system, raising questions about the exploitation of refugees by the legal system itself. The Immigration and Asylum Act 1999 marks a high point in the development of the oppressive regime for 'asylum seekers'. It institutionalises the Home Office's powers to require people to move anywhere across the country, and therefore legally entrenches the kind of dispersal programmes applied to the Ugandan Asians and Vietnamese. These developments raise questions about Britain's post-colonial commitment to multiculturalist realities that would be wished away by spurious law making enterprises.

96 *Secretary of State for the Home Department ex p Jammeh and Others* [1999] Imm AR 1.

CHAPTER 9

CONCLUSIONS

This book began with a historical analysis, in Chapter 2, of the reaction of the British State to the several groups which sought asylum in Britain from the Tudor to the Victorian periods. The treatment of gypsies was first contrasted with that given to European Huguenot refugees; while the gypsies were ordered to be expelled from the Kingdom, the Huguenots were positively welcomed. The contrast lay not only in the actual reception of the two groups, but also in their subsequent acknowledgment in the legal literature. This latter aspect has influenced modern perceptions of the law as being racially neutral since only the positive treatment by the State, which reflected the experience of European refugees, tended to be recorded. While gypsy experiences have been treated with silence, the Huguenots were metamorphosed into the exemplary group of refugees to which the State extended the principle of asylum and their experience was encoded into a foundation myth for the right of asylum in Britain. The economic benefits arising from Huguenot migration were emphasised, while such considerations did not seem to feature at all in the case of the gypsies. The experiences of gypsy groups in the Tudor period augured the harsh reactions to Asian people in subsequent periods right up to the late 20th century.

The involvement of Britain in slave trading from Africa had received official sanction, and led to the worst treatment of Africans under English law, and the principle of freedom was only gradually realised in Britain with the onset of the abolitionist movement. The main example of Africans seeking refuge in Britain came with the arrival of Black soldiers who had fought on the British side during the American war of independence. Their presence in Britain provoked a harsh reaction from official bodies which sought to degrade and then to 'repatriate' them to Sierra Leone. The experience of African refugees in modern Britain, therefore, finds an echo in these earlier periods of British history.

On the other hand, in the case of further waves of European refugees, the principle of asylum was catapulted to constitutional status in domestic and international discussions. Legislative powers were given to the executive to control their movements only intermittently and were hardly exercised. Despite the international embarrassment to Britain, the principle of asylum was defended against foreign countries, and when collusion between the British and foreign governments was suspected, it led to the resignation of a minister. The Orsini crisis of 1858 underlined the difficulty of pursuing politically active European refugees through the criminal laws. Some limits on the activities of European refugees were eventually set by the Extradition Act of 1870, although that Act protected 'political offenders' and was really only effective against anarchists. Generally, the freedom of movement remained intact for European refugees.

The principle of free movement, guarded at least rhetorically in the English common law, then began to wane as a result of a reaction by the Privy Council and judges in other parts of the Anglo-Saxon world who began to accommodate legislative demands for immigration controls. The Privy Council's Musgrove judgment can be identified as a turning point in legal thinking that has proved persistent to the present day in providing justifications for the exercise of arbitrary State power. At the time, this revisionism was directed to accommodating States' concerns about the settlement of blacks, Japanese, Chinese and South Asians in territories Europeans claimed to control exclusively. The judgment also showed how international law principles could be used against non-Europeans underlining their racist application. The evidence of continually reproducing reactionary attitudes in the legal system against the settlement of non-European groups of refugees before the 20th century is thus ample. As further chapters in this book have shown, such attitudes have been carried over to the end of the 20th century.

In Chapter 3, the reaction of the British State towards two ethnic groups was compared. The Aliens Act 1905, the first permanent legislation on immigration in Britain, was passed after a lengthy period of problematisation of the Jewish presence in Britain. However, by today's standards, the 1905 Act was not draconian, and at the time probably had more of a psychological impact given the resumption of Jewish migration in the aftermath of its passage to pre-Act levels. Further, the Anglo-Jewish leaders' success in obtaining several concessions from the British Government shows the extent of plurality observed in practice. There was no indication of such an attitude of co-operation in the case of the small number of gypsies, whose arrival coincided with the 1905 Act. Indeed, the reaction against the gypsies was draconian, culminating in their deportation.

While the two cases coincided more or less in time, and therefore provide a comparison of how racial factors could determine the reaction of the State, they are relevant for a further reason. There is evidence of a continuity of the quality of reactions to refugees based on their ethnic or racial background. Such continuity is evident in the case of the gypsies, who had also been rejected during the Tudor period, and has become evident again in the late 20th century with respect to Roma gypsies from Central and Eastern Europe. Continuity is evident in the case of the Jews also, although pointing in a different direction. The Anglo-Jewish community leaders managed to continue their relationship of co-operation with the British Government when another outflow of Jews from Europe began to gain prominence in the 1930s.

Although draconian controls were established against 'aliens' with the onset of the First World War, what Chapter 4 shows is the 'ethnic' Jewish influence in shaping the liberal regime that came about in practice which, in some respects, represented a continuation of the trend set in earlier stages of mass Jewish migration. Between the World Wars, one effect of this 'ethnic' factor was that refugees were classed as economic contributors, which was especially important during a time of depression. Preferential treatment towards Jews from Germany in British asylum policy was another outcome of that factor. Meanwhile, Jewish organisations in Britain prepared to help Britain fulfil its obligations undertaken in the Balfour declaration of 1917 by organising large scale settlement to Palestine. Jewish organisations in North America and Europe also managed to internationalise the refugee issue; the IGCR was set up especially to deal with the situation of Jewish refugees. Although the international response was generally poor, Britain itself remained a place of refuge for a much larger share, despite the knee jerk imposition of an internment policy at the outbreak of the Second World War in 1939.

The internationalising trend was given a massive push forward after the Second World War, and was further propelled by the Cold War. However, Cold War considerations do not by themselves explain the positive stance taken on the right of asylum. The British reaction was overwhelmingly motivated by the need for labour. Recruitment of 'European Volunteer Workers' from refugee camps in Europe and from demobilised Polish soldiers was undertaken while, at the international level, the IGCR and the IRO organised the process of resettlement. At this stage, both the economic and racial benefits to Britain were invoked simultaneously as a justification for allowing immigration. In the event, the 1951 Refugee Convention, so central to asylum debates today, was conceived of to legally protect European refugees who had already obtained asylum in another State. The deepening Cold War was also occasioned by a major outflow of Hungarian refugees and smaller numbers from other East European countries whom Britain generally supported by providing asylum. However, while Britain continued to support the new international framework, the Convention was never tested in the domestic courts, showing that an open asylum policy could be operated without resort to the legal system. On the other hand, the extension of the protection of the 1951 Refugee Convention to refugees coming from beyond Europe's borders had been premised upon the belief that there was no risk that substantial numbers of people from outside Europe would be seeking asylum there. As seen in subsequent chapters, the concept of asylum did not fare well in the face of movements of Asian and African refugees to Britain, which did in fact emerge.

In Chapter 5, the treatment of refugees from the British Empire and Commonwealth was discussed. While the formal distinctions between 'aliens' and 'British subjects' were preserved until recently, they provided a fictive and theoretical unity to the concept of Empire, rather then indicating the actual treatment received in the immigration context. Various British territories were ascribed certain nationality statuses corresponding to the formal relations of colonial domination by which they were categorised. On the other hand, in the immigration context, examples could be seen in the early 20th century of hostility to non-white British subjects, soldiers and seamen among them, in Britain. Thus, the myth of equality of British subjects was contradicted in practice. Further developments, notably the British Nationality Act 1948, also showed that the concept of Commonwealth unity was retained in theory, although when large scale migration from, among other places, the West Indies, the Indian subcontinent, West Africa and Hong Kong began to occur, controls were clearly introduced on racial grounds. The reaction to non-white Commonwealth migration can be contrasted with the favourable reception given to the European Volunteer Workers.

The case of the East African Asians provides the main example of a group forced to undertake asylum migration to Britain, which was seen as an obvious destination as many Asians still claimed a British nationality status. In the case of the Asians from Kenya, it was seen that, although the independence arrangements had evidently left open the possibility of unrestricted migration to Britain, this route was cut off by the Commonwealth Immigrants Act 1968. Instead, affected people were forced to obtain vouchers from British missions abroad before embarkation. The voucher scheme was an administrative device to limit the numbers arriving in Britain in the hope that frustrated applicants would look elsewhere for their future, at a time when other countries were also restricting migration routes to the Asian British nationals. Soon after the Kenyan Asians incident, Asians in Uganda were ordered to leave. The British reaction was to limit the numbers to be admitted by, at first, sticking to the voucher scheme, while airlines were requested not to carry those fleeing and other countries were called upon to receive the Asians. The UK could not escape accepting at least a proportion of those fleeing as it was bound to be held to accepting its own nationals by other countries. When the Asians arrived in Britain, official reluctance to admit them became transformed into the dispersal policy to spread people around the country. Although this strategy did not work, it was applied again to the Vietnamese refugees whose immigration was accepted from the late 1970s, but evidently also resented on cultural grounds. The Immigration and Asylum Act 1999 now institutionalises a dispersal strategy, showing the persistence of assimilationist thinking at the official level. In contrast to the treatment given by the State authorities to the inflow of Asian British nationals, no corresponding problematisation has been evident of successive waves of white British migrants who have relocated upon decolonisation. In fact, as seen in the case of the white British from Kenya, special arrangements were made for them to revert to British nationality if given up. These examples have been followed in the Rhodesian/Zimbabwean and South African cases as well on the transition to majoritarian rule in those countries.

When the challenges against maltreatment of Asians by the British officials were taken to the courts, the judges also showed a negative or hostile reaction. The voucher queue was obviously hurting Asian women applicants, but discrimination in the operation of the scheme was accepted by judges, who also ratified the freedom of the executive in this area by denying a right of appeal against adverse decisions and even by invoking the royal prerogative. Judges colluded with other officials in accepting the principle that Asian British passport holders may be expelled even if there were indications that another country would not accept the expellees. The case of Thakrar showed that, while responsibility had been accepted for the Ugandan Asians at the international level, judges would not accept an international legal principle obliging the UK to accept the Asians. More recent evidence indicates that Asians connected with East Africa have found it harder to maintain their transnational identity across continents as many families became divided, while governments continue to apply restrictions against their movements.

The East African Asians cases also showed what reaction could be expected from the human rights institutions in Strasbourg. Although the European Commission on Human Rights made a bold finding that the UK had discriminated against the East African Asians by passing the 1968 Act, the contested cases were then taken to the Committee of Ministers where no agreement could be reached after eight years. Further challenges before the Commission were frustrated, there being no sign that the Commission would revert to its previous views. Recent moves to incorporate the European Convention on Human Rights must be read in the light of the generally unfavourable reaction of the Strasbourg bodies on immigration and asylum matters, and it is thus questionable whether a real enhancement of rights for non-European refugees is involved. The reluctance in Europe to deal seriously with the problems of the East African Asians may also reflect wider concerns about the immigration of non-Europeans. Already, when the UK acceded to the European Economic Community from 1973, non-patrial British passport holders were excluded from the benefits of free movement. These incidents point to an early realisation of the need to close off migration routes to non-Europeans which have intensified in the direction of a 'fortress Europe' mentality, and indicate that membership of inter-governmental bodies with other European countries offers a chance for the UK to downgrade protection for refugees. These features have become much more pronounced by the 1990s.

Chapter 6 began with a discussion of the reasons behind the establishment of a new international regime for refugees under the Protocol of 1967 to the Convention on Refugees of 1951. The main effect of the Protocol was to widen the category of refugees recognised under international law by the elimination of the 1951 dateline. It was pointed out that the main reason for the establishment of the 1967 Protocol was to enable the UNHCR to intervene in refugee crises outside Europe with a reinforced legal basis. Thus, the main aim of the Protocol was not to cater for the requirements of non-European refugees in Europe. On the international level, these developments mark a splitting of the functions of the UNHCR from an agency designed to promote resettlement of European refugees to one concerned to pursue the aims of Western governments outside the West through 'aid' missions. These moves augur the more recent containment strategies pursued by the UNHCR. At the domestic UK level, it is especially remarkable that no discussion about the consequences of the 1967 Protocol for immigration policy in Britain took place. This may be explained by the fact that control of Commonwealth immigration was still the primary concern in Britain, and Commonwealth citizens, formally still British subjects, appear to have been totally excluded from the scope of the Protocol at this stage.

Motivated by the desire to control Commonwealth immigration, a legalised approach was created in Britain from the early 1970s. The Immigration Act 1971 apparently provided a comprehensive structure of control, including an appeals framework. Although the Immigration Rules made under the 1971 Act recognised refugees under international instruments, the retention of discretionary powers outside the 1971 Act enabled the question of Commonwealth refugees to be side stepped through the application of extra-Rules mechanisms such as the quota voucher scheme applied to the East African Asian refugees, through the granting of exceptional leave to remain, or by bringing them under non-asylum categories. The appeals system was designed to provide legitimacy to a system of immigration control which already deliberately targeted non-whites, mainly Commonwealth citizens. Distinctions between Commonwealth citizens and 'aliens' were carried over into the appeals framework as well, for example, by keeping the East African quota voucher applicants outside it altogether. Further gaps also appeared in the appeals system through declaring arrivals as 'illegal entrants' due for summary expulsion. Still, the Immigration Act 1971 provided a model of administrative justice, premised upon the assistance of legally qualified personnel, which was to be deployed intensively to control non-European refugees in the 1990s.

From the late 1970s, a rethink about the legal structures applicable to control refugees took place. At the international level, there was a consciousness that the intensification of refugee situations outside Europe would not escape the West. These developments were occurring in the context of a general curtailment of non-European migration across various western European countries. For the UK, commitments were undertaken to curtail primary immigration altogether by the late 1970s, while the legal system reacted against family reunification and formation, which was leading to further non-white settlement. On the asylum front, this meant the enactment of new Immigration Rules in 1980 and the institution of some new procedures to control refugee admissions. This change is significant for several reasons. First, it was a recognition that, while Commonwealth migration was being brought under control, the new refugee streams, which were already finding a course to Britain, were not restricted to the Commonwealth. This concern could explain the assimilation of Commonwealth citizens and 'aliens' under a single asylum regime. Secondly, it was thought appropriate to bring the intrusive legal mechanisms already in the Immigration Act 1971 to bear on the new refugees in order to control admissions more tightly. Thirdly, although the new practices did not involve a significant shift in the approach to refugee cases, they allowed the Home Office to monitor the numbers of applications by various nationality groups more closely.

In light of these trends to control non-European refugees, it was discussed whether the acceptance of over 15,000 refugees from Vietnam provides a counter-example. Yet, their treatment did reflect the underlying uneasiness about non-European settlement in Britain. It is clear that, on the one hand, the political capital gained against the regime in Vietnam was seen as outweighing the prevailing racist anti-immigration stance. On the other hand, although significant numbers were accepted, they were treated as though they constituted a cultural liability to Britain as seen in the dispersal policy which was designed to spread them across the country to minimise their visibility. That policy was applied with the awareness that a similar strategy applied to the Ugandan Asians had not worked, and it had disastrous consequences for the Vietnamese themselves. By the time the new Rules on asylum were published, a definite policy of restriction was also adopted against Vietnamese refugees. Ultimately, containment in Hong Kong's refugee camps came to be seen as preferable to undertaking further immigration commitments. It is significant that Ivor Stanbrook saw the new legal controls, which he, among others, advocated, as part of a strategy to avoid the type of non-white immigration commitments which were involved in the Vietnamese case.

By the early 1980s, therefore, non-European refugee migration was seen as the main threat to public policies premised around preventing further non-European settlement in Britain. Significantly, the new strategy involved deployment of legal resources which, from the point of view of the State, would legitimise such control strategies. This strategy came to be much more pronounced from the mid-1980s onwards when a new law on 'asylum seeking' developed. As the discussion in Chapter 7 shows, this law developed mainly in reaction to the settlement of Tamil refugees from Sri Lanka, and was then extended to cover other African and Asian refugee groups, again underlining the racialised basis for law and policy applicable to refugees in Britain.

The settlement of Tamils in Britain was a result of the colonial links established between Britain and Sri Lanka before they became visible as 'asylum seekers'. However, from the early 1980s, the settlement of Tamils was identified under a separate 'asylum seeker' category of immigration control. By 1985, the arrival of more Tamils who claimed asylum provoked the imposition of a visa requirement directed against their further settlement. In addition, the law was moving, with judicial support, to legitimise their official portrayal as 'bogus' refugees, as can be seen in the extension of the law on 'illegal entrants' to cover asylum seekers and through the imposition of systematic detention policies. Despite the uncertainty created by the State about the further acceptability of Tamils in Britain, further streams continued to arrive. The case of the 64 who arrived in February 1987 showed, again, the systematic nature of the detention policies supported by judges. Airlines were brought further into the process of immigration control under the Immigration (Carriers' Liability) Act 1987 which, in combination with the visa requirement, routine detention and the 'illegal entry' doctrine, pushed up the cost of travelling to Britain significantly. The Tamils' court battles to secure recognition of their status as refugees, after the Home Office's refusal to do so, were also not successful. Ultimately, the House of Lords ratified the Home Office perspective in the *Sivakumaran* case, which allowed the latter to proceed with repatriation policies.

The Tamils' case also helped to propel the question of the settlement of non-European refugees into Europe wide discussions. The UNHCR was quickly subordinated to the interests of its Western financier States who pushed for a repatriation orientated policy focus. Some European countries began to formulate common policies, including the application of carriers' sanctions and the doctrine of the 'safe third country'. These developments formed a backdrop to the *Vilvarajah* litigation in Strasbourg, where the European human rights organs were asked to determine the case of five Tamils who had been repatriated and ill treated. The European Commission of Human Rights, influenced by the UNHCR backed repatriation programme in India, did not find a breach of the norm against inhuman and degrading treatment in the European Convention on Human Rights. On this point, the Court of Human Rights agreed. On the other hand, the Commission's opinion that there was not an effective domestic remedy for rejected asylum seekers put the UK system of judicial review into question. Still, the Court did not ratify this view, and UK policy escaped unscathed in Strasbourg. The *Vilvarajah* decision left the way open for further repatriation measures, such as that instituted in Switzerland and backed by the UNHCR.

Other Asian and African refugee groups who followed the Tamils were also caught up in the restrictive asylum regime which was being erected. Visa requirements were extended to cover these groups as well. Detention policies which were being systematically applied hit Kurdish and Zairean refugees in particular, while the response of the courts was generally unfavourable. In fact, the number of asylum cases being litigated in the High Court, representing mainly Tamils and Kurds, was becoming increasingly politicised as the Home Office resented being obstructed in its aim of removing or detaining applicants, while judges themselves reacted against Asian and African refugees. By the early 1990s, there was also a considerable number of cases being built up by the Home Office, while applicants were placed in detention or were granted the precarious status of temporary admission. The case loads in the Home Office and the courts became primary considerations in the design of legislation in the 1990s.

Meanwhile, European harmonisation of asylum laws was proceeding upon two main considerations: the removal of barriers to the further settlement of Europeans and the prevention of further settlement of non-Europeans. While the initial spur to harmonising laws and practices on asylum centred around the settlement of Tamils, it was extended to controlling the movement of other refugee groups as well, and tended to justify and guarantee the restrictive policies of some States in Europe, notably Britain and Germany. The provisions of the Dublin and Schengen Conventions on asylum seeking provided for the quick removal of refugees who could be identified as having the slightest connection with another European State, but the 1992 Edinburgh Ministerial Conclusions showed that priority was to be given to finding States outside the European Community to which expulsion could be realised. Other aspects of harmonisation have justified the use of restrictive interpretations of refugee status and procedural devices to reject claims as quickly as possible. More recent departures include the targeting of migration flows as a matter of European Union foreign policy, or UNHCR policy, requiring intervention in third States to obstruct the possibility of migration to Europe or the West. Further, plans have been set in motion to end European countries' adherence to the 1951 Refugee Convention and its 1967 Protocol, with the likelihood that asylum seekers will be subject even more completely to the discretion of State officials in future.

A repatriation focused formula was incorporated in the Asylum and Immigration Appeals Act 1993, the accompanying Procedure Rules and the Immigration Rules. The Home Office then began to reject a huge number of claims outright, forcing applicants into the new appeals framework also introduced by the 1993 Act, and which necessitated their dependency on lawyers and State funded advice agencies. Experience of the appeals system has not been friendly and refugees were treated with suspicion, forcing many to resort to the courts. While this latter avenue may have led to some relief by way of gaining time, the reaction of the courts, which have endorsed the government plan of fast tracking appeals, has also been generally hostile. With the build up of further cases at the Home Office and continued resort to the courts, further changes were enacted in the Asylum and Immigration Act 1996, in order to fast track more cases, to deprive many refugees of State welfare benefits and public housing, and to introduce measures to further criminalise asylum seeking. Large scale expulsions, detentions and the mass creation of legally insecure statuses have become established features of refugee policy in the UK. Refugees are thus left as a marginalised class of people, without access to legal employment. With the Immigration and Asylum Act 1999, these features are strengthened. The 1999 Act also institutionalises a dispersal strategy of the kind already attempted in the case of the Ugandan Asians and the Vietnamese. Recent refugee policy in the UK has therefore reacted with authoritarian force against the settlement of Asian and African and Latin American refugees, and represents a high point of institutionalised racism against them. By marginalising non-Europeans in these ways, the British legal system continues to draw upon the firmly founded historical tradition of hostility against them, and sets its face against the de facto multiculturalisation of society.

BIBLIOGRAPHY

Adams, C (ed) (1987), *Across Seven Seas and Thirteen Rivers: Life Stories of Pioneer Syhetti Settlers in Britain*, London: Tower Hamlets Arts Project

Adam, HM and Ford, R (eds), *Mending Rips in the Sky: Options for Somali Communities in the 21st Century*, Lawrenceville, Asmara, Eritrea: Red Sea

Aga Khan III (1954), *The Memoirs of the Aga Khan: World Enough and Time*, London: Cassell

Aga Khan, S (1976), 'Legal problems relating to refugees and displaced persons', 149 *Hague Receuil*, pp 287–352

Aleinikoff, TA (1995), 'State-centred refugee law: from resettlement to containment', in Daniel, E and Knudsen, J (eds), *Mistrusting Refugees*, Berkeley, California: California UP, pp 257–78

Al-Rasheed, M (1994), 'The myth of return: Iraqi Arab and Assyrian refugees in London', 7(2/3) *Journal of Refugee Studies*, pp 199–219

Anker, D (1989), '*INS v Cardoza Fonseca*, one year later: discretion, credibility and political opinion', in Lydio, FT (ed), *In Defense of the Alien*, New York: Centre for Migration Studies, pp 120–30

Anwar, M (1979), *Pakistanis in Britain*, London: Heinemann

Aronsfeld, CC (1962), 'German Jews in Victorian England', in VII *Leo Baeck Institute Yearbook*, pp 312–29

Ashford, Mark (1993), *Detained Without Trial: A Survey of Immigration Act Detention*, London: JCWI

Asylum Aid (1995a), *No Reason at All*, London: Asylum Aid

Asylum Aid (1995b), *Adding Insult to Injury: Experiences of Zairean Refugees in the UK*, London: Asylum Aid

Asylum Aid (1999), *Still No Reason at All: Home Office Decisions on Asylum*, London: Asylum Aid

'Asylum in Europe' (1985), *Refugees*, July, pp 19–28

Asylum Rights Campaign (1996), *'The Risks of Getting it Wrong': The Asylum and Immigration Bill Session 1995–96 and the Determinations of Special Adjudicators*, London: ARC

Bailey, BA (1989), 'Conflicting trends in Western European refugee policies', in Nanda, VP (ed), *Refugee Law and Policy*, Westport, Connecticut: Greenwood, pp 55–64

Ballard, R (1994), *Desh Pardesh: The South Asian Presence in Britain*, London: Hurst

Bamber, D (2000), '3,000 Kosovars to seek asylum', *The Sunday Telegraph*, 26 March

Banham, D (1994), 'Anglo-Saxon attitudes: in search of the origins of English racism', 1(2) *European Review of History*, pp 143–56

Beloff, M (1995), 'Judicial review – 2001: a prophetic odyssey', 58(2) *Modern Law Review*, pp 143–59

Berkowitz, NP (1999), 'Employer sanctions and their impact on asylum seekers', in Shah, P and Doebbler, CF (1999), *United Kingdom Asylum Law in its European Context*, 1999, London: Platinium and Group for Ethnic Minority Studies, pp 114–29

Bevan, V (1986), *The Development of British Immigration Law*, London: Croom Helm

Bhabha, J and Shutter, S (1994), *Women's Movement: Women Under Immigration, Nationality and Refugee Law*, Stoke on Trent: Trentham

Bindoff, ST (1950), *Tudor England*, Harmondsworth: Penguin

Blake, C (1983), Case note on *Enwia and Others; AS v IAT, Journal of Social Welfare Law*, pp 303–04

Blake, C (1984), 'Recent developments in immigration law', *Legal Action*, pp 21–23

Blake, N (1988), 'The road to Sivakumaran', 3(1) *Immigration and Nationality Law and Practice*, pp 12–16

Blake, N (1990), 'Life after the Lords: developments in the case of *Sivakumaran and Others*', 4(1) *Immigration and Nationality Law and Practice*, pp 7–11

Boccardi, I (1993), *Towards a Common Asylum Policy: Options after Maastricht*, unpublished MA dissertation, Bruges: College of Europe

Bolten, JJ (1991), 'From Schengen to Dublin: the new frontiers of refugee law', *Nederlands Juristenblad*, 31 January, pp 165–78

Bridges, L, Mészáros, G and Sunkin, M (1995), *Judicial Review in Perspective*, London: Cavendish Publishing

Bristow, M (1976), 'Britain's response to the Uganda Asian crisis: government myths versus political and resettlement realities', 5(3) *New Community*, pp 265–79

Burgess, D (1991), 'Asylum by ordeal', *New Law Journal*, 18 January, pp 50–52

Burleston, L (1993), 'The State, internment and public criticism in the Second World War', in Cesarani, D and Kushner, T (eds), *The Internment of Aliens in 20th Century Britain*, London: Frank Cass, pp 102–24

Burrell, I (1998), 'Race relations "damaged by outcry over asylum seekers"', *The Independent*, 11 December

Busch, N (1999–2000) 'Fortress Europe', *Peace News*, December 1999–February 2000, pp 20–22

Bye, E (1999), 'Passport offenders following the *Adimi* case', 13(4) *Immigration and Nationality Law and Practice*, pp 136–38

Care, G (1998), 'Working with the asylum regime: an adjudicator's perspective', in Nicholson, F and Twomey, P (eds), *Current Issues of UK Asylum Law and Policy*, Aldershot: Ashgate, pp 158–75

Carro, JL (1986), 'Sanctuary: the response of an age old right or a dangerous misinterpretation of an abandoned ancient privilege?', 54 *Cincinnati Law Review*, pp 747–78

Carsten, FL (1984), 'German refugees in Great Britain 1933–45', in Hirschfeld, G (ed), *Exile in Great Britain*, Leamington Spa: Berg, pp 11–28

Castles, S, Booth, H and Wallace, T (1985), *Here for Good: Western Europe's Ethnic Minorities*, London: Pluto

Cesarani, D (1989), 'An embattled minority: the Jews in Britain during the First World War', 8(1/2) *Immigrants and Minorities*, pp 61–68

Cesarani, D (1993), 'An alien concept? The continuity of anti-alienism in British society before 1940', in Cesarani, D and Kushner, T (eds), *The Internment of Aliens in 20th Century Britain*, London: Frank Cass, pp 25–52

Chaudhuri, KN (1990), *Asia Before Europe: Economy and Civilisation of the Indian Ocean from the Rise of Islam to 1750*, Cambridge: CUP

Cheney, D (1993), 'Valued judgments? A reading of immigration cases', 20 *Journal of Legal Studies*, pp 23–38

Chimni, BS (1993), 'The meaning of words and the role of UNHCR in voluntary repatriation', 5(3) *International Journal of Refugee Law*, pp 442–60

Chitty, CW (1966), 'Aliens in England in the 16th century', VIII(2) *Race*, pp 129–45

Çiçekli, B (1998), *The Legal Position of Turkish Immigrants in the European Union*, Ankara: Karmap

Cohen, R (1989), The detention of asylum seekers in the UK, in Joly, D and Cohen, R (eds), *Reluctant Hosts: Europe and its Refugees*, Aldershot: Avebury, pp 145–61

Cohen, R (1994), *Frontiers of Identity: The British and the Others*, London: Longman

Cohen, R (1996), 'Review of Sherman, AJ (1995), *Island Refuge: Britain and Refugees from the Third Reich, 1933–39*, London: Frank Cass', 9(1) *Journal of Refugee Studies*, pp 107–08

Coles, G (1989), 'Approaching the refugee problem today', in Loescher, G and Monahan, L (eds), *Refugees and International Relations*, Oxford: OUP, pp 373–410

Collinson, S (1993), *Europe and International Migration*, London: Pinter

Commission for Racial Equality (1985), *Immigration Control Procedures: Report of a Formal Investigation*, London: Commission for Racial Equality

Connelly, M (1984), 'Refugees and the UK', 168 *Race and Immigration*, June, pp 8–16

Connelly, M (1985), 'A life of fear', *Amnesty*, August–September, pp 14–15

Cottle, TJ (1978), *Black Testimony: The Voices of Britain's West Indians*, London: Wildwood House

Craies, WF (1890), 'The right of aliens to enter British territory', 6 *Law Quarterly Review*, pp 27–41

Cruz, A (1995), *Shifting Responsibility: Carriers' Liability Laws in the Member States of the European Union and North America*, Stoke on Trent: Trentham and Group for Ethnic Minority Studies, School of Oriental and African Studies

Dalglish, C (1989), *Refugees from Vietnam*, London: Macmillan

Daniel, EV and Thangaraj, Y (1995), 'Forms, formations, and transformations of the Tamil refugee', in Daniel, EV and Knudsen, J (eds), *Mistrusting Refugees*, Berkeley, California: California UP, pp 225–56

Deakin, N (1969), 'The British Nationality Act of 1948: a brief study in the political mythology of race relations', XI(1) *Race*, pp 77–83

Dean, D (1993), 'The Conservative Government and the 1961 Commonwealth Immigration Act: the inside story', 35(2) *Race and Class*, October–December, pp 57–74

De Hart, EL (1886), 'The extradition of political offenders', 2 *Law Quarterly Review*, pp 177–87

De Jong, CD (1993), 'Co-operation in the field of aliens law; the granting of visas, passports and asylum and refugee status', in Schermers HG, Flinterman, C, Kellerman, AE, van Haersolte, JC and van de Meent, GA (eds), *Free Movement of Persons in Europe*, Dordrecht: Martinus Nijhoff, pp 183–98

Desai, R (1963), *Indian Immigrants in Britain*, Oxford: OUP

De Zwaan, JW (1993), 'Institutional problems and free movement of persons: the legal and political framework for co-operation', in Schermers HG, Flinterman, C, Kellerman, AE, van Haersolte, JC and van de Meent, GA (eds), *Free Movement of Persons in Europe*, Dordrecht: Martinus Nijhoff, pp 335–51

Dicey, AV (1915), *Introduction to the Study of the Law of the Constitution*, 8th edn, London: Macmillan

Dines, M (1973), 'Cool reception', II(4) *New Community*, pp 380–83

Dinnerstein, L and Reimers, DM (1988), *Ethnic Americans: A History of Immigration*, 3rd edn, New York: Harper & Row

Dirks, GE (1977), *Canada's Refugee Policy: Indifference or Opportunism?*, Montreal: McGill-Queen's UP

Dodd, V (2000), 'Dover, no port in a storm for refugees', *The Guardian*, 28 March

D'Orey, S (1984), *Immigration Prisoners: A Forgotten Minority*, London: Runnymede Trust

Drabu, K and Bowen, S (1989), *Mandatory Visas: Visiting the UK from Bangladesh, India, Pakistan, Ghana and Nigeria*, London: Commission for Racial Equality

Drzemczewski, A (1978), 'A "non-decision" of the Committee of Ministers under Art 32(1) of the European Convention on Human Rights: the East African Asians cases', 41 *Modern Law Review*, pp 337–42

D'Oliveira, HUJ (1993), 'Fortress Europe and (extra-communitarian) refugees: co-operation in sealing off the external borders', in Schermers, HG, Flinterman, C, Kellerman, AE, van Haersolte, JC and van de Meent, GA (eds), *Free Movement of Persons in Europe*, Dordrecht: Martinus Nijhoff, pp 166–82

D'Souza, F (1980), *The Refugee Dilemma: International Recognition and Acceptance*, London: Minority Rights Group

Dummett, A and Nicol, A (1990), *Subjects, Citizens, Aliens and Others: Nationality and Immigration Law*, London: Weidenfeld & Nicolson

Dunstan, R (1998a), 'A case of ministers behaving badly: the Asylum and Immigration Act 1996', in Nicholson, F and Twomey, P (eds), *Current Issues of UK Asylum Law and Policy*, Aldershot: Ashgate, pp 52–72

Dunstan, R (1998b), 'United Kingdom: breach of Art 31 of the 1951 Refugee Convention', 10(1/2) *International Journal of Refugee Law*, pp 205–13

El-Solh, CF (1991), 'Somalis in London's East End: a community striving for recognition', 17(4) *New Community*, pp 539–52

Ephimenco, S (1985), 'Sri Lankan Tamils: a parliamentary debate', *Refugees*, July, pp 36–37

Farah, N (2000), *Yesterday, Tomorrow: Voices from the Somali Diaspora*, London: Cassell

Feria, M (1996), 'Commentaries on the Social Security (Persons from Abroad) Miscellaneous Amendments Regulations 1996', 10(3) *Immigration and Nationality Law and Practice*, pp 93–100

Fernhout, R and Meijers, H (1993), 'Asylum', in *A New Immigration Law for Europe? The 1992 London and 1993 Copenhagen Rules on Immigration*, Utrecht: Nederlands Centrum Buitenlanders & Standing Committee of Experts in International Immigration, Refugee and Criminal Law, pp 8–24

Ferris, EG (1993), *Beyond Borders: Refugees, Migrants and Human Rights in the Post-Cold War Era*, Geneva: WCC

Findlay, A (1996), 'Extra-Union migration: the South-North perspective', in Rees, P, Stillwell, J, Convey, A and Kupiszewski, M (eds), *Population Migration in the European Union*, Chichester: John Wiley, pp 39–50

Ford, R (2000), 'Ministers nervous as asylum alarm grows', *The Times*, 15 March

Fortin, C (1978), *Third World Political Refugees in the United Kingdom*, Institute of Development Studies and World University Service

Fox, JP (1984), 'Nazi Germany and German emigration to Great Britain', in Hirschfeld, G (ed), *Exile in Great Britain*, Leamington Spa: Berg, pp 29–62

Frank, IL (1977), 'Effect of the 1967 United Nations Protocol on the Status of Refugees in the United States', 11 *International Lawyer*, pp 291–305

Fransman, L (1989), *Fransman's British Nationality Law*, London: Fourmat

Fraser, A (1992), *The Gypsies*, Oxford: Blackwells

Fraser, CF (1940), *Control of Aliens in the British Commonwealth of Nations*, London: Hogarth

Fryer, P (1984), *Staying Power: The History of Black People in Britain*, London: Pluto

Fullerton, M (1988), 'Restricting the flow of asylum seekers in Belgium, Denmark, the Federal Republic of Germany and the Netherlands: new challenges to the Geneva Convention Relating to the Status of Refugees and the European Convention on Human Rights', 29 *Virginia Journal of International Law*, pp 33–114

Füredi, F (1998), *The Silent War: Imperialism and the Changing Perception of Race*, London: Pluto

Gainer, B (1972), *The Alien Invasion: The Origins of the Aliens Act of 1905*, London: Heinemann

Garrard, JA (1971), *The English and Immigration 1880–1910*, Oxford: OUP

Gartner, LP (1973), *The Jewish Immigrant in England*, 1870–1914, 2nd edn, London: Simon

George, V and Millerson, G (1966), 'The Cypriot community in London', VIII(3) *Race*, pp 277–92

Ghai, YP and Ghai, D (1971), *The Asian Minorities of East and Central Africa*, London: Minority Rights Group

Ghai, YP (1973) 67 *Proceedings of the American Society of International Law*, p 123

Gilbert, G (1994), 'Tackling the causes of refugee flows', in Spencer, S (ed), *Strangers and Citizens: A Positive Approach to Migrants and Refugees*, London: Institute for Public Policy Research and Rivers Oram, pp 18–43

Gillan, A (2000), 'Glasgow chill wind is better than home', *The Guardian*, 29 March

Gillespie, J (1996), 'Asylum and Immigration Act 1996: an outline of the new law', 10(3) *Immigration and Nationality Law and Practice*, pp 86–90

Gilroy, P (1993), *Small Acts: Thoughts on the Politics of Black Cultures*, London: Serpent's Tail

The Glidewell Panel (1996), *The Report from an Independent Enquiry into the Implications and Effects of the Asylum and Immigration Bill 1995 and Related Social Security Measures*, 16 April

Goodwin-Gill, GS (1983), *The Refugee in International Law*, Oxford: Clarendon

Goodwin-Gill, GS (1996), *The Refugee in International Law*, 2nd edn, Oxford: Clarendon

Goodwin-Gill, GS (1999), 'Refugee identity and protection's fading prospect', in Nicholson, F and Twomey, P (eds), *Refugee Rights and Realities: Evolving International Concepts and Regimes*, Cambridge: CUP, pp 220–49

Grahl-Madsen, A (1966), *The Status of Refugees in International Law, Vol I: Refugee Character*, Leiden: AW Sijthoff

Grahl-Madsen, A (1972), *The Status of Refugees in International Law, Vol II: Asylum, Entry and Sojourn*, Leiden: AW Sijthoff

Grahl-Madsen, A (1980), *Territorial Asylum*, Stockholm: Almqvist & Wiksell International

Grahl-Madsen, A (1982), 'International refugee law today and tomorrow', 20 *Archiv des Voelkerrechts*, pp 411–67

Grant, L and Martin, I (1982), *Immigration Law and Practice*, London: Cobden Trust

Grenier, M (1995), *Beyond Belief: The Home Office and Nigeria*, London: Refugee Council

Grenier, M (1996), *The State of Asylum: A Critique of Asylum Policy in the UK*, London: Refugee Council

Grenier, M (1997), *Protection Denied: Sri Lankan Tamils, the Home Office and the Forgotten War*, London: Refugee Council

Guest, I and Keel, P (1985), 'Tamils "are not genuine refugees"', *The Guardian*, 31 May

Guild, E and Martin, D (1996), *Free Movement of Persons in the European Union*, London: Butterworths

Guild, E (1993), 'Towards an European asylum law: developments in the European Community', 7(3) *Immigration and Nationality Law and Practice*, pp 88–92

Gurung, M (1992), 'New Bill means added misery for oppressed', 65 *Leicester Rights Bulletin*, November–December 1992, pp 7–11

Hammar, T (ed) (1985), *European Immigration Policy: A Comparative Study*, Cambridge: CUP

Harlow, C and Rawlings, R (1984), *Law and Administration*, London: Weidenfeld & Nicolson

Hartley Booth, VE (1980), *British Extradition Law and Procedure*, Alphen aan den Rijn, the Netherlands: Sijthoff & Noordhoff, 2 vols

Hartley, TC (1978), *EEC Immigration Law*, Oxford: North-Holland

Hartley, TC (1980), 'The new immigration rules', 43 *Modern Law Review*, pp 440–44

Harvey, A (1998), 'Researching "The risks of getting it wrong"', in Nicholson, F and Twomey, P (eds), *Current Issues of UK Asylum Law and Policy*, Aldershot: Ashgate, pp 176–97

Hathaway, JC (1990), 'A reconsideration of the underlying premise of refugee law', 31(1) *Harvard International Law Journal*, pp 129–83

Hathaway, JC (1991), *The Law of Refugee Status*, Toronto: Butterworths

Hawkins, F (1989), *Critical Years in Immigration: Canada and Australia Compared*, Montreal: McGill-Queen's UP

Haycraft, TW (1897), 'Alien legislation and the prerogative of the Crown', 13 *Law Quarterly Review*, pp 165–86

Helweg, AW (1979), *Sikhs in England: The Development of a Migrant Community*, Delhi: OUP

Henriques, HSQ (1906), *The Law of Aliens and Naturalisation*, London: Butterworths

Hensman, R (1993), *Journey Without a Destination: Is There a Solution for Sri Lankan Refugees?*, London: Refugee Council

Hiro, D (1991), *Black British, White British: a History of Race Relations in Britain*, 2nd edn, London: Grafton

Holborn, LW (1938), 'The legal status of political refugees, 1920–38', 32 *American Journal of International Law*, pp 680–703

Holborn, LW (1956), *The International Refugee Organisation. A Specialised Agency of the United Nations: Its History and its Work 1946–52*, Oxford: OUP

Holborn, LW (1975), *Refugees – a Problem of Our Time: The Work of the United Nations High Commissioner for Refugees: 1951–72*, Metuchen, New Jersey: Scarecrow, 2 vols

Holdsworth, WS (1938), *A History of English Law*, Boston: Little, Brown, vol 10

Holmes, C (1980), 'The German-gypsy question in Britain, 1904–06', in Lunn, K (ed), *Hosts, Immigrants and Minorities: Historical Responses to Newcomers in British Society, 1870–1914*, Folkestone, Kent: WM Dawson & Sons, pp 134–59

Holmes, C (1988), *John Bull's Island: Immigration and British Society, 1871–1971*, London: Macmillan

Hondius, FW (1993), 'The last frontier: movement of persons in Greater Europe. The role of the Council of Europe', in Schermers, HG, Flinterman, C, Kellerman, AE, van Haersolte, JC and van de Meent, GA (eds), *Free Movement of Persons in Europe*, Dordrecht: Martinus Nijhoff, pp 154–65

Hoole, R (1993), 'Tamil refugees in Sri Lanka and the West', *Tamil Times*, 15 July, Pt 1, pp 16–18 and 15 August, Pt 2, pp 16–18

Home Office (1997), *Asylum Statistics: United Kingdom 1996*, London: Home Office Research and Statistics Directorate

Howell, RC (1987), *The Royal Navy and the Slave Trade*, London: Croom Helm

Humphry, D and Ward, M (1974), *Passports and Politics*, Harmondsworth: Penguin

International Commission of Jurists (1968), 'United Kingdom: second class citizens', 34 *The Bulletin*, p 1

Independent Commission on International Humanitarian Issues (1986), *Refugees: The Dynamics of Displacement*, London: Zed

Jackson, D (1996), *Immigration: Law and Practice*, London: Sweet & Maxwell

Jagmohan, J (1996), *The Short Procedure: An Analysis of the Home Office Scheme for Rapid Initial Decisions in Asylum Cases*, London: Asylum Rights Campaign

James, W and Harris, C (eds) (1993), *Inside Babylon: The Caribbean Diaspora in Britain*, London: Verso

Jeffery, P (1976), *Migrants and Refugees: Muslim and Christian Families in Bristol*, Cambridge: CUP

JCWI (1976), *Annual Report 1975–76*, London: JCWI

JCWI (1979), *Annual Report 1978–79*, London: JCWI

JCWI (1984), *Annual Report 1983–84*, London: JCWI

JCWI (1985), *Annual Report 1984–85*, London: JCWI

JCWI (1986), *Annual Report 1985–86*, London: JCWI

JCWI (1987a), *Annual Report 1986–87*, London: JCWI

JCWI (1987b), *Out of Sight: The New Visit Visa System*, London: JCWI

JCWI (1989), *Annual Report 1988–89*, London: JCWI

JCWI (1993), *Annual Report and Policy Review 1992–93*, London: JCWI

JCWI (1997), *Annual Report and Policy Review 1997*, London: JCWI

Jones, R and Welhengama, G (2000), *Ethnic Minorities in English Law*, Stoke on Trent: Trentham

Juss, SS (1993), *Immigration, Nationality and Citizenship*, London: Mansell

Justice, Immigration Law Practitioners' Association and Asylum Rights Campaign (1997), *Providing Protection. Towards Fair and Effective Asylum Procedures*, London: Justice, Immigration Law Practitioners' Association and Asylum Rights Campaign

Kadish, S (1992), *Bolsheviks and the British Jews: The Anglo-Jewish Community, Britain and the Russian Revolution*, London: Frank Cass

Katsapaou, C (1997), 'Refugee Kurds from Turkey: an analysis of the Secretary of State's refusal of asylum', 11(4) *Immigration and Nationality Law and Practice*, pp 124–26

Kaye, R (1992), 'British refugee policy and 1992: the breakdown of a policy community', 5(1) *Journal of Refugee Studies*, pp 47–67

Kenrick, D and Puxon, G (1972), *The Destiny of Europe's Gypsies*, London: Heinemann

Khan, VS (1977), 'The Pakistanis: Mirpuri villagers at home and in Bradford', in Watson, JL (ed), *Between Two Cultures: Migrants and Minorities in Britain*, Oxford: Blackwells, pp 57–89

Kimball, A (1973), 'The harassment of Russian revolutionaries abroad: the London trial of Vladimir Burtsev in 1898', VI *Oxford Slavonic Papers*, pp 48–65

King, M (1993), 'The impact of Western European border policies on the control of "refugees" in Eastern and Central Europe', 19(2) *New Community*, pp 183–99

Kochan, M (1993), 'Women's experience of internment', in Cesarani, D and Kushner, T (eds), *The Internment of Aliens in 20th Century Britain*, London: Frank Cass, pp 147–66

Kochavi, A (1991), 'British policy on non-repatriable displaced persons in Germany and Austria, 1945–47', 21 *European History Quarterly*, pp 365–82

Krajewski, M and Rittsteig, H (1996), 'German nationality law', in Nascimbene, B (ed), *Nationality Laws in the European Union*, London: Butterworths and Milan: Giuffre Editore, pp 357–85

Kruijtbosch, EDJ (1993), 'Benelux experiences in the abolition of border controls', in Schermers HG, Flinterman, C, Kellerman, AE, van Haersolte, JC and van de Meent, GA (eds), *Free Movement of Persons in Europe*, Dordrecht: Martinus Nijhoff, pp 31–39

Kushner, T (1993), 'Clubland, cricket tests and alien internment', in Cesarani, D and Kushner, T (eds), *The Internment of Aliens in 20th Century Britain*, pp 79–101

Landa, MJ (1911), *The Alien Problem and its Remedy*, London: PS King

Lane, AJ (1992), 'Putting Britain right with Tito: the displaced persons question in Anglo-Yugoslav relations 1946–47', 22(2) *European History Quarterly*, pp 217–46

Lane, T (1994), 'The political imperatives of bureaucracy and empire: the case of the Coloured Alien Seamen Order 1925', 13(2/3) *Immigrants and Minorities*, pp 104–29

Lauterpacht, H (1948), 'The Universal Declaration of Human Rights', 25 *British Yearbook of International Law*, pp 354–81

Lavenex, S (1999), *Safe Third Countries: Extending the EU Asylum and Immigration Policies to Central and Eastern Europe*, Budapest: Central European UP

Lawyers Committee for Human Rights (1991), *The UNHCR at 40: Refugee Protection at the Crossroads*, New York: Lawyers Committee for Human Rights

Layton-Henry, Z (1992), *The Politics of Immigration*, Oxford: Blackwells

Lipman, VD (1990), *A History of the Jews in Britain Since 1858*, Leicester: Leicester UP

Lloyd Jones, D (1979), 'The role of habeas corpus in immigration cases', 95 *Law Quarterly Review*, pp 171–74

Loescher, G (1993), *Beyond Charity. International Co-operation and the Global Refugee Crisis*, Oxford: OUP

Loescher, G and Scanlan, JA (1986), *Calculated Kindness: Refugees and America's Half Open Door, 1945 to the Present*, New York: Free Press and London: Collier Macmillan

London, L (1989), 'British government policy and Jewish refugees', 23(4) *Patterns of Prejudice*, pp 26–43

London, L (1990), 'Jewish refugees, Anglo-Jewry and British government policy, 1930–40', in Cesarani, D (ed), *The Making of Modern Anglo-Jewry*, Oxford: Blackwells, pp 163–90

London, L (1991), 'British immigration control procedures and Jewish refugees', in Mosse, WE (ed), *Second Chance: Two Centuries of German Speaking Jews in the United Kingdom*, Tübingen: Mohr, pp 485–517

Macdonald, IA (1972), *The New Immigration Law*, London: Butterworths

Macdonald, IA (1983), *Immigration Law and Practice in the United Kingdom*, London: Butterworths

Macdonald, IA (1987a), *Immigration Law and Practice in the United Kingdom*, 2nd edn, London: Butterworths

Macdonald, IA (1987b), 'The growth and development of modern immigration law', 2(3) *Immigration and Nationality Law and Practice*, pp 54–59

Macdonald, IA and Blake, NJ (1991), *Immigration Law and Practice in the United Kingdom*, 3rd edn, London: Butterworths

Macdonald, IA and Blake, NJ (1995), *Immigration Law and Practice in the United Kingdom*, 4th edn, London: Butterworths

McDowall, R (1989), 'Co-ordination of refugee policy in Europe', in Loescher, G and Monahan, L (eds), *Refugees and International Relations*, Oxford: OUP, pp 179–86

McDowell, C (1996), *A Tamil Asylum Diaspora: Sri Lankan Migration, Settlement and Politics in Switzerland*, Oxford: Berghahn

McGrory, D (1998), 'Kenyan woman's claim "could open door for millions"', *The Times*, 12 December

McGuire, K (1999), '"No Entry" – a critical reading of the Asylum and Immigration Act 1996', in Shah, P and Doebbler, CF (eds), *United Kingdom Asylum Law in its European Context*, 1999, London: Platinium and Group for Ethnic Minority Studies, pp 66–74

McKee, R (1996), 'The Asylum Appeals (Procedure) Rules 1996 – a survey of the main changes and their likely effects', 10(4) *Immigration and Nationality Law and Practice*, pp 136–38

McKee, R (1997), 'A survey of some recent tribunal determinations in asylum cases', 11(3) *Immigration and Nationality Law and Practice*, pp 79–86

McKee, R (1999), 'Safe third countries', in Shah, P and Doebbler, CF (eds), *United Kingdom Asylum Law in its European Context*, London: Platinium and Group for Ethnic Minority Studies, pp 103–13

McNair (Lord) and Watts, AD (1966), *The Legal Effects of War*, Cambridge: CUP

Mamdani, M (1983), *Imperialism and Fascism in Uganda*, London: Heinemann

Manson, E (1902), 'The admission of aliens', VI(1) *Journal of the Society of Comparative Legislation*, pp 114–27

Marshall, B (1996), *British and German Refugee Policies in the European Context*, London: Royal Institute of International Affairs

Mattausch, J (1998), 'From subjects to citizens: British "East African Asians"', 24(1) *Journal of Ethnic and Migration Studies*, pp 121–41

May, TE (1878), *Constitutional History of England*, London: Longmans, Green, 3 vols

Mayall, D (1988), *Gypsy Travellers in 19th Century Society*, Cambridge: CUP

Menski, W (ed) (1995), *Coping with 1997: The Reaction of the Hong Kong People to the Transfer of Power*, Stoke on Trent: Trentham and Group for Ethnic Minority Studies, School of Oriental and African Studies

Modood, T (1992), *Not Easy Being British: Colour, Culture and Citizenship*, Stoke on Trent: Trentham

Mongia, RV (1999), 'Race, nationality, mobility: a history of the passport', 11(3) *Public Culture*, pp 527–55

Moore, R and Wallace, T (1975), *Slamming the Door: The Administration of Immigration Control*, London: Martin Robertson

Morgenstern, F (1949), 'The right of asylum', 26 *British Yearbook of International Law*, pp 327–57

Mortimer, E (1997), 'The treatment of refugees and asylum seekers: an essay on a Ditchley Foundation conference held at Ditchley Park, Oxfordshire, UK, 27–29 September 1996', 10(2) *Journal of Refugee Studies*, pp 199–207

Murray, AL (1962), 'The extradition of fugitive slaves from Canada: a re-evaluation', XLIII *Canadian Historical Review*, pp 298–314

Murtagh, P (1987), 'Hurd forced to back down on asylum Tamils', *The Guardian*, 3 March

Nadelhaft, J (1967), 'The Somersett case and slavery: myth, reality and repercussions', 52 *Journal of Negro History*, pp 193–208

Nanda, VP (ed) (1989), *Refugee Law and Policy*, Westport, Connecticut: Greenwood

Ng, KC (1968), *The Chinese in London*, Oxford: OUP

Oliver, B (1966), *The British Red Cross*, London: Faber & Faber

Owers, A and Shutter, S (1984), 'MPs and immigration cases', *Legal Action*, January, pp 7–8

Panayi, P (1993), 'An intolerant act by an intolerant society: the internment of Germans in Britain during the First World War', in Cesarani, D and Kushner, T (eds), *The Internment of Aliens in 20th Century Britain*, London: Frank Cass, pp 53–75

Parry, C (1957), *Nationality and Citizenship of the Commonwealth and of the Republic of Ireland*, London: Stevens

Patterson, S (1978), 'The Poles: an exile community in Britain', in Watson, JL (ed), *Between Two Cultures: Migrants and Minorities in Britain*, Oxford: Blackwells, pp 214–41

Paul, K (1997), *Whitewashing Britain: Race and Citizenship in the Post-War Era, London*: Cornell UP

Payne, HC and Grosshans, H (1963), 'The exiled revolutionaries and the French political police in the 1850s', 68 *American Historical Review*, pp 954–73

Pearl, D and Menski, W (1998), *Muslim Family Law*, 3rd edn, London: Sweet & Maxwell

Pellew, J (1982), *The Home Office 1848–1914: From Clerks to Bureaucrats*, London: Heinemann

Pfeiffer, NP (1988), 'Credibility findings in INS asylum adjudications: a realistic assessment', 23 *Texas International Law Journal*, pp 139–51

Philips, R (1994), 'Self-determination in Western melting pots', *Tamil Times*, 15 May, pp 11–14

Phillips, M (1987), 'Why the Tamils are the last straw', *The Guardian*, 4 September

Plaut, WG (1995), *Asylum: A Moral Dilemma*, 1995, Westport, Connecticut: Praeger

Plender, R (1971), 'The exodus of Asians from East and Central Africa: some comparative and international law aspects', XIX *American Journal of International Law*, pp 287–324

Plender, R (1972), 'The expulsion of Asians from Uganda: legal aspects', 1(5) *New Community*, pp 420–27

Plender, R (1988), *International Migration Law*, 2nd edn, Dordrecht: Martinus Nijhoff

Porter, B (1979), *The Refugee Question in Mid-Victorian Politics*, Cambridge: CUP

Porter, B (1980), 'The *Freiheit* prosecutions, 1881–82', 23(4) *The Historical Journal*, pp 833–56

Porter, B (1983), 'The British Government and political refugees c 1898–1914', in Slatter, J (ed), *From the Other Shore: Russian Political Emigrants in Britain, 1880–1917*, London: Cass, pp 23–45

Porter, B (1987), *The Origins of the Vigilant State: The London Metropolitan Police Special Branch Before the First World War*, London: Weidenfeld & Nicolson

Qureshi, S (1988), 'Opening the floodgates? Eligibility for asylum in the USA. and the UK', *Anglo-American Law Review*, pp 83–107

Ramdin, R (1999), *Reimaging Britain: 500 Years of Black and Asian History*, London: Pluto

Randall, C (1994), 'An asylum policy for the UK', in Spencer, S (ed), *Strangers and Citizens: A Positive Approach to Migrants and Refugees*, London: Institute for Public Policy Research and Rivers Oram, pp 202–31

Refugee Legal Centre (1996), *Annual Report April 1995–March 1996*, London: Refugee Legal Centre

Refugee Legal Centre (1997a), *Annual Report 1996–97*, London: Refugee Legal Centre

Refugee Legal Centre (1997b), *Reviewing the Asylum Determination Procedure: A Casework Study*, London: Refugee Legal Centre

Richmond, AH (1994), *Global Apartheid: Refugee, Racism and the New World Order*, Oxford: OUP

Robertson, AH (1973), *European Institutions: Co-operation, Integration, Unification*, London: Stevens and New York: Matthew Binder

Robinson, N (1953), *Convention Relating to the Status of Refugees: A Commentary*, New York: Institute of Jewish Affairs

Robinson, V (1996), 'Redefining the front line: the geography of asylum seeking in the new Europe', in Rees, P, Stillwell, J, Convey, A and Kupiszewski, M (eds), *Population Migration in the European Union*, Chichester: John Wiley, pp 67–88

Roche, TWE (1969), *The Key in the Lock*, London: John Murray

Rodney, W (1982), *How Europe Underdeveloped Africa*, Washington, DC: Howard UP

Rose, D (1986), 'Tamils protest over "shuttle" of refugees', *The Guardian*, 5 March

Rose, D (1987), 'Home Office ignored court move by refugee', *The Guardian*, 6 January

Ruchames, L (1969), 'The sources of racial thought in colonial America', 52 *Journal of Negro History*, pp 251–72

Ruff, A (1989), 'The United Kingdom Immigration (Carriers' Liability) Act 1987: implications for refugees and airlines', 1 *International Journal of Refugee Law*, pp 481–500

Rufford, N (2000), 'Giant barracks to cut queues', *The Sunday Times*, 19 March

Ruth, E (1998), *'Give Them a Wash and Send the Gyppos Back': Walzer, Kymlicka, Concepts of the Foreigner, and the Experiences of Slovak Roma Under the New UK Asylum Procedures*, unpublished MA dissertation, Colchester: University of Essex

Sachdeva, S (1993), *The Primary Purpose Rule in British Immigration Law*, Stoke on Trent: Trentham and Group for Ethnic Minority Studies

Salomon, K (1991), *Refugees in the Cold War: Toward a New International Refugee Regime in the Early Post-War Era*, Lund: Lund UP

Saunders, D (1985), 'Aliens in Britain and the Empire during the First World War', 4(1) *Immigrants and Minorities*, March, pp 5–27

Scannell, R (1987), Case note on *R v Secretary of State for the Home Department ex p Sivakumaran and Others*, *Legal Action*, December, pp 17–19

Scannell, R (1989), 'Recent developments in immigration law', *Legal Action*, November, pp 17–19

Schermers, HG (1993), 'Human rights and the free movement of persons: the role of the European Commission and Court of Human Rights', in Schermers HG, Flinterman, C, Kellerman, AE, van Haersolte, JC and van de Meent, GA (eds), *Free Movement of Persons in Europe*, Dordrecht: Martinus Nijhoff, pp 235–47

Shah, P (1995a), 'Access to legal assistance for asylum seekers', 9(2) *Immigration and Nationality Law and Practice*, pp 55–58

Shah, P (1995b), 'British nationality and immigration laws and their effects on Hong Kong', in Menski, W (ed), *Coping with 1997: The Reaction of the Hong Kong People to the Transfer of Power*, Stoke on Trent: Trentham and Group for Ethnic Minority Studies, School of Oriental and African Studies, pp 57–119

Shah, P (1995c), 'Refugees and safe third countries: United Kingdom, European and international aspects', 1(2) *European Public Law*, pp 259–88

Shah, P (1998a), 'Rewriting the Refugee Convention: the Adan case in the House of Lords', 12(3) *Immigration and Nationality Law and Practice*, pp 100–04

Shah, P (1998b), 'Post-*Chahal*: the Special Immigration Appeals Commission', 12(2) *Immigration and Nationality Law and Practice*, pp 67–69

Shah, P (1999), 'Taking the political out of asylum: the legal containment of refugees' political activism', in Nicholson, F and Twomey, P (eds), *Refugee Rights and Realities: Evolving International Concepts and Regimes*, Cambridge: CUP, pp 119–35

Shah, RKD (1992a), 'Britain and Kenya: some immigration and nationality issues', 6(2) *Immigration and Nationality Law and Practice*, pp 35–39

Shah, RKD (1992b), 'Britain and Kenya's citizenship law: a conflict of laws?', 6(4) *Immigration and Nationality Law and Practice*, pp 120–25

Shearer, IA (1971), *Extradition in International Law*, Manchester: Manchester UP and Dobbs Ferry, New York: Oceana

Sherman, AJ (1995), *Island Refuge: Britain and Refugees from the Third Reich, 1933–39*, 2nd edn, London: Frank Cass

Sibley, NW and Elias, A (1906), *The Aliens Act and Right of Asylum*, London: William Clowes

Sjoberg, T (1991), *The Powers and the Persecuted: The Refugee Problem and the IGCR, 1938–47*, Lund: Lund UP

Smith, P (1993), 'Reducing legal aid eligibility criteria: the impact for immigration law practitioners and their clients', *Civil Justice Quarterly*, pp 167–87

Somerset, F (1983), 'Vietnamese refugees in Britain: resettlement experiences', 10 *New Community*, pp 454–63

Spencer, IRG (1996), 'Open door, labour needs and British immigration policy, 1945–55', 15(1) *Immigrants and Minorities*, pp 22–41

Spiro, B (1983), 'The role of the MP in immigration cases', *Legal Action Group Bulletin*, November, pp 137–38

Stadulis, E (1952), 'The resettlement of displaced persons in the United Kingdom', 5(3) *Population Studies*, pp 207–37

Stanbrook, I (1982), *British Nationality Law*, London: Clement

Stanbrook, I and Stanbrook, C (1980), *The Law and Practice of Extradition*, Chichester and London: Barry Rose and Justice of the Peace

Starkey, T (1997), *Black Liverpool: Law and Disorder*, unpublished LLB dissertation, London: School of Oriental and African Studies

Steel, D (1969), *No Entry: The Background and Implications of the Commonwealth Immigrants Act 1968*, London: C Hurst

Steen, A-B (1993), *Varieties of the Tamil Refugee Experience in Denmark and England*, Copenhagen: Minority Studies, University of Copenhagen and Danish Centre for Human Rights

Stevens, J (1992), *The Case Law of the European Convention on Human Rights Relating to Immigration, Asylum and Extradition*, London: Immigration Law Practitioners' Association and The Law Society

Storey, H (1997), 'United Kingdom case law on the "Internal Flight Alternative"', 11(2) *Immigration and Nationality Law and Practice*, pp 57–66

Sunkin, M, Bridges, L and Mészáros, G (1993a), 'Trends in judicial review', *Public Law*, pp 443–46

Sunkin, M, Bridges, L and Mészáros, G (1993b), *Judicial Review in Perspective: An Investigation of Trends in the Use and Operation of the Judicial Review Procedure in England and Wales*, London: The Public Law Project

Sunkin, M, Bridges, L and Mészáros, G (1996), *Judicial Review in Perspective*, 2nd edn, London: Cavendish Publishing

Supperstone, M (1983), *Immigration: The Law and Practice*, London: Oyez Longman

Sword, K, Davies, N and Chiechanowski, J (1989), *The Formation of the Polish Community in Great Britain 1939–50*, University of London: School of Slavonic and East European Studies

Sword, K (1996), *Identity in Flux: The Polish Community in Britain*, University of London: School of Slavonic and East European Studies

Tabori, P (1972), *The Anatomy of Exile: A Semantic and Historical Study*, London: Harrap

Takkenberg, A and Tahbaz, CC (1989), *The Collected* Travaux Preparatoires *of the 1951 Geneva Convention Relating to the Status of Refugees*, Amsterdam: Dutch Refugee Council and European Legal Network on Asylum, 3 vols

Tambs-Lyche, H (1980), *London Patidars: A Case Study in Urban Ethnicity*, London: Routledge

Tamil Information (1993) 'Tamils fear UNHCR involvement in Sri Lanka will lead to refoulement', *Tamil Information* – Special Issue, January

Tang, TTL (1994), 'The legal status of the refugee in the United States', 42 *American Journal of Criminal Law*, pp 577–615

Tatla, DS (1999), *The Sikh Diaspora: The Search for Statehood*, London: UCL

Taylor, D (1994), *The Symbolic Reconstruction of the Sri Lankan Hindu Tamil Community in Britain*, unpublished PhD thesis, University of London: School of Oriental and African Studies

Thackray, R (1998), 'UN intervenes in flight to keep "suicidal" refugees in Britain', *The Independent*, 5 July

Thompson, D (1938), 'Refugees: a world problem', 16(3) *Foreign Affairs*, pp 375–87

Thomson, D (1966), *Europe Since Napoleon*, Harmondsworth: Penguin

Toal, R (1997a), 'Applications for political asylum by Somali nationals and the 1951 Convention relating to the status of refugees', 11(1) *Immigration and Nationality Law and Practice*, pp 3–12

Toal, R (1997b), 'Applications for political asylum by Somali nationals and the 1951 Convention relating to the status of refugees: the judgment of the Court of Appeal in Adan and Nooh', 11(2) *Immigration and Nationality Law and Practice*, pp 43–45

Toal, R (1998), 'Applications for political asylum by Somali nationals and the 1951 Convention relating to the status of refugees: the decision of the House of Lords in *SSHD v Adan*', 12(3) *Immigration and Nationality Law and Practice*, pp 94–98

Tolstoy, N (1977), *Victims of Yalta*, London: Hodder & Stoughton

Travers, M (1999), *The British Immigration Courts: A Study of Law and Politics*, Bristol: Policy

Trost, R and Billings, P (1998), 'The designation of "safe" countries and individual assessment of asylum claims', in Nicholson, F and Twomey, P (eds), *Current Issues of UK Asylum Law and Policy*, Aldershot: Ashgate, pp 73–99

Turley, DM (1980), '"Free air" and the fugitive slaves: British abolitionists versus government over American fugitives, 1834–61', in Bolt, C and Drescher, S (eds), *Anti-Slavery, Religion and Reform*, Folkestone, Kent: Wm Dawson and Hamden, Connecticut: Archon, pp 163–82

Vernant, J (1953), *The Refugee in the Post-War World*, London: Allen & Unwin

Verzijl, JHW (1972), *International Law in Historical Perspective. Part V: Nationality and Other Matters Relating to Individuals*, Leiden: AW Sijthoff

Vincenzi, C (1985), 'Aliens and the judicial review of immigration law', *Public Law*, pp 93–114

Vincenzi, C (1992), 'Extra-statutory ministerial discretion in immigration law', *Public Law*, pp 300–21

Visram, R (1986), *Ayahs, Lascars and Princes: The Story of Indians in Britain 1700–1947*, London: Pluto

Voutira, E and Harrell-Bond, BE (1995), 'In search of the locus of trust: the social world of the refugee camp', in Daniel, EV and Knudsen, JC (eds), *Mistrusting Refugees*, Berkeley, California: California UP, pp 207–24

Wade, HWR (1983), *Administrative Law*, 5th edn, Oxford: Clarendon

Wahlbaeck, Ö (1999), *Kurdish Diasporas: A Comparative Study of Kurdish Refugee Communities*, London: MacMillan and New York: St Martin's

Walvin, J (1971), *The Black Presence: A Documentary History of the Negro in England, 1555–1860*, London: Orbach & Chambers

Wasserstein, B (1984), 'The British Government and the German immigration', in Hirschfeld, G (ed), *Exile in Great Britain*, Leamington Spa: Berg, pp 63–81

Webber, F (1997a), 'Asylum seekers caught by the Act', 38(3) *Race and Class*, pp 73–75

Webber, F (1997b), 'Governing racism: the corruption of the executive', 39(1) *Race and Class*, pp 19–35

Webber, F (1998), 'Kurdish refugees: pawns in a deadly game', 39(4) *Race and Class*, pp 77–80

Weil, S (1974), 'Bene Israel in Britain', III(2) *New Community*, pp 87–91

Weis, P (1953), 'Legal aspects of the Convention of 28 July 1951 relating to the Status of Refugees', 30 *British Yearbook of International Law*, pp 478–89

Weis, P (1967), 'The 1967 Protocol relating to the Status of Refugees and some questions of the law of treaties', 42 *British Yearbook of International Law*, pp 39–70

Weis, P (1979), *Nationality and Statelessness in International Law*, Alphen aan den Rijn and Germantown, Maryland: Sijthoff and Noordhoff

Weis, P (1982), 'The development of refugee law', in *Transnational Legal Problems of Refugees, Michigan Yearbook of International Legal Studies*, New York: Clark Boardman, pp 27–42

Weis, P (1995), *The Refugee Convention 1951: The* Travaux Preparatoires *Analysed*, Cambridge: Grotius

White, RCA (1974), 'When is a British protected person not a British protected person?', 23 *International and Comparative Law Quarterly*, pp 866–73

White, RM (1987), 'The new visa controls', *Public Law*, pp 350–56

Winterbourne, D, Shah, P and Doebbler, C (1996), 'Refugees and safe countries of origin: appeals, judicial review and human rights', 10(4) *Immigration and Nationality Law and Practice*, pp 123–35

Witherow, R (1995), 'Detention of asylum seekers: a continuing cause for concern', 9(2) *Immigration and Nationality Law and Practice*, pp 59–63

Yaansah, E (1987), 'Refugees, race and recent developments in the law', 1(4) *Immigration and Nationality Law and Practice*, pp 115–19

Young, C (1998), 'Political representations of geography and place in the introduction of the UK Asylum and Immigration Act 1996', in Nicholson, F and Twomey, P (eds), *Current Issues of UK Asylum Law and Policy*, Aldershot: Ashgate, pp 34–51

Zolberg, AR, Suhrke, A and Aguayo, S (1989), *Escape from Violence: Conflict and the Refugee Crisis in the Developing World*, Oxford: OUP

INDEX